# 15:

# THINGS

# *EVERY*

# SELF-BUILDER

# SHOULD

# KNOW

## By Barry Sutcliffe

# INTRODUCTION BY THE AUTHOR:

**Multiple choice question:**

*You are thinking about going on holiday, but you want to go somewhere new. Do you:*

> a) *Download tour guides / street maps / and "Things to do" guides of hundreds of different resorts / villages / cities and read them all, before you make up your mind where to go?*
> b) *Download a few brochures of countries or regions you might like to visit, learn a bit about them. then decide whether or not to go to one or more of them?*

The answer would nearly always be "b)".

This book is "*answer b)*" for anyone who is thinking about self-building. This is the "**Should we go there?**" book that you need to read, before you decide whether or not self-build is right <u>for you.</u>

Most self-build books presently available (*including my own "Self-Build Simplified"*) head out on the journey together with the reader, from start to completion. Highlighting, explaining, and tutoring as they go. This book does a different, but just as important job, in not only helping you to decide whether or not the whole venture would be a good idea in the first place, but if it is, also being there with you *every day*, reminding you what you need to do, think about and look out for. In that respect it mimics my role at the many live self-build events I have been invited to attend over the past ten years or so, as "Self-Build Expert".

In that role I get either 15 or 30 minutes consultations (*depending on which show it is: Grand Designs or Homebuilding and Renovating*), seeing up to 15 clients per day, over 2 to 4 days. During these consultations, I listen to each guest's problems, worries and queries related to their own projects, and to try to solve them.

Following along those same lines, **151 things** presents the reader with short, concentrated, subject related, easy to understand sections, full of ideas, facts, figures, suggestions, advice and warnings, covering important subjects, such as preparation, research, finance, planning, programming, finding trades people…. (*and so on*). It also dispels many of the myths related to the self-build process, and shines a bright light on inherent threats *to*, or weaknesses *in* the readers own ideas and plans, that they may not yet be aware of yet, but that could trip them up at any time.

*This book could become the most important, and most used tool in your self-build tool kit.*

**Note:** The way the book is formatted occasionally results in information in one section overlapping with one or more other sections. Where this happens it is not an error. It is simply to make sure that each section is in itself complete and doesn't require the reader to try to think or look back to another part of the book for answers to the specific problem that they are considering at that moment.

My style of writing is friendly and informal, but also honest and straight to the point. This is how I communicate on site as a Construction Project Manager and have done for the past 40+ years. My ethos, related to my job has always been:

*"Bring me a problem, I'll try my best to help you to solve it, then hopefully, you can get on with what you were doing".*

*So, with that, I will let you get on with what you were doing!*
*(which was, I think, beginning to read this book)*

**I hope you enjoy it and I look forward to hearing from some of you soon.**

*Barry S.*

## Additional:

### The book includes three extra features:

*Amazon Books* works in a way that allows updates to be made to a book at any time. As I intend to publish an updated edition of this book each year, I thought it might be a good idea to try out some ideas I have been toying with for a few years. So here are three extra features I have added at the back of the book:

1. **I have published my personal email address**. I have done so with the aim of promoting dialogue between myself and the book's readers. Sharing information and ideas that could be useful to us both, as well as others. Useful and/ or interesting ideas and facts gathered from these interactions, could find their way into future editions of this book, or be included in future titles in this series (*The Self-Build Simplified series*).
2. I am offering a limited number of bookings for **"one to one" full day Consultancy Sessions**, either at The Self-Build Centre in Swindon, or other suitable locations . At these face to face meetings, any aspects of *proposed* or *live* projects can be discussed and investigated. The meetings can then be followed up by further contacts by emails if required.
3. In a separate section at the back of the book, titled *"**The Self-Build Trade List**"*, I have compiled a list of over 200 useful self-build related contacts, drawn from various sources, including my own. The index will be updated with each new edition of the book.

# INDEX

## SECTION 1:

## PLANNING THE PROJECT AND FINDING LAND

## SECTION 2:

# PLANNING PERMISSION, DESIGN AND COSTING

## SECTION 3:

# BUILD METHODS

## SECTION 4:

# BUILDING

**EXTRAS:**

## SECTION 1:

# PLANNING YOUR PROJECT AND FINDING LAND

### THING 1: BE WELL PREPARED, BUT AVOID OVER RESEARCHING

*"Taking on a self-build project will change your life.*
*It may do so for a few months, a couple of years, or permanently.*
*Usually for the better, but very occasionally, maybe not so much!"*

*As soon as you start looking into the possibly of building your own home, your lives will probably start to change. Your free time can quickly become dedicated to doing everything you need to do and learning everything you need to learn, to turn your dream in to reality. That would be your first error.*

**Lesson one:** (*and one of the most important things I am going to say in this book*):

### *"Do ONLY what you need to do and learn ONLY what you need to learn".*

If you don't strictly follow that piece of advice, there is a good chance that you will spend the next five years researching, studying, travelling to shows and events and learning everything there is to be learnt about self-build. In doing so, you will probably scare yourself half to death! So much so, that there is a good chance that you will never actually get around to building *anything*.

I have been designing and building houses for over 40 years. I have a good level of knowledge on the subject. Everything I have learnt over those years probably means I can sensibly answer most questions, and solve most problems, related to house designing and building. However, all that knowledge and experience didn't stop my most recent build from being an absolute pig of a job, and doing its best every day, to go pear shaped. I could now carry on building houses for another 20 years, get another 20 years of experience, and still get another *pig of a job* at the end of that period.

**In this business, more knowledge does not necessarily link directly to more success. The things that link most directly to success for a self-build project are:**

I. Having *enough* knowledge.
II. Being well *enough* prepared.
III. Being able to react to and solve problems.
IV. The ability to stick to a plan.
V. The ability to stick to a budget.
VI. Determination.
VII. A healthy bank balance.

*Being equipped with those assets is far more important than endlessly researching into the subject. If you concentrate too much of your time on becoming a theoretical expert, on everything related to this subject, as soon as you try to turn your expertise into practical results, you will, more times than not, panic and fail.*

**Here is a practical example of what I mean by this:**

In my role as Self-Build Expert at the live shows, I have come across countless people who have become information junkies, knowledgeable on *every* aspect of *every* related subject. These people ask me questions along the lines of:

*"We can't make up our minds on the best way to build. Can you tell us, is Traditional build better than Timber Frame? We like really SIPS and Closed Panel systems but are afraid to go for either, because they are not as popular or widely used as some of the other methods. What about green building? Should we be using one of those systems to keep our carbon footprint down? We have been researching and trying to decide which method to use for months, and we still can't make up our minds. So, we have come to the show to ask you which is the best one to use."*

My answer starts with a few questions: 1) Have you researched <u>all</u> of those options? 2) Are they *all* suitable for your build? 3) Which one do you prefer? and 4) Can you afford that one?

If the answers to those questions is Yes, my response will simply be: *"Go for the one you prefer"*.

What I am saying here, is that all the established house building systems are ok. They all do a job, some are more expensive than others, some are more difficult to use, some are faster than others, but once you have carried out a reasonable amount of research on all the systems that interest you, the one that you prefer, will probably be the best one FOR YOU. It is as simple as that.

Far more important to the success of your project are:

I. Having *enough* knowledge to make the decision that is right *for you.*
II. Once you make that decision, you need to prepare to use *that* system. So, get to know more about <u>*just that one*</u> system.

III.    You can guarantee that there will be problems along the way, so spend some time investigating what they might be, so that you can hopefully avoid some of them and know how to fix the rest.

IV.    Once you have made your decision, stick with it.

V.    Make sure that your choice is going to be affordable for you.

*So, as you embark on this huge adventure, keep this principle in mind and, if at any point in the process you find yourself knowing all about how to wire up a charger point for an electric car, or what the chemical composition of mortar plasticizer is, you probably need to stop researching and get on with doing something useful!*


## THING 2: **IT DOESN'T NEED TO BE SCARY**

A Self-build is a major commitment for any person, couple, or family to take on. Government statistics indicate that around 12,000 such projects are presently being completed each year, whilst the same set of statistics state that an estimate of the number of people who would like to take on a self-build, amounts to around 53% of the total UK house buying market.

Why are there so many more people who would like to self-build, than there are actually doing so? There are many answers to that question and I will be touching on some of them later in the book. The one I am looking at in this section is *Fear*.

When I first started self-building, some 34 years ago (ouch!), there were around 22,000 completions per year, and the whole process was much simpler. At the time there was only really one accepted method house building: *Brick and Block* (*also known as Traditional build*).

Timber frames had not really entered the market at that time. There were a few companies who were thinking about introducing it, and one or two that were testing the market, but nothing had yet been seriously promoted. Land was cheap in most places, Planning Permission was a lot easier to achieve than it is now, mortgage choices were limited, so you simply took what was available, or you didn't bother. Windows were *plastic* or *wood*, there were no solar panels, it was hard to find underfloor heating systems. Bathrooms were basic and reasonably cheap, so were kitchens (*for the older readers, these were the days when "MFI" was the king of furniture!*). It was all just much simpler and less scary for would be self-builders.

Jump forward to today, and you find a huge difference in just about every aspect of the self-build process and industry. Planning Permission is complicated and onerous, there are now many different systems available to build a house, different types of foundations, land is horrendously expensive in most areas, there are a huge range of mortgage products, Architects will try to get you to use *this* new render, or *that* new drainage system, or *these* new recyclable products. No wonder the people I wrote about earlier get bunged up on information and find it hard to make up their minds on anything. There are simply far too many *shiny things* to think about, and we don't know enough about any of them to be certain of their benefits, drawbacks, or whether they are actually of any use at all.

So, as everything got more complicated and expensive, we (*self-builders*) started to get more fearful about making definite choices on *anything,* just in case those choices prove to be wrong.

> **Question:** *Have you noticed a similarity between Section 1 and Section 2 of this book?*
> **Answer:** *They are both related there being too many choices available to self-builders and how that can end up making the whole process more complicated and stressful.*

### Just as the problems are similar, so is the solution.

If you happen to be in the fortunate position of having an unlimited pot of funds to spend on your project, by all means, have what you want to have, and pay what you want to pay for it. If you have a large budget available for the build, the chances are that you will employ an Architect to work with you, to guide you through the process, from start to end, and to *(for a fee)* answer any questions you have, on any subject related to your project. If they don't know answer immediately, they will search heaven and earth to find one *(again, for a fee)*. They will, not surprisingly, usually guide *(or push)* you towards the decisions that they consider are the best, depending on what they are used to doing in any given situation.

However, if you are one of the mere mortals out there, who like me, does not have that sort of luxury, we still have all the options and the multitude choice of shiny things in front of us to choose from, but we are not always sure which ones are good, which are bad and which are worth paying extra for. That is the scary bit for most self-builders.

Think about older houses (*30+ years old*) and how they are built. How would you compare them to the houses the national house builders sell these days? Which would you rather have for quality, size, strength, soundproofing and longevity? You would probably agree that the older houses are a much better built, bigger, stronger and will probably last longer. **However:** New houses are warmer, they have nice kitchens, bathrooms and tiles, and those things are *nice to have.*

### Now think about this:

Why are you considering self-building?

In most cases, it is to get a better, bigger, stronger, more solid, warmer house with better soundproofing, ***and*** nice kitchens bathroom and tiles!

**So, why not consider this:**

If you could stick with the older style of house, build it bigger and stronger, using materials that have been used, tried and tested for many years, and then put nice kitchens, bathrooms and tiling inside them, and make them warmer, would that be a good result?

Now, which of all the *tried and tested* systems would you use?

Ok, brick and block would be the obvious answer, as it was most commonly used in the old days. However, when we are talking about *tried and tested*, most of the other systems now also fall into that category. Brick and block building is now quite expensive, slow, hard to insulate and scores low on the recyclability / carbon footprint scale. So is not the most obvious choice anymore.

Bearing that in mind, most of the new systems are ok. Some are better than others, but they all work, they are all strong and they will all last a long time. So, given that there are no particularly bad choices, your choice should simply be made based on what you like, what the reputation of the supplier is like, whether the products are of a good enough quality and are they warrantied, can you get them when you need them, and what are the prices like? **That's pretty much it.**

Once you break it all down in to simpler, smaller chunks, none of the decisions you need to make need to be particularly difficult or stressful.

*If you use this type of thinking for all the choices you will need to make throughout the project, you shouldn't lose too many night's sleep in the process, and who knows, you might even enjoy it!*


## THING 3: DON'T FOOL YOURSELVES ON THE COSTS

I always used to be one of the worst offenders when it came to the subject of overspending on building projects. I always seem to have to fight to keep myself in check and the build within budget.

My full time job is designing and building houses, usually for other people, but sometimes for myself, or for my development business. I couldn't even try to count how many houses I have worked on over my career, probably upwards of a couple of hundred. Why then can I still not get the pricing bit right? Why do I always underestimate the cost? (*The annoying thing is that I know exactly why, but I will probably continue to do the same thing, every time until I retire*).

I do it because I am human. I do it because I am an optimist. I do it because, at the start of the project I cannot possibly anticipate how many problems are going to occur, or how much they are each going to cost. I do it because I like to set myself *targets* for the costs, which, by default, usually tend to be lower than reality.

OK, yes, like the professional, responsible cost estimator that I am, once I have come up with a list of all the basic cost estimates, I then add a percentage for contingencies *(between 5% and 10%)*. I am also a good Site Manager, so throughout the build, I watch the costs, I barter and bargain with all the subbies and suppliers from day 1, until completion, so why do I end up over budget nearly every time?

**Here's why** *(and this is what you need to remember)*:

I. **On every new build project, large or small, there are always unforeseen costs.** Even if you are building two *identical* houses next door to each other, one can cost significantly more than the other. The major culprit is usually related to anything that goes on below ground level, but things can go wrong with any part of the build, at any time.

II. **The weather** can play havoc with progress and costs, and often does. Machinery on hire is charged by the time on site, not the time in use. Workers are often paid by the hour, not by how much work they are able to do. Scaffold hire can include the first 6 weeks on site but can sometimes be there for a year or more. The list of areas where prices *could* and often *do* rise, includes pretty much *everything* involved with the project.

III. **Price increases:** Materials usually increase in price twice a year. When estimating the costs, sometimes many months before work starts, we naturally tend to use the prices we get at that time for our cost build up. They can then go up 5% - 10%, either before work starts, or whilst the build is underway.

IV. **Building Regs Inspectors** have the power to request extra works, or for work to be redone if they don't think it is up to standard. It is hard to argue with them. Their word tends to be final, whether or not we think they are right.

V. **Architectural mistakes:** As with anything new, the first time something is done, mistakes can be made. Architects are not computers and they do make mistakes. Unfortunately, it is usually the builder who pays the cost of those mistakes. A small mistake made on a drawing at the start of a job, if it is not discovered quickly, can have huge cost and time implications later on.

VI. **Supplier and manufacturer mistakes:** Builders Merchants often make mistakes with deliveries *(wrong quantities, wrong items etc)*. If something is on a lengthy delivery time from the Merchant, and is in some way incorrect when it arrives, time and money can be lost, whilst the corrections are made and items are re-ordered, and delivered.

VII. **Subcontractor mistakes:** Any mistake made by a contractor as the building works proceeds, unless it is found very quickly, can have expensive consequences.
For example: Say an electrician forgets to fit an important electrical socket, and no-one else either checks, or notices. If the error is not discovered until the end of the project, the result could be that tiling, plasterboard and insulation have to be removed, cables extended from another socket to the correct location *(which could be a few metres away)* and the fitting retrospectively fitted. The reinstatement

works could then be significant and costly. *And all for what would appear to initially have been a single, minor error.*

VIII. **Estimating mistakes:** If Estimators or Quantity Surveyors hit the wrong button on their calculators, the unless they double check everything they do, the result could be that the total price for the job is either under or overestimated.

**Example:** When I was training to be a Site Manager, a friend of mine *(Hi David, if you read this!)* was asked to price up a job for *half a mile* of hardcore road inside a steel works. The road was needed to enable the company to bring a large new piece of equipment into the factory. My friend did the estimate, but accidentally hit the wrong button on the calculator and priced the *"supply, lay and compact hardcore"* item at **£1.80** / sq m. instead of **£10.80** / sq m.

The company (*not surprisingly*) won the job. No one picked up the error until it was time to start work, then the proverbial *muck hit the fan,* when someone happened to look at the amount of money available to pay for all the stone!

The only way the company got round the problem, was to send <u>every item</u> of excavating plant, from all the jobs in the area, down to that job, on a Friday afternoon. Everyone then worked solidly all weekend, day and night. That was the most efficient and most economical way to react, for trying to keep the cost as low as possible.

I remember my friend, who I was sharing digs with at the time, arriving back at the house after being on site for around 60 hours straight through (*grabbing a couple of hours sleep during that time, by lying on the drawings desk with his coat over him*). I remember him looking like the walking dead!

IX. **Breakages:** Things get dropped, fittings break, packaging and products get damaged. Like it or not, these things are always going to happen. Some estimators add up to 5% of the build cost for damage, loss, waste, and theft

X. **Health and safety:** This item is now adding significantly to the cost of building works. Overall, that is a good thing, but Estimators and Site Managers on both small and large projects, have not all fully got to grips with the financial impact this change is having. The cost of health and safety issues on any site have probably multiplied by a factor of at least 2 or 3 over the past few years.

XI. **Initially invisible costs:** (*These little critters are a pain in the backside*). Unexpected things that happen below ground level can add extra cost. Many of these will not have been allowed for in the original estimates. Here are two examples:

1) When the foundations are being excavated, if the ground is bad, the sides of the excavations can fall in. On site, that is just accepted as *what happens*, and no-one really takes any more notice of it than that. The muck is dug out, the area cleaned up and the men get on with what the job. The bill then goes to the office and is quietly paid.

2) As the required depth is reached on the foundations, sometimes the ground is too soft for a foundation to sit on. Where this is the case, the excavation has to be

deepened until the base *is* suitably hard. On a large building, the extra concrete needed to fill the extra depth can be significant.

Here is a theoretical, but very plausible example: Say the extra depth excavated is 1m, and the width of the trench has increased from 600mm to an average of 700mm, as earth has fallen in during the excavation. Let's assume we are building a reasonably sized 5 bed detached house, with a few internal loadbearing walls. In that scenario, instead of the foundation being 0.225m deep, it is now 1.225m deep, and instead of being 600mm wide, it is now 700mm wide. Let's also say that the concrete is around the £100 / cubic metre, and that there is a total of 100m length of foundation trench. The extra quantity of concrete needed would be in excess of 110 cubic metres, costing an extra £11,000. *Oh yes*, and don't forget to add the extra labour and plant costs for the extra excavating and laying the extra concrete, to that figure! **– Ouch!**

Luckily, major extra costs like this don't happen very often, but you do need to be aware of potential for them to keep popping up here and there.

**So, if that is how things can go wrong, how do you get your pricing as near to being realistic as possible?**

This is a difficult one. An experienced estimator can look at a site and think *"This should be an easy one"*, or *"Bloody hell, this is going to be a pain"*. Self-Builders don't tend to have the experience to be able to do that, so they just have to make sure there is a generous allowance for *what if's* and then keep their fingers crossed.

It is also a good idea to make sure you have a decent *emergency fund* to turn to, if it is needed (*on top of your contingency allowance*).

**Ignore this advice at your peril.**

## THING 4: ARE YOU READY FOR A GOOD DOSE OF STRESS?

To take on a self-build project requires money, time, organisational ability, intelligence, patience, foresight and the ability to put up with a lot of pressure without buckling, for what can be a significant period of time (*measured in months, if not years*).

There is no such thing as the perfect house build. There never has been. No matter what you try to do to make sure yours is the first perfect build ever, you will not succeed! I am afraid that is just a fact that we are all stuck with.

So, bearing that in mind, if you go ahead with your project, the chances are that you are going to be stressed, possibly _very_ stressed. So is your wife / husband / partner and, thanks to being around **_you_** *miserable lot*, so is the rest of your family! The stress factors will multiply if you all move into temporary accommodation or move away from the area where you presently live, while you build.

Overall, once it is has all been finished, when you look back on what you have accomplished, you will probably get to the point where you think that it was a fantastic experience, one of the highlights of your life, but while it is going on, you are probably going to lose quite a lot of sleep.

**So, how do you prepare for this, and how do you cope when, and if things start to go a bit pear shaped?**

One important factor in keeping a family team together during a self-build, is keeping everyone in the loop. Kids are going to get worried and scared if their world is suddenly changing around them, and they can't see either why, or when it will all be ok again. It is sometimes not too difficult to keep them on board once you have started all the exciting site works, but *getting* them on board in the first place, might be a bit harder. You have got to do it though!

The best way to smooth the way, is to include them in as much of the process as possible (*or at least as much as they want to be involved*) from day one. Let them have some input into activities and choices and try to get them excited about how much better their lives are going to be, once you have all worked together to complete the house.

To keep your own stress levels as low as possible, you need to prepare thoroughly (*but, as I said earlier, do not *over* prepare*). Work out what you need to do in plenty of time, before you need to do it, try to do it as well as you can, and when it is done, check it for errors and then move on to the next thing. Worrying about everything you are going to do or have just done won't do you, or anyone else any favours.

One good way to help to reduce the likelihood of bad thing happening on your project, is to try to learn from *other people's* experiences and mistakes, *before* you start your own project.

I would suggest that you buy some of the self-build magazines, and one or two of the books, but when you read them, don't try to learn how to build a house. Instead, look for the things they did wrong. By finding out what mistakes other people make and how they solve them, you might be able to equip and prepare yourselves for dealing with the problems that occur on your own project.

If you look back to section 1, this is one of the areas where the 5 attributes /abilities mentioned, come into play. If you are well prepared, and can react and adjust to problems, you will tend to suffer less stress when they do.

*Also, if you are in charge of the project and _you_ don't appear stressed, there will be less likelihood that the people around you start to worry and get stressed themselves.*

**One important thing that you should keep telling yourselves, is this:**

*"This is a major venture that we are undertaking. Not many people would be brave enough to take it on.*

*We have prepared properly, we are adequately funded, we have got a good team working with us and we have planned and allowed for problems and mistakes to occur. So, when they do, no matter how big they are, let's just all pull together, do whatever we need to do to get through them, and move on.*
*When this is all finished, it will be a fantastic place to live, and we will all be able to say:*

**"We built that!".**


## THING 5: ARE ALL THE FAMILY ON BOARD?

I can recall occasions at the self-build shows where I have been sat round a table with all the members of families who have been planning to take on their own project. Mum, Dad, kids and maybe even Gran and Grandad (*who will sometimes be moving in with the rest of the family, once the build has been completed*).

There are three general scenarios for such meetings:

1) Wife / Husband / Partner / Kids happy, excited, all in agreement about the idea, and enjoying their day at the show, looking at lots of shiny things. - *No problem there.*
2) Wife / Husband / Partner happy, kids not sure, but willing to be convinced. – They just need some reassuring. – *Not a major problem there, they just want to hear some positives about how it will make their lives better. Attending the show can be a big help with that.*
3) Wife / Husband / Partner / Kids all at loggerheads – Nightmare!

With *Scenario 3*, I can find myself sitting with 5 or 6 people around the table, one trying to be positive and upbeat, whilst the rest of the family are sitting there with (*as my dad used to say*) *faces like smacked backsides*!

Assuming *you* are the one who is going to be spearheading this adventure, it is very important that, in your own enthusiasm for how much this could benefit you all as a family, you don't just going dashing ahead, planning everything on your own, assuming everyone has the same picture in their minds that you have. Simply telling everyone "*It's going to be great*" as, day by day their lives are being turned upside down more and more, is not going to work for long, especially if they can't see the same light at the end of the tunnel that you can.

Remember that this will be a major event in your life, and it will be just as much of a major event in the lives of *everyone around you*.

From those family meetings at the shows, if I have picked up just one fact, it is that "*If your family is not on board, you haven't really got a project*".

Getting people on board is not usually too difficult. I have done it myself, on my own projects (*ok, we only had one child to consider, so maybe had it easy*).

For the project to succeed, you have got to get everyone to realise that if they want their lives to be better than they presently are, they will need to accept some change. You can all stay as you are, where you are, or you can all rough it for a while, to end up with a bigger, nicer, better place to live.

As we all know, change is part of life and part of growing up, but you still need to make the pill a bit easier to swallow for them where you can. If you manage that, the chances are that you will needs fewer pills of your own to get you through it all!

**Here are a few tips for if and when you find yourself in this situation:**

I.      Letting kids get involved with the choice of plot, early on, is probably not a good idea. Plots are hard to find and there are lots of considerations that will have to be made before making an offer on something suitable. This first part of the negotiation process to buy a plot of land is more of a business transaction than it is the start of realising the first part of your dream. You will need to talk about Planning Permissions and prices, which is not a conversation that is going to excite many people, especially kids.

II.     Once you have found the plot and there is a good chance that you will be buying it, *then* take the kids to have a look, and also show them some sketches of the sort of house that you envisage being able to build on it. That sort of thing will help to bring the idea to life for them

III.    Once you have secured the land, let each member of the family contribute to the discussion about the design and appearance of the house.

IV.     Try to give them bedrooms that are bigger and better than the ones they presently have and let them choose their own paint colours and furniture.

V.      Maybe think about giving them an en-suite each.

VI.     Little things like remote controlled dimming lights in their bedrooms can earn you lots of browny points and don't cost much. (*have a look at* tlc-direct.co.uk *and find your way to remote controlled lighting*).

VII.    Tell them that their bedroom walls and the floors will be sound insulated, so they won't be getting told *"Turn that down"* as often!

VIII.   Take them with you when you choose the bathrooms, kitchens, tiles, and carpets

It is not always a difficult task to get the kids on board, but you will usually need to use a bit of psychology and forethought. You will obviously know your own situation, your own kids and what you will be asking of them, but hopefully, with a bit of patience and understanding, everything might turn out to have a happy ending.

**Note:** By the way, I haven't mentioned so far, that Mum and Dad both need to be fully on board with the idea. Don't even think about starting a project unless the "top team" are fully in sync!

*Additional:*

*Something to bear in mind: If, no matter what you do, or offer as incentives, the whole family is really fighting you, and if everyone is falling out over the whole self-build idea, it might be better to shelve it, at least for a while.*

*If you push it too hard, by the time it is all finished, it could end up with your, by then **ex**-partner / wife / husband living in and enjoying the fantastic new house, while you are living in a grotty 1 bedroomed flat somewhere, on your own!*

## THING 6: **BE CAREFUL AT THE TRADE SHOWS – LEARN TO "FLOAT"**

Before I took on my first self-build project, and later became professionally involved in the self-build industry, I was a standard *"Wannabe self-builder"*. My dream was to build a spacious, attractive, sturdily built home, with a decently sized garden, in a nice location, whilst spending a lot less than I would have to, to buy one of the lousy matchstick and sticky tape offerings from the mainstream housebuilders.

So, I bought a book: Murray Armor's *"Building Your Own Home"*. As I remember, this was the only book of its type available at the time (early 1970's). Then I decided to hit the one and only self-build show each year, held at Alexander Palace, London.

In those days, a trip to London was a major adventure for me, a quiet lad from the North West, heading for the Big City. The show was not like the exciting events that we are now used to. The brightest stand would only be bright because the stand holder might have splashed out on some balloons! Nevertheless, to me, dull or not, the show was an Aladdin's cave of wonders. Hundreds of new things to look at, poke, prod and get excited about. It was great!

Coming up to date, there must now be getting on for at least a couple of dozen shows each year, large and small, up, down and across the UK. All the same big companies attend all the shows, plus a mixture of smaller local businesses. If you have been to one self-build show, you have really been to them all. But they are still great places to go, **and they are addictive!**

When you go to these huge shows, they are full of glitz and glamour, they have every new gadget on show, every system of building, all the environmental products that you will be told that you <u>are</u> going to need (*whether or not, when you arrive at the show, <u>you</u> think you do!*), beautiful kitchens, bathrooms, instant boiling water taps, Architects, windows, doors...... You name it, it is there, in *multiple choice* format!

One problem with this all this, is that once you have been to one show, although you know they will all be just about the same, you usually want to go to more, *just in case you missed anything exciting*. The fact is that you probably didn't. You may have missed some shiny thing or other, but whatever you missed will almost certainly not be something important.

So, at each show you attend, you learn more about each of these fantastic products, demonstrated by smart, clever looking people, who can seemingly work out all the complicated bits without even breaking a sweat! And you start to think:

*"How could I, a mere amateur, ever be able to decide sensibly between all the choices, and then how would I manage incorporate all my choices into just one project? And then there is the cost! It all looks expensive and I have a limited budget. – But I **<u>NEED</u>** it all,*
**<u>*including*</u>** ***the instant boiling water tap!***
*Maybe I would be better forgetting the whole thing, rather than risking messing it up. After all, if I don't try, I can't fail!"*

**It doesn't need to be like that.**

The trick with shows, is not to go to too many, and to teach yourself to see the shows as *"A nice day out where you'll see some nice stuff"*.

If you can separate the shows from reality and from the realistic target of building what 90% of self-builders actually <u>do</u> end up building: *A nice, decent sized four or five bedroomed family house, with a few features and extras thrown in*, then you can go to as many shows as you like, without them giving you an inferiority complex.

The key word to take note of in the title of this section is *"Float"*. That is what I taught myself to do, and it is what you need to do. Just try to *(virtually)* float over the stands, and instead of focussing on every detail, try to take a bird's eye view of everything on offer, thinking as you go: *"It is a good idea? Would it be advantageous to my project? Is it practical? Is it reasonably priced? Do I need it?"*

The answer to all those questions, 95% of the time will be:
*"No, you don't, but if it something that makes sense, is something worth having, will improve the project for you and your family, and you can afford it, maybe treat yourself,*
***just this once"***.

**After you have done that a couple of times, GO HOME, and don't go to any more shows!**

## THING 7: VIST THE SELF-BUILD CENTRE AT SWINDON

*After advising you to go easy on going to self-build shows, now, just to be confusing I am going to recommend that you go to a show.*

In case you haven't heard of the *National Self-Build and Renovation Centre* at Swindon, it is a permanent large exhibition and conference centre, just off Junction 16 of the M4. It has been there for many years (*it has probably been open for over 15 years*) and has continually re-invented itself during that time.

The centre is free to enter, and once inside, according to the brochure, you will find more than 250 stands, of all types, sizes, and varieties. There is a full scale, fully built house, and also an exhibition which walks you through a complete house renovation, cleverly set up inside a *full scale* purpose built exhibition building on three levels.

This particular attraction is set up so that you move from room to room, you are taken from a derelict building, stage by stage, through a full renovation, with each exhibit / room visualising what happens at each stage of the process, all the way through to completion.

You can pick up a set of headphones at the entrance to the exhibit, so that as you walk around, you can listen to a recorded soundtrack explaining what has been done, and how they did it.

At the opposite end of the hall there is another large exhibition area, filled with full sized examples of different types of foundations, detailing how they are constructed and where they would be used. If you haven't seen an *actual* foundation being constructed, this area could provide you with some valuable information to help you to make informed decisions related to your own project.

There is also a funding / mortgage centre (where you can pre-book an appointment to discuss funding for your own project), a coffee and snack bar, and a sitting area where you can spread out your drawings, or just sit and have a rest.

The centre also runs a number of self-build related courses. There are 5 available, including a general self-build course, land finding, heating, renovation, and Project Management. If you wanted to sign yourself up for one of the courses, there are hotels within walking distance of the centre.

When you sign in at the centre, you will be given a handheld scanner that you can simply "point and click" at bar codes, found on each stand. The stands are not generally staffed, apart from during special events, so if you are interested in any particular product, you click on the bar code on the stand, and the centre automatically lets the stand owners know that someone is interested in their product, and would like some information. You can request emails, posted information or phone calls.

Each time I have visited the centre over the years, there is always a stand full of one or two month old self-build magazines for you to help yourselves to, free of charge.

Well I think I have given the centre enough free advertising! Please note that I am not doing free plugs for any other company, but I really do think that if you are considering taking on a self-build project of your own, a visit to this centre is something that could prove very worthwhile, as well as interesting.

*At the back of the book, I am offering a "Consultancy Service", which will hopefully usually be arranged at the centre, so that once we have finished our own meeting, I can show clients around the centre itself.*

**Go to:** www.nsbrc.co.uk for more information on the centre.

## THING 8: LEARN A BIT ABOUT PROJECT MANAGEMENT

If you have little or no previous experience of running any sort of building project, the thought of taking on a full self-build project can be incredibly daunting. However, it is possible to equip, and prepare yourself to run such a project without too much drama.

There are various ways to acquire the basic knowledge and management skills you will need. Three of the best are:

I.   **Research:**
This could involve you spending time sitting in front of the computer, watching videos, reading on-line articles, self-build magazines and books, visiting shows, and possibly joining a Self-Build Club, such as BADSBA (*standing for Build a Dream Self-Build Association*) based in the South West (*but remember, don't go over the top with these activities*).

II.  **Find a local self-build project and visit it.**
If you are feeling brave, you could try to locate an ongoing self-build project in your own area, then simply call at the site during a working day and see if you can get to speak to the people working there. If there is no-one working, but there is a caravan on site, go and knock on the door (*or leave a note with your phone number*). There is nothing like talking to people who are actually "doing it" to quickly give you a realistic picture of how it all works. You may even be able to help each other out, by you offering to do some work on the site, in return for being able to pick up tips on how a *real life* self-build project is run.

*(By the way, if you think that walking on to a live self-build site is a bit rude, or that the people will be too busy to talk to you, don't worry. One thing self-builders love to do is to talk about their project. The fact is that most self-builders tend to morph into self-build bores leading up to and during the build. Not surprisingly, the project fills our lives, and anyone venturing anywhere near us tends to find out all about it, whether they want to or not!)*

If you do manage to find a site somewhere near you, the first time you call round, maybe just introduce yourselves to the owners, and ask if it would be ok for you call round some other time for a quick chat about how have planned, and are running the project (*only do this with the owners, <u>not</u> the builders*). They will almost certainly be more than happy to arrange something with you.

III.   **Take a course on the subject:**
In the previous section I talked about the Self-Build Centre in Swindon. That is one of the places you can go to take a course in Project Management. There are not many of these types of courses available in the UK, but here are a few more contacts:

**Short Self-build courses:**
https://www.cat.org.uk
https://www.potton.co.uk/courses

**Self-build course to gain qualification in Project Management or Construction and the Built Environment:**
https://www.ucas.com

For anyone considering taking on a self-build, I would personally advise doing a bit of mix and match of both research and a course. Watching videos is a good way to learn about a subject quickly. Here are a few links:

https://www.potton.co.uk

https://www.homebuilding

https://www.youtube.com/watch?v=q7NrO-4f4v8

There are plenty more videos on-line, just search "Self-Build videos".

**Join the BADSBA club:**
Joining BADSBA (see above) could be a sensible move to consider. Valerie Bearne runs the club and is great. The meetings tend to be in the South West, but there are site visits organised and just having this connection to other self-builders could help you to feel that you are not alone.

## THING 9: HOW MUCH HOUSE WILL WE NEED?

Below is a list of the rooms and average room sizes that self-builders would tend to include when they design their own, decently sized, 4 or 5 bedroomed house.

To work out the potential square footage of the sort of house that you and your family might design, you simply need to add up the square footage of all the rooms in the list that you would include in your own design, then multiply that figure by 1.1 (*to allow for circulation spaces and internal wall thicknesses*).

If you think the sizes that I have used below are either too small or too large, increase or decrease them as you wish, for your own calculation.

**Hint:** If you are struggling to estimate the sizes of rooms you might need, try this:

1) Measure all the rooms in your present home and write the figures down.

2) Stand in each room and use the existing room measurements to estimate out how much more (or less) space you would like in the same rooms, in the new build.

**Here are my estimated room sizes for a reasonably sized four or five bedroomed house:**

| | |
|---|---|
| Living room: | 18ft x 13ft = 234 sq ft |
| Dining room: | 14ft x 12ft = 168 sq ft |
| Kitchen: | 14ft x 12ft = 168 sq ft |
| Utility: | 10ft x 7ft = 70 sq ft |
| Family room: | 12ft x 12ft = 144 sq ft |
| Study: | 8ft x 8ft = 64 sq ft |
| W.C: | 8ft x 5ft = 40 sq ft |
| Bed 1: | 16ft x 14ft = 224 sq ft |
| Bed 2: | 12ft x 12ft = 144 sq ft |
| Bed 3: | 12ft x 12 ft = 144 sq ft |
| Bed 4: | 9ft x 7ft = 63 sq ft |
| Bed 5: | 9ft x 7ft = 63 sq ft |
| Attic room: | 25ft x 12ft = 300 sq ft |

Once you have listed all the room sizes, add them all together, and don't forget to multiply the figure by 1.1. The figure you end up with, will be a rough estimate of the potential size, in square feet, of your new home.

You can now use that figure for all sorts of tasks, such as estimating your build costs, applying for funding, looking at plots and plot sizes etc.

*Note:* *If you prefer to work in square metres, divide the square footage by 10 (there are roughly 10 square feet in one square metre).*

## THING 10: DO NOT DESIGN YOUR HOUSE UNTIL YOU HAVE YOUR PLOT

In an enthusiastic rush to get their project going, self-builders tend to want to do something practical. The show visiting, internet browsing, and information gathering are some of the first things on the list of *to do's*, and another activity everyone tends to have a go at straight away, is designing a house. Just on some scrap paper, *"Just to get an idea of what we would want"*. Nice thought, lousy idea.

If you think about it, once you make the decision to go ahead with the project, and are fairly sure that you will get the funding you need, one of the first actions you are going to take, is to try to find a suitable building plot.

If there is one thing I can almost guarantee, it is this: The plot you find, and want to buy, **will not** be a standard 25m x 35m, flat, clear plot of virgin ground, adjacent to a main road, with nothing around it but fields, and with Full Planning Permission for your ideal home. Sadly, that simply does not happen (*or at least I have never come across it happening in 40+ years of doing this stuff!*)

It is more likely that the plot you find will incorporate any number of the following attributes:

- Sloping.
- Oddly shaped.
- TPO'd trees (*Tree Preservation Order*).
- Mature trees that will affect the positioning of buildings.
- Neighbours close to its boundary (with windows on your side).
- Underground drainage, or other underground development restricting characteristics.
- Restricted access.
- Restricted planning (*conditions, limitations etc*).
- Old buildings, or foundations already on it.
- Bad ground.
- Legal restrictions to certain types of development.
- Protected wildlife scheme in place.
- Rights of way.

So, if I were to sit down and design my new home before I am ready to go out and look for plots, I'd bet a pound to a penny that when I find one that I would like to buy, my lovely house design (*the one I have just spent many hours fine tuning*) will either not fit on it, or will fit but won't suit some other feature of the land. So, I'll end up having to start the design all over again. This time using the *actual plot* that we want to buy, taking all its unique physical characteristics in to account, together with any relevant physical, legal, and planning restraints in to account, as I do so.

Having said that there is some value in having a play around with house designing early on. If you have access to software such as *Sketchup,* or one of the other simple house design packages, it won't do any harm to try to get at least a basic idea of the sort of building size and layout that is going to suit you and your family. In the previous section, I gave you a quick way to get an idea of the likely square footage of living accommodation you will be looking to achieve, so there is nothing stopping you from using that information to sketch out some ideas on floor plans, or even elevation designs. Just don't do anything at this stage that costs you money, takes up too much of your time, or that can't be thrown in the bin later, without you bursting in to tears at thought of all your wasted effort.

Once you find your ideal plot, being able to transfer your early sketch ideas into a simple, basic design layout for the house, showing where it would sit on the plot, could save you time and money when you hire the house designer (*How? The first job any house designer will usually do on a new project, is to draw up and send you some design ideas in sketch form, from which you can get an idea of the sort of house you like and would want. Their time preparing these sketches will cost you money. So, it will be much better for you and for your wallet if **you** can give **them** the ideas instead*).

## THING 11: HOW MUCH WILL IT COST TO BUILD?

This is *the* big question. The one question that every single self-builder wants an answer to. I wouldn't be surprised if you came straight to this section after reading the index! This is also by far, the most common question I am asked at the shows. It normally goes something like:

*"We are just wondering if you can give us a rough figure of how much it costs to build an average 4 bedroom detached house, on an average plot. - Nothing special, just normal sized rooms, with normal kitchens and bathrooms. We need a figure, or something to be able to work out whether we can afford to do our own project, but we can't find anything in the magazines. So, we thought we'd come and ask you. There must be some sort of average build cost for a 4 bedroomed house. Do you know what it is?"*

Unfortunately, my answer, every single time has to be:

*"Unless I knew a lot more about your project, I would have no idea"*

I then add:

*"But I can help **you** to work out some sort of ball-park figure for yourselves"*.

The first line of that statement is not me being glib, it is the truth. There is no way that I could or would even attempt to answer that question, in those circumstances. As you carry out your research, you may find somewhere, maybe in one of the self-build books or magazines, someone saying *"This is roughly how much it should cost to build a house"*, without going into any detail about how they justify making the statement. If you do, bin the book straight away!

Having said that, at this stage of the process, it's no good just saying *"Nope, No chance!"*, you do need to find a way get *a rough* idea of costs, if you want to be able to move forward with a realistic plan for the development. If you don't have something at least *in the right ball-park* you will always be trying to plan, possibly the biggest project that you will take on in your lifetimes, pretty much blindfolded.

So, how do we fix this problem? At this stage, for what we are doing, and to give us enough information to move ahead with, there is a way, and it is not too difficult. It is however, not something you can ask someone like me to do, you have to do it yourselves.

### How do you estimate the build cost yourselves?

You should already have a rough idea of the sort of *floor area* your house will cover (*from the calculation you did in section 6*). Now you need to use that figure to work out a rough build cost:

### First:

If you have worked out the floor area in square feet (*let's say it is 2000 sq ft*), multiply the floor area by 130 (we are using *£130 per sq ft as a build cost*) = £260,000.

Or, if your measurements are in metres, there are roughly 10 square feet in a square metre, so, 2000/sq ft would equal 200/sq m. The build cost per square metre will be 10x the cost compared to a square foot, which makes it £1300/sq m.

So, 200 sq.m x £1300 = £260,000

That £260,000 figure is a **very** rough guide price to the build cost of your 2000 sq ft house.

How can I say that, after saying that you can't guess this figure?

When I talk to house builders, Quantity Surveyors and Estimators, around £130 / sq ft is the guide figure they presently tend to use for the development cost of new homes. However, the variations in build prices between areas of the country, or even between local areas can be significant, and different finishing specifications can also make a big difference to costs.

So, in reality the question of *How much will a house cost to build*, is a bit like asking *How long is a piece of string?* Nevertheless, for a one off house build, on a one off plot, this is probably the best *basic guide figure* you are going to get to start you off.

### Next:

What you need to do with that figure once you have it, is to try to fine tune it to the best extent you can, to suit your own build, so now ask yourselves these four questions:

1. Is your house going to be a simple or complicated design?

2. Is the ground ok to build on, or could there be any costly problems attached to it? (*You might not know this yet, but as soon as do, build it in to the equation*).
3. Will the house be of low, medium, or high spec?
4. How much are your borrowing costs likely to be (*set up costs and interest payments on your borrowing*)?

Depending on the answers to those questions, you can adjust the £130 per sq ft figure up or down, based on your own "gut" feeling. After doing all that, the figure you end up with, if you prepare the figures diligently, will probably be about as close as you will get before you start getting detailed quotes for the labour and materials.

**Working out your plot budget:**

Now you can use the rough figure you have just calculated, to work out approximately how much you can afford to spend on your building plot, using a bit of simple maths:

*(Maximum build budget – Estimated build cost + 10% contingency) = The maximum you can pay for your plot.*

## THING 12: SMALL STEPS

How you set the project up at the pre-build stage is important, but it doesn't have to be complicated. You simply need to make a list of all the pre-build activities that need to be completed, sorting the items into a practical order of first, second, third and so on (*use this book to help you to compile that list*). Then, starting with number 1, give each item on the list, a strictly limited amount of attention.

Once you have done that for each item, it should become apparent whether or not more attention needs to be given to any single item. If it is, give it more, if it isn't, bank the information you have, note what you need to do next on that subject, and when you need to do it.

Repeat this process, each time narrowing down the number of tasks that need further attention, until you get to the point where every subject has been adequately dealt with, and you have started to formulate a comprehensive *to do* list (*better known as a "programme"*) for getting project itself started.

Here are some suggestions for where to concentrate your efforts.

I. **Talk to your family:** Ask some basic questions like: Do they think self-building is a good idea? / Will they be ok roughing it for a while, so you can *all* get something nice out of doing so? / Where would they like to live? / Would they like to live on site, or rent somewhere while you build? / Would they prefer to get started now, or to leave it for a while?

If the answers are all pretty much what you hope they would be, move forward, if not, consider putting the brakes on for a bit, while you find out what the hesitancy or resistance is due to, and try to fix the problem(s), before taking things too much further.

II. **Check your finances:** Are you financially robust enough to take on this sort of project? Is your job secure? Would you have access to a financial buffer if you went over budget? How much do you think you could afford to spend in total? Make sure you are on a sound financial footing before you commit yourselves.

III. **Think about what you would _need_ to achieve, and what you would _like_ to achieve:** Work out a plan for how to meet as many of those goals as possible and then try to stick to that plan. Don't get side-tracked in to adding extra goals, or changing course part way through, unless you are forced to do so by some fact or event.

IV. **Investigate the _existing_ housing in the areas you would like to live:** Have a browse through the online estate agents, find the properties you like the look of, and see what prices they are selling for. These days, mainly due to the price of land, the cost of self-building does not necessarily save you a lot of money. The benefits of self-build now tend to be in achieving a high quality, high spec build, a unique, bespoke home, on a good sized plot, and if you are lucky, a bit of "_on paper_" profit.
Once you find out how much houses in the areas where you would like to live are selling for, ask yourself: "_If we thought we would end up paying out the full market value to be able to build our own home in this area, would we want to go through all the hassle, and would we be able to afford it?_"

V. **Do the research and the footwork:** Now is the time to visit one or two self-build shows. Also get hold of some self-build related magazines and read the articles about people who have already completed their projects. If you have time, also read a couple of the Self-build _guides / manuals_, to get a more rounded view of the whole subject.

VI. **Consider the house design:** Correlate everyone's ideas for what your new home should look like, how big it should be, and what it would need to include to keep everyone at least _reasonably_ happy. A good way to do this is to look round local housing developments, especially the ones that include show homes. Once you have come up with a design and layout that everyone would be happy with, bank that option and move on.

VII. **Decide where you would like to live:** It will be beneficial if you can be flexible about where you would all be happy to live. Plot prices (_and therefore full build prices_) vary hugely from area to area, so the more flexibility you give yourselves, the more likely you are to find a suitable plot, at the right price. Compile a short list of maybe 3 or 4 suitable areas and stick with those, at least to start with. If you can't find what you are looking for within a reasonable time, widen your search parameters.

VIII. **Stick to your original plan where you can:** Proceed on the basis that, if your initial plan seems to be working, stick with it and only change to "Plan B" if you have to.

**Important note:**
**You should not go past this point in the process until you are confident that the project is viable and affordable.**
**You should be able to get here without spending a lot of money.**
**If everything looks good up to now, your *next step* would be to go and speak to funders and house designers.**

## THING 13: **COULD WE BUILD IT OURSELVES?**

**No. - Please go to the next section!**

Ok, I am joking (well *sort of*).

Back in the seventies, eighties, and probably up to the early 2000's, most mortgage lenders allowed self-builders to physically build their own homes, using a standard self-build mortgage to fund the build, *even if* they had no previous personal experience of anything related to house building. Many of these projects, predictably went pear shaped, and ultimately failed. But the practice continued for many years.

Then came the recession, and the whole housing market pretty much dried up completely. Self-build mortgages almost disappeared from the market and when we came out of the recession, lenders were so nervous about losing money, that (*pushed to some extent by the Government*) they dramatically tightened the qualifying requirements for self-build mortgages. At that time, I remember the availability of these types of mortgages reducing to literally and handful, maybe 10 or so, down from what had been around 200 mortgage products prior to the recession.

So, as things panned out, the big change after the recession was that lenders decided that they needed self-builders to be a lot more professional. To achieve that goal, anyone applying for funding had to prove that they would be able to manage the project competently and professionally, before they would be offered a mortgage.

This meant that qualifications that might have been accepted a couple of years previously, such as someone having built and wired up a garden shed, or fitted a kitchen, were not now acceptable as proof of competence, and an application from someone who simply "*speaks like they know what they are talking about*", from the recession onwards, would now be rejected out of hand (*and yes, it really was that easy in the old days!*).

So, the answer I gave at the top of this section to the question: *"Could we build it ourselves?"* is, thankfully, 90% of the time **NO!**

However, there are exceptions. If for example, you are a fully qualified tradesperson or general builder, whose job is building extensions and houses, then, as long as you have all the necessary training, first aid and safety certificates that you should have, and if your finances stand up to scrutiny, you will stand a good chance of being accepted for a *hands on based* self-build mortgage. The rest of us mere mortals, whether we like it or not, now have to hand most of the process over to professionals.

**(That was the reality check, now for a bit of better news)**

Once you have set the project up professionally, there *are* things you can still do yourselves, such as:

- Keeping the site clean and safe.
- General labouring (*you can cut the cost of some of the trades by, for example loading out the blocks and bricks, loading out the building with floorboards, plasterboards etc*).
- Fitting the insulation into external and internal walls (*a major task these days*).
- Fitting timber strengthening pads (*pattresses*) to the walls, for all the different electrical and plumbing fittings that will be fitted later.
- Fixing vapour barrier to timber frames.
- Painting the render (*only needed if you use traditional sand and cement renders, not the modern self-coloured renders*).
- Fitting skirtings, architraves, and doors (*don't do this unless you have experience and are fully competent*).
- Fitting window boards (*cills*).
- Fitting boxing ins (*there are usually a number of these needed, to hide exposed pipes*). Again, a certain level of skill / experience is required here.
- Decorating.
- Wall tiling (skill needed).
- Floor tiling (skill needed).
- Kitchen fitting (*don't try this unless you have some knowledge and previous experience of the correct ways to fit all the different parts, including scribing the worktops*).
- Carpeting / laminate flooring etc (skill again!).
- Gravel footpaths around the house.
- Patios / decking (strong back needed!).
- Landscaping.
- Fencing.

There has always been a natural tendency for people who take on self-build projects to want to get physically involved with the building work. I honestly think that limiting the amount of work the self-builder can do without being qualified, is a far better, safer, and more practical way to set things up.

**Authors note:** From this point onwards, we are starting to move away from the theoretical aspects of the project, and beginning to make decisions that you will be sticking with for the rest of the job. These decisions could therefore have major consequences for the future of the project, as well as your own future.

------------------------------------------------------------------------------

## THING 14: BE FLEXIBLE WITH YOUR PLOT AND ITS LOCATION

*(I touched on this topic in Section 12, here, I will go into more detail).*

Up to now we have been pondering over and tinkering with some general principles, thoughts, and ideas about *"plots, houses and other stuff"*. Now we are going to start to formulate a plan the whole thing **for real**.

*(Don't panic, you can still dump everything you are going to decide over the coming sections, and start again, but, unless you do that, you will now be drawing up a road map / plan of action that, should you decide to go ahead with the project, could be what guides you and dictates your actions from now on).*

Your first big decision to be transferred from the *general thoughts' category,* to becoming *a final decision*, is:

### Where are we going to live?
*(This decision is HUGE!)*

Where you decide to build your new home will have an impact on just about *every* aspect of the future lives of you and your family. As you start to investigate different areas and plots, you should therefore seriously consider:

- Would you be allowed to build the house that you want to build in that location?
- Would you be able to use the materials that you want to use on the external walls?
- Could there be further development around you, spoiling your views?
- What is the access like?
- What are the ground conditions like?
- Would the plot require special foundations?
- Where are the nearest service connections (*drainage, gas, electricity, water, BT*)?
- Is the plot in a designated flood area, or could it be in a few years?
- Is there Himalayan Balsam or Knotweed anywhere locally, or even on the site (*see later for more details*)?
- How much parking space would there be?
- Would there be extra parking close by for visitors if you needed it?
- Could there be local problems that you might not be aware of yet?
- What are the *surrounding* areas / neighbourhoods like?

- What are the neighbours like?
- Are the surrounding areas generally safe for children?
- Are you near schools, shops, sports facilities etc?
- What are the schools like?
- Would you be near work?
- How much would a decent plot cost?
- How big a plot do you need?
- What would the completed value of your home be? And would that value make it worthwhile building?

I'll stop there and pick up on that last point.

The price you pay for your plot, how much it will cost to build the house that you want, and what the property will be worth once it is complete, are all parts of an important equation that you need to try to get to grips with _before_ you part with any money (_see section 12_).

We have previously worked out roughly how big the house could be, and approximately how much it could cost to build. Those figures then gave you a maximum price that you should pay for your plot. That bring us to the point where it can get a bit complicated.

Land is expensive, pretty much wherever you go. If the land is not expensive, then the property values are normally roughly proportional to the land price.

If you were to find a very cheap plot of land and go to a lender for funds, you could be turned down due to the fact that they will look at the completed value, the land cost and the likely build cost before they decide whether or not to lend.

You tend to find that the cost / value of the land has an out of proportion effect on the end value of the property, in this respect:

**The more you spend on the land, the better chance you have of making a decent profit.**

**Examples:**

i)      If the land costs £80,000, the build costs around £200,000 and the end value on completion would be around £250,000, no-one is going to lend you any money for that project. Why? You would have spent **£280,000,** to get **£250,000** worth of house.

ii)     If you paid £130,000 (_an extra £50,000_) for the land and £150,000 (£50,000 less) for the build (_possibly the same design of house, but at a lower finishing spec_) and the end value was £300,000, you would still have paid out **£280,000** in total, but now you would have **£300,000** worth of house.

In the second example, because of the higher land value, a lower spec house built on it, was worth £50,000 more on completion, for the same _overall_ financial outlay.

That example is a simplistic way of looking at the equation, and in reality there are many more factors that come into play, but before you make a decision to buy a plot of land, this is an equation you should try to calculate.

That *single point* that I have just considered is just *one* from the list of 21 (*above*), which itself is only a partial list of the things that you might need to consider when buying your plot.

*By the time you finish reading this book (maybe a couple of times), hopefully you will have a clear picture in your mind of how the whole equation works, and will be able to use that knowledge to your advantage.*

## THING 15: FINDING A GOOD PLOT AT THE RIGHT PRICE

Finding a good quality plot of land, that won't be expensive to build on, but that will maximise the end value of the house, is not an easy equation to make work, especially if you live in the South East (*or a number of other areas across the UK*).

Where I live, in Wales it is not too bad for land prices, but overall, since well before the 2009 recession, building land has been overpriced. The reasons? 1) There is not much of it available and 2) A lot of people would like to build their own home, so often have to compete financially, for the few bits of land that are available.

The results of the demand, and the consequential cost increases is that the self-build cost equation that worked in the eighties and nineties, of: *33% for the land / 33% for the build / 33% for profit*, went out of the window a long time ago. I am pretty sure, never to return.

So, like it or not, most self-builders are simply stuck with having to pay a lot of money for their land. However, there is hope!

I have come across (*or pinched would be a better word*) a trick that you might like to have a think about using. It can potentially get you a decent plot of land at a decent price. It will usually involve quite a bit of work and patience, but it can be successful.

**This is how it works:**

- **First, you choose an area where you would like to live.** The wider the area of choice, the more chance you will have of finding something suitable, at the right price.
- **Next, go online** and find your way to the section of the Government's Planning Portal that deals with the geographical areas where you would consider living (*type "Planning Portal / your chosen location"*) .
- **Work your way through the system to the "New Planning Applications".** All new planning applications, for everything from a signboard to a housing estate, in the area you choose, are all listed together in this database.

- **Spend as long as you (sensibly) can going through that database.** Look at all the planning applications for land, new homes, and even conversions / renovations, going as far back as your available time allows. With a bit of luck, what you will find hidden away, will be applications for (for example) *"4 Bedroomed Detached Property"*, or *"Single building plot"*.
- **Open the file:** When you come across these applications, you should be able to go into the file and see the full details, including the full address, contact details of whoever has made the application, what the application includes, when it was lodged, who is dealing with it, etc. Make notes from the files, on anything that interests you.
- **Using those notes, you can usually then contact the applicant / owner / agent** (*depending on how much information they have included in the application*). Once you contact someone, you can ask if they would be interested in selling the plot, on the basis that they are successful at achieving Planning Permission.

This is a system that is used all the time in the commercial building industry. There are housing development companies large and small, who pay research companies to gather the information from planning applications across the country and send it to them each week or month. They then do *exactly* what I have just suggested that you do, either on a small or large scale. *You can simply cut out the middleman by doing it yourself.*

The beauty of this system is that you, as a self-builder (*as opposed to a commercial builder*), would probably be happy to pay a significantly more generous price for the plot than a commercial builder (*who would always be looking to make a decent profit*), whilst possibly still paying well under its full market value.

**This system can also be used for multiple plots:**

If you happen to find a planning application on land that you like the look of, which is for multiple houses, by considering *buying in bulk*, the individual price per plot could work out to be significantly lower than the market value of one similar *individual* plot.

How could you buy in bulk? You would need to find other people to join with you to purchase the whole parcel of land (*by putting ads online or in the local press to find other potential self-builders in the area*), or you could consider seeing if the owner would enter into an *"Option Agreement"* with you (*see next section*).

## THING 16: **WHAT IS AN OPTION AGREEMENT?**

If someone owns a piece of land, whether it is for one house or many, and they want to sell it, an option agreement is one of the options available to them.

The normal way of buying a plot of land is by:

*Offer / acceptance / legal and financial process / sale.*

We are all used to using that system for buying houses and it is pretty much the same when you buy land. But how about if you own some land that doesn't have Planning Permission, that you would like to sell? And let's say you haven't got the time, or cash available to be able to take it through the planning application process yourself? An option agreement is one way you could choose to go.

Or, what if you had land *with* Planning Permission for multiple plots, and you wanted to sell it, but would need to get all the services installed and spend a lot of time and money sorting out all the legal aspects before you could do so. And what if you couldn't afford to do that yourselves. - *Option agreement to the rescue again!*

As I write this book, I am also working on getting a project started using an Option Agreement. So, rather than trying to explain the theoretical logistics of how it all works, I will summarise this real life case:

A few years ago, we were looking to start one or two small new housing developments. I found a nice parcel of land which had previously (*before the recession*), had Planning Permission for 4 detached houses, which had now lapsed. The land was owned jointly by 3 people.

We liked the land, the plots were spacious and the land itself
was gently sloping in the right direction for natural drainage. There were open fields to the rear, it was near to a motorway junction, but in a quiet area, with schools nearby. I could see good potential in it, but it was basically at the time just a field, overgrown in places, and with no services or entrance drive into it.

The land was up for sale as a *job lot*, without Planning Permission. That would mean that whoever bought it as it stood, would have to apply for and achieve a new Planning Permission before they could develop it, and they would therefore be taking a financial risk by buying it. If an application failed, they would have just bought a very expensive paddock!

I approached the owners and made an offer:

We would pay them £X for each plot if they would enter in to a three year option agreement with us. We would then pay all the costs to re-apply for the Planning Permission. If we were successful, we would then market the land as individual plots, as part of a "Custom Built New Homes" package, to the general public.

We would only pay for each plot as it was sold (*or if we had the cash available to buy it, and wanted to do so*). We would pay for the shared driveway construction and all the service connections etc after buying the first plot.

The price we offered per plot was slightly higher than the price it was being market as multiple plots, but much lower than each plot would be worth if sold individually, with Planning Permission and services installed. We would only have to pay for each plot as we sold it to a client (*so we would use their purchase funds to pay for the plot and have some left to start the build*). We would then realise our full profit on each house, as it was completed.

Our risks on this deal were 1) Losing the costs of re-applying for Planning Permission, if the application failed, and 2) Losing whatever we paid for the legal fees, if the application failed. The potential benefits were that we could eventually build 4 houses on the land, and make 4 profits by doing so, without needing to have a large sum of cash available to pay for the land upfront.

The sellers agreed to sell, using the proposed system. The Option Agreement was set up in a few months and we *did* manage to obtain the new Planning Permission. (*As I am writing this book, we are marketing the plots as "New Custom Finished Homes"*).

**So, how could this system work for you?**

1) If you find land without Planning Permission, but which you think might achieve it, an Option Agreement could enable you to *reserve* the plot (*probably at a low price*) until you found out whether or not the application would be successful, without you having to buy it upfront. The most you could lose would be the costs associated with applying for the Planning Permission, and your time.

2) If you found land for multiple plots, you could use the same system that we used to set up our latest site, then advertise locally, to find other people to join you in the venture (*of course, if you had the cash available to buy all the land, you could build one plot for yourselves and sell the other plots at full market value*).


# THING 17: **WHAT TO LOOK FOR IN A BUILDING PLOT**

The total cost of building a house can be split into four main areas of expenditure:

1) Everything related to the plot, the services, and the drainage.
2) Everything related to Planning Permission & Building Regulations.
3) Everything involved with foundations and slab.
4) The rest of the job.

Your choice of plot will determine the likely costs related to the first three of those cost centres, so making sure that you do your homework and don't end up buying *a lemon* is of critical importance to the whole project.

**How do you choose the right plot?**

One of the biggest problems that faces every builder is to try to guess upfront, what will be found once we start investigating a plot, its history and, even more difficult to predict is what will be found once you have cleared the site and start to *dig holes*.

The only way you can at least *try* to minimise risk of extra expense once you start work, is to know what problems to look for at the outset, and to learn as much as you can about the land itself.

The following inherent criteria are important to include in your investigations when you assess potential building plots:

- Level or sloping ground?
- Previously undeveloped?
- Good geological properties (a good load bearing strata)? Trial holes should be excavated, and samples taken and tested from any potential dubious ground.
- Good natural drainage.
- Not near a surface water course (*100m+ away, or possibly less if the water course is significantly lower than the plot*).
- No underground water courses running across it, or close by.
- No overhead cables nearby or running across the site.
- No large (*especially TPO'd*) trees on, or close to where you would want to situate the house (*TPO = Tree Preservation Order. - In other words, the tree is protected. – Keep away!*)
- All services close by.
- Mains drainage close by.
- Good, fairly level entrance access (*for bringing materials in*).

There are other *not related* to the physical properties of the plot, that will also influence your final choice of plot, such as:

- Location of Schools.
- Restrictions on the position of the house on the plot.
- Size or layout restrictions on the house design.
- Height restrictions on the house.
- Restrictions on materials used for appearance.
- Restrictions on building caused by bats, foxes, badgers, butterflies, or other protected species.
- Affordable Homes planning conditions (*you will usually have to contribute to affordable housing, as part of your planning application*).

**The plot needs to be purchased at the right price, taking in to account all those criteria**.

**Additionally:** You also need to make sure the plot has enough time left on the Planning Permission, to allow you to get through what could be a protracted planning application period. (*they say it should take 8 weeks to process a planning application. In 99% of cases, they lie!*)

*So, when you start looking for your ideal plot, don't just consider its location, how attractive it is, what the views are like, and all the other surface considerations. To avoid buying that "lemon" of a plot, you need to give serious attention to investigating all of the potential inbuilt physical, legal, and financial traps that could be hiding just round the corner (or just as importantly, **under the ground**).*

## THING 18: SERVICES / DRAINAGE CONNECTIONS

Working out how you are going to organise your service and drainage connections is one of the tasks that needs to be given attention well before work starts on site. That doesn't mean that you actually need to connect everything before you start, but you need to carefully think through the build process, in order to work out when you are going to need: 1) Running water, 2) An electricity supply, 3) A working drainage system 4) Gas connection 5) Telecoms connection.

The first three of those (*water / electricity supply / drainage*) may be required at the start of, or during the building works. The other two are not normally needed until towards the end of the project.

Organising the service connections are one of the jobs that can easily be overlooked during the planning phase. At that stage, you tend to be concentrating more on Planning Permissions, mortgages, Building Regulations, Warranties, Insurances, finding subbies, and planning the start date for the work.

In your cost estimates, you will allow money for the services, and for making the connections, but then that particular part of the project will often be forgotten in the rush to get, what seem to be the most important things organised. However, one day, as you continue to concentrate on all those other tasks, the subject of service connections will raise its head, and you'll suddenly think to yourself, *"Oh, b\*\*ger, I forgot about all that, I'd better get it sorted fast"*.

The two main factors you need to consider when programming in the service connections are:

1. **Where are the incoming services and drainage runs, related to the build, and how could their location affect the job?** You might have unknowingly planned to build your house right over where the new drains need to run, or the existing drains do run. Or, the nearest mains drainage connection could be 100m away from the site. You might not have even realised that there is no mains gas supply to the plot (*ok, I am being a bit of a devil's advocate a bit here, but you see what I mean*). You need to gather all the information you can on where everything is, as early as possible in the project planning phase. That way, you can make informed decisions on how and when to get everything connected up.

2. **Will you need a water and / or electricity supply, or mains drainage for the building work?** There are ways to set up the site so that you don't need either water or electricity. You can:

- Hire site cabins with built in generators to run their electrics, power a water supply pump to feed the sink and provide heat for the cabin itself.
- Hire other generators to provide power for the site works.
- Hire a water bowser and get it refilled as required, during the works

However, if you are going to be living on the site in a caravan, or don't want to pay out for hiring generators, you will need to think about, and plan for getting at least the water and electric connections made, as one of the first jobs you do on site.

**Water:** You can request temporary services for both water and electricity. For water, you will excavate a trench (*where the permanent trench will be if possible*), then lay the permanent pipework in the trench and get the water connection made at the site boundary. At the same time, choose a suitable location somewhere along the trench, to construct a *lockable* timber or brick housing for a temporary stop tap, which will then provide for your temporary water requirements while you build.

Once you get to the point at which you need the house to be permanently connected, you will cut off the temporary supply, extend the pipework to the house and connect it to the internal plumbing system.

**Electricity:** Similar to the temporary water supply, you will excavate the service trench (*this can be the same trench as the water, but the pipes go in at different depths*), choose a suitable location, and build a lockable electricity box, into which a temporary meter is fitted, along with 120v power outlets (*you cannot use 240v power on a building site*). Extension cable are then used to supply power to where you need it on the site. Again, when it is time to make the permanent connection, the meter is disconnected, extended to the house, and connected to the permanent meter.

**Drainage:** If you are going to be living on site, you may need to make a temporary connection into a mains foul drainage system. As with the electricity and water, you would need to make the temporary connection to wherever you need it whilst you build, then at the appropriate time, cut that facility off and re-route the pipework to suit the permanent, approved drainage design.

**What services do you have and where are they?** To find out where all the services routes and drainage runs are, relative to your plot, you can contact the various suppliers individually, tell them what you are proposing and where you are, and then follow their procedures to access the records you need to.

You can also use companies such as *"National One Call"* who can do everything for you in one hit (https://www.national-one-call.co.uk/). There will be a charge for this service, but it could save you a lot of time and messing around.

**Note:** A very important job that needs doing as early as possible in your planning phase is to find out the *"invert level"* of the main drain into which you will connect your new system (*in other words, what is the depth of the existing drain?*). The level at which you will build your house will be partly dictated by the ground floor slab having to be high enough above the main drainage connection, to give the required fall from the house to the connection.

You will need to take a level survey on the invert levels (*the levels of the bottom of the drainage pipe*), of the existing manholes *either side* of the point where you will need to connect your own drainage system to the main system. You (*or your Surveyor / Groundworker / Site Engineer*) can then *interpolate* (work out) the readings, to ascertain the invert level at the point where you will need to connect. From that calculation (*using the Building Regulations figures for "required falls for mains drainage"*), you can work out the level that you will need to set the ground floor slab of the house at.

*(Don't worry if that all sound complicated, there is a good chance that you probably won't be involved in that job, but it is handy to know what needs to happen and how to do it, just in case)*

Give this subject some thought early on in your planning process, so that you can make appropriate decisions as to how and when you will plan in all the various connections.

Doing so will help you to avoid that *"Oh b\*\*gger"* moment later on.


## THING 19: ONLY BUY A PLOT IF YOU CAN BUILD WHAT YOU WANT ON IT

If there is one situation you need to keep as far away from as possible, it is having to deal with a stubborn Planning Department, to either apply for a new Planning Permission, or change existing permissions to suit your own ideas, before you get to start work on your project. Pretty much the worst case scenario, is for any self-builder to buy a plot of land that doesn't already have some form of planning approval for new housing, that would allow them to start work as soon as they are ready.

I have met people (*thankfully not many, but more than there should be*), who have bought land that doesn't have any form of Planning Permission when they buy it. Someone might have told them that it *"should get it, no problem"*, or they are persuaded to part with their cash simply because *"We think it will get planning, and it is cheap"*.

If you are a planning specialist who wants to become a self-builder, you are possibly in the best position to take a punt on buying land without it already having suitable Planning Permission, but even if you are, the risk is still high that you could lose your investment.

So, bearing that in mind, there are three rules that I suggest you follow when it comes to buying land:

1) **DO NOT buy land that does not already have Planning Permission (*Option Agreements are ok though*).**

   Not many sellers would try to pull off this scam. They would realise that people who are in the position to be able to buy land, will be intelligent enough not to get caught out.

   The fact is that only a fool would sell a piece of land that *could get* Planning Permission, without trying to get it, and increase its value by up to a factor or 10 when they do so.

   Another fact is that, only someone who doesn't understand how the planning system works would buy a plot of land that doesn't already have Planning Permission, simply hoping it would be able to achieve it.

   **Here is an example of someone trying to sell me some land that didn't have Planning Permission:** When I was in my twenties, and still new to all this land buying and house building malarkey, I was offered a field, for £5000. I was told that it had Planning Permission for (*as I remember*) 15 houses. £5000 then is probably equivalent to £100,000 now. It was a stupidly low price even then, but being a bit green, I was initially tempted.

   We didn't have the internet in those days, and I couldn't afford to carry out extensive legal investigations, so instead, I visited the local Planning Office and searched the records, to see if the land did indeed have planning approval. Of course, it did not. When I broached the person trying to sell it, he made up an excuse, saying that he was selling it for a friend who had told him that it had planning. Anyway, luckily, I didn't fall for it.

   *Think about it:*

   i.  Coming up to date: If you were to ask a farmer if you could buy a field from him to keep a horse in, he would charge you maybe £5,000, maybe £10,000? (*I really have no idea to be honest, but I don't think it would be a lot*).

   ii. If you were to try to buy that same field with Planning Permission for 10 houses on it, what would you pay for it? No-one in their right mind would sell it significantly under its realistic value. They may sell it cheap if they needed the money, but even then, maybe asking £1,000,000 instead of £1,200,000 (*or a lot more depending on where it was situated*).

   So, if anyone ever tries to sell you a piece of land for way below the price that it you would have thought it should be sold for, and they can't fully prove that it has a valid Planning Permission, tell them to go take a hike!

2) **DO NOT buy land that has Outline Planning Permission for residential construction, without first looking closely at all the conditions attached.**

This scenario is a bit different from the previous one. This land has Outline Planning Permission, which means it can have *something* (*in this case a house*) built on it, but many of the details still need to be approved. The problem with this situation is that, until you check through all the conditions, you won't know:

I.    Whether the Outline Planning is for the type of building that you want to build.

II.   How much time is left on the Planning Permission before it lapses, or if there will be enough time to prepare your application and submit it before the existing permission runs out.

III.  Whether there are any other onerous restrictions on the land.

*Make sure you always do full due diligence before you commit yourselves to anything, especially if the land is for sale at a low price*

3) **As with the previous point, DO NOT buy land that has Full or Reserved Matters Planning Permission, without first checking the conditions attached to it.**

Be aware that Reserved Matter and Full Planning Permission are a lot more specific than Outline Planning. Where Outline Planning says: "*Something along these lines can be built here*", Reserved and Full Planning says: "***This** particular building can be built here*".

A Reserved / Full approval document will normally include detailed drawings of the property and the site plans, showing the position and size of any buildings along with a lot of other details. If you want to change anything significantly from what is detailed in the approval doc, you may have to go through the whole planning process again, and you could potentially be turned down, resulting in you either having to build what is already approved, or sell the land to someone else.

## THING 20: MADE UP GROUND & GROUND SURVEYS

It is now getting harder to find building land that has never been anything other than *open ground* or *field*, especially in the South East. If land hasn't already had a building of some form or other on it, it will often have had some other sort of use, possibly commercial, resulting in some form of contamination. Maybe as refuse tip, or it may have previously been excavated and then backfilled with loose earth, or even worse, fill from somewhere else, with no recorded history. Land with this sort of history could be a nightmare to develop.

House foundations need to have strong, solid ground directly underneath them, that can easily cope with supporting whatever is built on them, without even settling as little as half an inch. Just *half an inch* of underground settlement could result in the foundations cracking, and the walls that are sitting on them also settling, causing horizontal or vertical cracking above ground. **This is NOT a good thing!**

Depending on how severe, or widespread the settlement is, it could result in your house being almost worthless, or slightly less dramatic, but still not very nice, could cost you tens of thousands of pounds to rectify.

Before you purchase any building plot, make sure you investigate its history, and geological makeup. To do this properly, you really need to carry out a ground investigation, for which you would possibly need to hire a local ground investigation company. You would also need to get permission from the owners, for the investigators to gain access to the site to excavate some trial holes.

There are different types of ground surveys that can be carried out, and they vary in their levels of intrusiveness. Starting with a low key investigation, which can comprise a number of small boreholes being dug or drilled, using a spade or a small *auger* tool. Samples of the ground are taken and analysed at a laboratory and you would be sent a report and the results a week or two later.

A more dramatic type of ground investigation would involve hiring an excavator for a day, to excavate some larger trial holes. These excavations should not be where the foundations could eventually sit, as the holes will be creating their own little areas of made up ground, which you need to avoid. The holes should be close to the area where the building will be situated (*but not less than around 5ft – 6ft away*). The investigators will know where to excavate and will usually take samples from the digs. They will test the samples and you will then get a written report.

**What do the reports try to establish?** All these types of investigation set out to establish the physical and chemical makeup of the ground, and to ascertain what type of foundation would be suitable to take the building that the client hopes to build.

The reports are, however, not infallible. It could be that the trial holes completely miss a troublesome area of the site, or they don't go quite deep enough to find a layer of ground that could cause a problem.

Before they arrange to come to site, the investigators will often carry out a desktop Survey. They will usually have on file, records of ground strata from across the UK, and from that information they can often work out whether or not a full site survey is even necessary. If they don't think you need the site investigation, you might only need to pay for the desk survey, which, on its own, should satisfy whoever needs to see it (*Lenders, Planners, Warranty providers, Building Regs etc*).

**A couple of other possible options:**

I.     The owner may have already done a survey of some type, and may be willing to give, or sell it to you. This is fine, but the survey may not be to a high standard, and you may not feel 100% happy that it will be sufficient for the purpose you need it for. If so, get your own survey done.

II.    If the ground is expected to be good, you could ask if you can carry out *your own* survey. If the owner agrees, you, yourself could bring a groundworker and excavator in for a couple of hours, to dig some trial holes. An experienced local groundworker will often know what the quality of the ground is likely to be in the local area. They will also recognise good or bad ground as soon as they excavate, so they will tell you whether or not they think there are any problems.

Take some photos of the excavation and keep them in case you do buy the land and need them to send to the Building Inspector at a later date.

*The condition, make-up, and nature of the ground are very important aspects of any self-build project. Making sure, one way or another, that everything is as it needs to be, should not be an operation that is skimped, just to try to save a bit of money.*

*Your ground investigation, in whatever form it takes, should furnish you with the best information you can get, to help you decide either to buy the land, or walk away.*


## THING 21: **WHAT PROBLEMS DO SLOPING SITES PRESENT?**

I live in Wales. Finding a flat building plot in Wales is not an easy thing to do. Round here, we don't ask *"Does it slope?"*, We ask *"How much does it slope?"* On the other hand, 30 years ago, I lived in Cheshire, and we had the Cheshire Plain (*flat as a pancake*).

So, although I love living in South Wales, when it comes to building houses, living here tends to introduce some complicated and often expensive aspects to any new build project. Developers are used to it and know how to deal with it, but new self-builders can get caught out.

So, wherever you live, how do you deal with sloping plots and what challenges do they present?

My first advice would be to get a *site level and geographical survey* carried out as soon as possible, possibly soon after you make an offer for the plot. That leaves you time to find any inherent problems before you hand any money over.

You could hire a Land Surveying company to carry out this, which should cost you between £200 and £500, depending on its complexity. A Site Surveyor would come to site to carry out the survey, recording features and land levels, which are then plotted on to a drawing, copies of which are sent to you to use as you wish.

Before you decide on the ground floor level for the house on a sloping site, you need to make sure that the new drainage will be able to flow at the required gradients and that the driveway gradient also conforms to regs. The obvious level for the ground floor slab, to suit those two considerations, may mean that you end up reducing the level of part of the plot that may be too high, and/or building up another part of the site that may be too low.

Trying to get all these different parts of the equation to work together can get a bit complicated, and may result in the house not being positioned quite where you originally wanted it to be, or you not being able to get the perfect view that you had hoped to make the most of.

You don't need to get involved in working out how the problems caused by the slopes, will be solved. If you have the level survey, using that and their own skills, your house designer should be able to take care of everything, simply checking that you are happy with their solutions before adding the details to the Building Regulation drawings.

**Here are a few other aspects of the job that sloping sites could affect:**

1. Ground floor levels will need to take into account any potential overlooking of neighbour's properties.
2. Retaining walls may be needed to hold up steep parts of the plot. These can be expensive to construct.
3. Where possible, you should try and avoid rainwater running down slopes, towards the house. If this is unavoidable, you will have to install drainage channels around the house to intercept the flow, and divert it to the surface water drainage system or soakaways.
4. Soil or lawns that slope down towards the rear of a retaining wall will require the retaining wall to have land drainage installed behind it, and possibly *through* it. This may be required to avoid the possibility of the weight of water building up behind the wall, potentially causing damage to it (*trying to push it over*).
5. Bad landscaping design, with poorly calculated sloping areas, could cause boggy areas in the garden, which can be very annoying, especially if they are in the lawned areas
6. Gravel is a good material to help garden drainage.
7. Soakaways are a good tool to take excess water from potentially boggy areas, store it and then let it dissipate into the surrounding area, over time.

*OK, that was section was a bit complicated, but don't worry if you don't think you could understand or coordinate all those complicated factors, just do what most people do and pay the professionals to do all the hard bits. You will have plenty of other important things to do.*

## THING 22: **GET QUOTES FOR SERVICES ASAP**

Nearly everything below slab level is difficult to estimate prices for, until you start work and begin excavating for the foundations. No matter how much research you do and how many surveys you carry out, you really can't be sure what problems you are going to come across. You could pay the best Quantity Surveyor to prepare all of your cost estimates, and they would still have to add disclaimers like: "*Subject to remeasure on completion*" and "*based on information available*" because, as good as they are at their jobs, they will basically be guessing a lot of the prices, for a lot of the works underground. That is just a fact. We all do our best, but at the end of the day this is how it is with groundworks.

On the more positive side, there is one small part of the groundworks section of the job that you can get, at least *partly* fixed prices for: The services. You might not be able to accurately estimate the cost of excavating the service trenches, but you *can* get fixed quotes for the connections themselves.

One worthwhile exercise for you to carry out early on, when you are compiling your initial cost estimates, is to apply for quotes for all the service connections. Here are two good reasons why:

1.  Standard service installations have become a lot more expensive over the past few years, and the costs can vary significantly from site to site. It is therefore difficult to estimate how much the connection quote will be for any of the main service providers, except, for BT (*which is usually free*), so don't even try. Simply by filling in an online application form in, you will be able to get a fixed quote within a few days (*which last at least 3 months and shouldn't change significantly if a requote is necessary*). Getting quotes for the gas, water and electricity will take away the guesswork and help you to estimate the *full build costs* more accurately.

2.  One of the big problems with services is that they are not necessarily all going to be ideally placed at the end of your driveway. They could be 50m or more away and require a footpath to be taken up, and a trench excavated from their present location, to your driveway before the connection can be made. Or, there could already be too many other existing cables, ducts, and pipes at the location where yours should be made, resulting in your connection being re-routed from a different source point somewhere else. On my most recent project the footpath was so full of existing service cables and pipes, that there was physically no room to get even small excavating tools between them without risking damaging them. Our supply therefore had to be re-routed, taking an extra 3 days to do the work. There was no extra charge

So, by taking a couple of hours early on, to fill in three application forms, you could get rid of a potential messy and tricky job and get some definite build costs for your spreadsheet. This would not only help you to plan better financially, you will also impress the mortgage lenders with your professional approach.

# THING 23: PREPARING ACCURATE / FLEXIBLE COST ESTIMATES

Any professional business plan needs to include a realistic financial plan, which should contain reasonable contingency allowances to cover unexpected or overlooked costs.

A Self-Build is, by definition an amateur project, but the way that the financial planning is approached should be no different to how it is done on a multi-million pound development: Sensibly, professionally, and as accurately as possible.

Ok, nice idea, but the slight problem with this fact that a self-build project is not usually a multi-million pound development, and it doesn't have professional Estimators and Quantity Surveyors on hand, who will work for weeks or months to prepare the cost estimates. It will most likely be just you and/or your partner who takes on that task, doing your best, getting as many prices on labour and materials as you can, reading reference books and other relevant *pricing related* information, trying to come up with something that, when you send it to a potential mortgage lender, as part of your mortgage application, the lender will think: *"Fair play, this application has been professionally produced, the figures look about right, and everything appears to be within our lending guidelines. Give these folks their money!"*.

However, no matter how well a building project is planned financially, one thing is almost guaranteed: *The estimate will miss some items, things will go wrong on site, and putting those things right will cost extra money.*

The problems could be underground, or could be caused by bad weather, mistakes made by you or anyone on site, breakages, accidents, price rises, changes of mind, theft, or any of a hundred other reasons. But be assured, some things **will** go pear shaped on the cost front.

So, taking that into account, plus the fact that you are probably not professionals at this type of work, and that you could even be get things wrong on some of the easy parts of the costing, *it is not just common sense* to make sure you spend adequate time preparing the estimates, and that you allow enough of a contingency sum. **It is vital.**

The best way for you to approach the price estimating process is:

> Do your best to get the pricing right first time, but to try to make sure that you don't catch a cold later in the project, add around 10% - 15% for "what if's" to each price.

> Then, if you think your borrowing limits will stand the strain, or if you could get it, if required, somewhere else, add *another* 10% to the final total as a *"pull the red chord"* emergency fund (*if you don't need it, you won't have to borrow it, so everyone will be happy*).

This might seem a slightly odd, inaccurate, and possibly unprofessional way of approaching the task, but if you have watched any of the TV house building programmes, how many of them, despite all their planning and preparing, ever keep within their budgets? I can't remember seeing even one.

The main reasons for most self-builds going over the original target spending figures are that, although we are all intelligent people, and are very keen to get it right, we are all amateurs. We also tend to be optimists (*which is something we need to be, just to even think about taking a project on in the first place*). We tend to look on the bright side, telling ourselves: "*That should be plenty of allowance for the scaffolding hire, we should have it up and down within 10 weeks*", only for it to rain every day for the next 3 months, adding another couple of thousand pounds to the scaffolding bill.

If you agree with what I have said here and if you make those sensible allowances within your initial cost estimates, who knows, you may become one of the first of a whole new breed of *super self-builders* whose projects don't eat through their budgets well before the job is finished.

*Then, one day, the viewers of the TV shows might even have good reason to think that we might actually know what we are doing!*

**<u>Seriously though: This is important!</u>**

## THING 24: REFURBISHING AN OLD BUILDING v KNOCKING IT DOWN AND BUILDING NEW

If you live in an area where good quality building land is expensive and/or scarce, possibly in the South East, parts of Cornwall, or various other sought after places, you may be keen to take on your own self-build, but find yourself being stymied by the fact that you simply can't find a decent plot of land that you can afford, in the areas where you would like to live.

In these circumstances, many self-builders turn to the option of buying an old house that may be derelict, or might just be outdated and not in particularly good order. They then have to decide between renovating the existing house, or knocking it down and building a new one. At that point they usually need to get some advice, and that is when I usually get to see them at the self-build shows.

At those meetings, the first thing they usually want to do, is to show me photos of the existing house, and some of their own sketches visualising what they think they could do with it. In the South East especially, these properties, even though they are derelict, or need a lot of work, can still be very highly priced. In some areas, even ramshackle shells of old houses can be sitting on very valuable plots.

After I have been shown the photos and sketches, my guests then generally want to hear my thoughts on their ideas, and what I think would be their best option between renovating and starting again.

The first thing I do is ask them what the asking price of the property is, whether they think they could get the price any lower, how happy are they with their own sketch designs for adapting the existing house?

The answer is almost always, whilst casting a despondent look at each other, before they say: *"Well it's not perfect, but if it is the best option, it would be ok, and we are not sure if we would get planning for a re-build"*.

So, here I have, sat in front of me, people who are so desperate to be able to do their own house build or renovation project, that, if there was no other practical or affordable option, they would be prepared to accept (*basically*) sprucing up an old wreck of a house, in order to to try to get something as near to what they really wanted, as possible.

I can't remember any time when my response has been *"Just do it up, I am sure it will be fine"*. My immediate response is always *"If you can get Planning Permission, if you are not in a hurry, and if you can afford to, I suggest you apply for planning to knock it down, and start again"*.

Why am I so definite about my response? Because, if you think about it, if <u>you</u> were to ask yourself:

*"Why am I seriously considering going through all the effort, stress and upheaval to take on a self-build project?"*

I bet your answer would almost certainly be something along the lines of:

*"So that we can live in house that is exactly what we want, built the way we want it to be built, with the rooms, the fittings, the garden and everything else just how we want them all to be"*.

**No matter how much you spend, or how hard you work, doing up an old shell of a house *will not* give you that result.**

What I normally end up advising these people to do is, before they buy old property, and accept that they will have to either decide to do the renovation, or try for Planning Permission for the new build, why not give the idea that I detailed in Section 15: *"Finding a good plot at the right price"* a try?

It could be that there are properties to be found in those areas where they would like to live where, although self-build plots are in short supply, builders still seem to be building new homes. They just need to find them.

## THING 25: **WATCH OUT FOR JAPANESE KNOTWEED AND HIMALAYAN BALSAM**

I am not going to including many images in this book (*they seem to confuse the Amazon book formatting machine, and I apologise if these two , or any of the others have done so*), but I think it is worthwhile adding two images here. The first one is Japanese Knotweed and the second one is Himalayan Balsam.

If you haven't come across these nasty little b**gers yet, if and when you start getting involved in building houses, there is a good chance that you will. If you happen to find them on a plot you are thinking about buying, turn round and run a mile!

These two "weeds" are becoming the scourge of land sellers and house builders in many parts of the country. They are both highly invasive, and once you have them on your land, they can decrease its value substantially.

They usually grow near water (*riverbanks and streams*) but can spread quite a distance from the water course itself. They grow in Spring, flower during the summer months and then voraciously seed in the Autumn, then they die back to hibernate in the ground over winter.

One of the reasons they are so dangerous is that because of their aggressive seeding, they spread quickly. Another is that they are difficult to eradicate. I have seen Himalayan Balsam close up in the Autumn. If you catch it just at the right time, as summer turns to Autumn, and you shake a plant sharply, the seed pods will literally *explode* and fire the seeds over a wide area (*up to a radius of around 15ft from the plant*). Once that happens, you are going to have a very much larger crop the following year, and as they spread, they kill off a lot of the other plant growth around them.

If you want or need to get rid of them, you will usually need to hire a specialist company to do the job. There are now companies that concentrate only on *these two* species, suggesting that the problem is becoming a more widespread. Getting rid of them is not a one off operation either. They may need three or four years of treatment before you can officially be declared free of them.

You may wonder why a weed is getting so much attention? Well, for a start it can grow through concrete! It is very strong as well as being very invasive and aggressive. If you have spores (seeds) in the ground underneath a driveway, in a couple of years you could start to see a crop of Knotweed growing through it!

The problem these two weeds are creating has become so serious, that there is now a question about knotweed on the legal forms that you fill in when you are selling a house or land. You are now *specifically* asked if knotweed is present on the property that is being sold. If it is, there is a good chance that no mortgage company will be interested in lending on that land until it has a certificate to say that the problem has been dealt with, and the land is now certified as being clear. This is playing havoc with people trying to sell land for both self-build and commercial development.

So, when you get around to plot hunting, keep an eye open for any sign of anything that looks like either of these weeds. If you find something similar, but you are not sure about it, ___don't___ take one home to check against the photos above, instead, take a photograph of it where it is, and compare that photo to the ones above, or on the internet. And also **clean the soles of your shoes / boots** asap after moving off the land where you find them. The spores could get into the treads on the soles, then fall out on some other ground and start a new crop.

## THING 26: **TREE ROOTS AND PROTECTED TREES**

Staying on the subject of *things that grow that can cause you headaches*, trees and tree roots can have a significant impact on what you can build and where you can build it.

**Two things:**

I.   When you find a plot that you would like to buy, make note of where trees are located (*especially mature trees*), both on the plot itself, and close to the perimeter, on adjacent land.

If the plot is small, awkwardly positioned, large trees, could severely limit your build options, and/or dramatically increase build costs. For example: If there is a chance that, at some time in the future, tree roots could undermine your foundations, the foundation trench will need to be excavated down to below the level that any root growth could potentially reach.

The way this potentially expensive problem is normally solved, is to try to design the development so that trees are far enough away from buildings so that roots won't be a problem. That could result in the location of the building having to be moved from its ideal position on the plot, either that, or the cost of increasing the depth of the foundations will have to be built into the budget.

II.  A Tree with a Tree Preservation Order (TPO) on it could cause more significant problems. Where there is a TPO in force, whether you want to or not, you will be required to keep any building works outside a calculated protected radius around the tree, so that neither foundations, nor any building works will interfere with the roots.

As part of the TPO, the tree will have legal protection against damage, known as a "Root Protection Area" (RPA). During any type of development, these trees must be protected from *anything* that could damage their roots (*1.8m high fencing is the normal way to exclude them from the working / building zone*).

The RPA is worked out using the width of the tree trunk as a starting point. A calculation has to be done to ascertain the distance from the centre of the trunk that needs to be protected (*if a tree has multiple trunks, each trunk forms part of the calculation*). The calculation works as follows:

*Measure the diameter of the trunk at 1.5m above ground level. Multiply the measurement by 12. That gives you the radius of the RPA from the centre of the trunk.*

RPA's could not only cause problems with the locations of the building on the land, they could also restrict where driveways can be constructed. I came across this problem on one of my own sites: I was building some large houses along a main road frontage that included several large TPO'd trees. I needed to construct driveways through the gaps between the trees. After some discussion, I managed to agree with the Planning Officer that I would construct a *breathable, permeable* driveway over any roots areas that were within the RPA's. It was not too much of a pain to do, but it all added to the build cost and time taken to do the job.

(*search "Permeable Driveways" for more information*).

Here are some other points to think about, related to large and/or protected trees within your plot boundaries:

- You would need to get a report compiled by an Aboriculturalist (tree specialist), detailing all the pertinent facts about the protected tree(s), usually also including reports on other trees on the site. This can be a time consuming and costly exercise.
- TPO's could restrict the size of the house you are able to build.
- The position on the site where you are allowed to build might end up being in permanent shade of a tree.
- Trees may be partly on your property, and partly on someone else's, so anything that you plan on doing with or to them, would have to first be agreed with the neighbour affected.
- The impact of trees being where they are, could increase your build costs and lengthen build times.
- Leaves from trees close to the house could fill the gutters of the house every year, requiring cleaning out.
- A tree, or large branch could potentially one day fall on to the house.


## THING 27: **BADGERS, BATS, BUTTERFIES AND OTHER ASSORTED WILDLIFE**

The protection of wildlife has now become an important aspect of all types of new building work. Self-build is particularly susceptible to being affected by its implications, due to most self-build projects being for just one house, but potentially having to deal with protecting various species of wildlife in just the same way, and to the same extent as large, mutli-plot commercial sites. So, where a commercial builder may be restricted from building one particular house, or from building on one particular area of a site, if there are any wildlife restrictions imposed on a self-build project, they can stop the whole job, sometimes for months.

My company has recently gone through the planning application process for a fairly rural site which has a derelict house on it. The site has previously had Planning Permission, to knock down the house and build 4 detached new homes, on good sized plots. The permission had lapsed.

Even though planning approval had previously been granted, our new application involved us in having to jump through some more hoops and learn more about wildlife considerations than any other project I have previously been involved with. We have also had to agree to make a significant monetary contribution towards the protection of butterflies.

Here is what we had to do as part of the planning process (and *it stands to reason that you may be affected to the same sort of extent, wherever you build, so you might need to make appropriate allowances in your build cost estimates*):

1) **Bat Survey:** We had to hire a specialist to monitor whether and when bats use the derelict house. As it turned out, they don't, at least not regularly, so we were ok on that one. If they did use the house, I am not sure what restrictions we would have had imposed on us, and what effect that would have had on the job overall, but I am sure there would have been some (*has any reader had experience of this?*)
2) **Butterfly Survey:** This also proved to be negative, but in a planning approval condition, we were obliged to pay over £4,000 towards a *"Butterfly Mitigation"* scheme.
3) **Badger Survey:** Again, negative. There was no sign of badgers, however, there was evidence of them found at our previous development a couple of years ago. As with this new site, we had been required to get a badger expert in to check for badger sets. If they found live sets, depending on how far from the actual building work they were found, we could have had our building start times restricted, so that we would not disturb their mating season. That could potentially have lost us months of progress, and massively curtailed our income potential for that year.

Each of the reports mentioned above cost around £500 - £600. If they had revealed that we did have badgers, bats or butterflies, the impact, both financially and timewise could potentially have threatened the project itself.

I fully understand these actions by the planning authorities, I just think that when they get ideas like this, they tend to go a bit over the top with them. They don't take local factors into account; they just tend to blanket cover everything and everyone with the same rules. Nevertheless, I reckon we are all stuck with it until we can come up with better solutions.

Because of the importance that is now placed on wildlife, I would strongly suggest that, once you find a plot you are interested in buying, you should check the Planning Permission documents, to see what conditions have been included. When you add up all the restrictions due to trees, animals, and the other potential factors, you might end up thinking twice about buying it.

## THING 28: **MAKING AN OFFER**

When it comes to making an offer for a plot, it helps if you know how to play the game.

Here is an example of one case I was involved in many years ago. The prices have changed, but the principles are still the same:

Around 30 years ago, I working as a Self-Build Consultant in the North West of England. I was asked to locate a suitable building plot, design the house to go on it, and manage build. I started by looking for plots. It was a time when the market was reasonable, but not fantastically busy. Generally, most of the plots I saw had been on the market for two or three months, while the best new ones that appeared week to week, were selling within month or so.

I found a nice, fairly flat, generously sized plot, on a hill, with good views. The asking price was £100,000. I checked the details and found that it had been on the market for over three months. I couldn't see any major problems with it, apart from it needing a long private driveway from the plot boundary to the main road. Overall, I liked the plot, which had planning for a large detached bungalow, exactly what the client was looking for.

I took the client to see the plot, and he immediately decided he wanted it. This was the first plot he had tried to buy, and he was keen not to lose his chance to get it. He said he was happy to pay the asking price.

I explained to him that the land had been on the market for a while and there were not a long line of people fighting for it. I suggested that, if he was willing to take a bit of a chance, he should make a low offer, on the basis that if they declined it, he could always increase it an hour later, continuing to doing so until they accepted. He agreed and asked what price to start at. I said, *"Go for £70,000, you have got nothing to lose"*. He did and his first offer was accepted.

After having that one short conversation with me, the client saved £30,000 on the plot *(and I didn't even get a pint out of it, although I did then build the house for him)*.

The lesson to be learnt from that experience is that *you*, as a buyer have no idea what is happening at the other end of the selling / buying chain. The owner of that plot accepted the £30,000 reduction in price without even bartering, which would suggest that they needed to get some cash in quickly, and decided, for whatever reason that £70,000 would be acceptable.

Ok, that was a long time ago and the market has changed since those days, but, as I said at the top of this section, the theory *can* still work, at least in some areas of the country.

So, how should you approach making an offer when you find your ideal plot?

The approach varies, depending on where you are situated in the UK. If you are in the popular, expensive areas of the South East, where good quality plots are hard to find, and can sell in the blink of an eye, I suggest not messing about with haggling, and make your best offer straight away. If you have a mortgage offer ready to go, that will help, and if you can tell the seller that you should be able to complete in about 4 weeks, that will give you even more bargaining chips.

Things are not quite so competitive in other areas of the country, where there is not quite the *panic station* situation, so you could possibly think about testing out the idea that I detailed above (*but perhaps not quite so dramatically*).

It is easy to check online how long a plot has been up for sale for (*it is usually included in the sales details on sites like Right Move, Zoopla and On the Market),* but unless a plot is has major problems, it will be rare to find one still available three or four months after it was first marketed.

As very rough rule of thumb, for good quality plots, you could consider offering 5% less than the asking price as soon as it goes up for sale (*but be prepared to go to full price or more if you are turned down, but really want it*). After a plot has been for sale for a month, you could offer 5% - 10% under asking price, after 2 months, 10% - 15%, and reduce by a further 5% per month after that, up to about the 6th month. If it hasn't gone by then, it has problems, so if you like it, find out what the problems are, then it might be worth making a more audacious daring offer. If you do, think about including a letter with the offer, that lists the problems you have found out about, suggesting how much those problems could cost to put right. Doing so could help you to justify your low offer.

**Here is a summary of things to consider / research before you decide how much to offer on a plot of land:**

i. Check how long the land has been on the market.
ii. Talk to the selling agent, ask how much interest there has been, and If they know whether the seller would be open to sensible offers?
iii. Have your funds ready if possible. If you can, make sure the seller knows that you should be able to make a quick completion.
iv. Look for potential problems with the land. You need to know about anything that could cost you time and/or money, and you can potentially use what you find as bargaining tools.
v. Have a look at the Planning Permission and see if there is anything onerous in it, that would justify you asking for a price reduction.
vi. Find out where the services are located. If they are anywhere else apart from at, or close to the plot boundary, it could cost you a lot of money to get them all connected. If that is the case, a price reduction may be a reasonable thing to ask for, to help cover that extra cost.
vii. What it the ground condition like? Is it level, or sloping, or a mixture of the two? Sloping sites are more difficult to build on and more costly. Poor ground might need special foundations.

viii.    How far is the build area from the main road? Is the driveway going to be expensive to construct?

ix.    What is the access like? Are suppliers going to have problems getting large loads to site, and charge you more for delivering everything on small loads?

x.    Is there any sign of wildlife living on, or adjacent to the land?

By the way, don't go over the top trying get the price down. Keep all negotiations short, polite, and sensible. The seller could get fed up after receiving more than two or three unacceptable offers from you, and may simply say *"No thank you, I'll wait for another buyer to come along"*.

## THING 29: BUYING LAND AT AUCTION

In 40 years working in the self-build industry, I have never come across a self-builder who has bought land at auction. I would not do so either. However, some self-builders do at least consider this option, especially in the South East.

Why do I have a negative view on buying a building plot at an Auction?

One of the main reasons is that I have never found a convincing answer to the question:

*"Why would any seller want, or need a potential buyer to have to make a quick decision on buying their land, when good land is in such poor tight supply and selling at auction will not get them the best price for it?"*

Ok, all the legal paperwork is available prior to the auction for potential bidders to view, so it is all above board, and there may also be some surveys and other accessible information included in the pack, but why not give people the chance to go through the usual process of viewing the site, checking Planning Permissions and the site's history, checking boundary lines, making sure there are no ransom strips (*see section 39*), making sure the land is not going to be liable to flooding, possibly talking to the neighbours, the Building Regs department, service providers, and even talking to groundworkers about it. Plus, checking it's true value against other recently sold plots in the same area.

I simply would not consider buying land that I had not had the chance to fully investigate before I parted with any money.

### Why would _anyone_ do that?

If that question were ever adequately answered, I might consider the idea of buying land at auction, but I would still be hesitant.

*(which is the one thing you can't be, if you are buying land at auction!)*

### Comments invited

# THING 30: FUNDING AND MORTGAGES

Most self-builders need to find suitable finance before they can take on their own project. The standard form of funding for the self-build industry is the **Self-Build Stage Mortgage**. When I began writing this book, I looked up the figures, and there were around 12,000 of these mortgages being agreed each year. That figure is down significantly from 20,000 or so, 20+ years ago, but up significantly since the 2008 recession, when the numbers reduced to almost nil.

A stage mortgage basically does what it says on the tin. It gives you the money to build your home, in stages. This (*theoretically*) supplies you with an adequate cash flow to hire and pay all the subbies, to buy all the materials, get the services connected, and to complete the job.

> (**Note**: I use the word "theoretically" on the basis that all self-builders seem to have a natural, built in ability to overspend on anything and everything related to the build, sometimes dramatically, which can scupper the "adequate cash flow" part of that equation!)

**This is way most self-build mortgages work:**

1. You find a suitable plot of land.
2. You agree a purchase price.
3. You contact the mortgage broker (*see below*).
4. You may need to have a telephone interview, or even a face to face interview, where the lender will decide on whether they think you are suitable candidates and you may need to produce evidence to prove past experience of you being involved with some other building related projects, also proving that that you possess relevant skills and/or qualifications in management / supervision.
5. You will also need to prove that you are financially *able and stable* enough to run such a project, alongside your other day to day responsibilities.
6. If the interview has a positive outcome, you will complete and submit the application form.
7. If that goes ok, you would usually then be approved for the mortgage.

**The setup of the funding:**

Different lenders work in slightly different ways, but all stage mortgages tend to follow these same basic principles:

1. If you need funds to buy the land, as long as it has the necessary Planning Permissions, and if there are no legal or other problems, depending on the mortgage product you use, you will be able to drawdown up to 100% of the price of the land.
2. You will then be able to make 4 or 5 further drawdown claims over the course of the build, normally at the following stages:

i)      At completion of the foundations.

ii)     Once the building reaches wall plate level (top of the upstairs windows).

iii)    There may be another payment once the roof is completed and the building is fully weathertight.

iv)     Once the building is plastered.

v)      At completion.

If you were to run short of cash prior to reaching the pre-set drawdown points, with some lenders, it may be possible to get an *interim* drawdown, although there will usually be charges associated with doing so.

That's it. It is normally quite simple. Some lenders may want more information and charge more fees or higher interest rates than others, but that, in a nutshell, is a stage mortgage.

Where can you find these mortgages?

Here are a few contacts (*also see: The Self-Build Trade List*):

**Build Store:** https://www.buildstore.co.uk/

**Mary Riley Self Build Mortgages:** https://www.maryrileysolutions.co.uk/

**Ecology Building Society:** https://www.ecology.co.uk/

**Money Supermarket:** https://www.moneysupermarket.com/mortgages/self-build/

**Remember these points when the time comes to apply for your mortgage:**

- It is worth you talking to more than one provider, they all have their own different ways of working, charge different fees and have varying interest rates.

- If, and when you go to meet their representative, be as professional as you can. Treat this as a job interview. The self-build lenders caught a cold, not only during the recession, but also before that, by granting mortgages to people they should have refused, who stood little chance of succeeding, and who often failed. All lenders now make sure that they are fully confident that the person managing the build has *all the right boxes ticked*, and one thing they are looking for, is a professional approach to the subject.

- Make sure that you have a list of questions for *the lenders* to answer. They like people who want to be aware of all the facts, and who ask the right questions. It shows they are preparing for the project in the right way.

- Expect the interest rates to be higher than for standard mortgages. This is because there is more risk involved in this type of lending, and because they want you to get the job completed as quickly as possible. However, once the project has been completed, you can usually change to one of their standard mortgage products within a couple of months, and benefit from normal interest rates.

# SECTION 2

# PLANNING PERMISSION, DESIGN AND COSTING

## THING 31: GET YOUR FINANCES AND CASH FLOW SORTED BEFORE YOU START WORK.

I have already talked about how it is a good idea to have a provisional mortgage offer on the table when you are negotiating a purchase for land. So, as soon as you decide to take on a project, looking at mortgages and, if possible, getting an *In Principle* offer, should be near to the top of your list of priorities.

So, assuming that your mortgage is sorted, you now need to formulate a plan to create a cash flow that will allow you to maintain progress on site from day one, all the way through to the completion.

The first task is to work out how much cash you will require, and when. Stage mortgages usually pay in arrears, so, after you have received funds to pay for the plot itself, *you* will need to fund the first part of the build, before you get your next payment (*which is usually when the foundations have been completed*). If you think cash flow could be a problem, search "*Buildstore Accelerator Mortgage*", which makes the stage payments up front rather than in arrears, but charges higher fees for this service.

To work out how much cash you are going to need to get you to your first payment stage, you will need to use your cost estimate figures. It would also be useful if you have already lined up your groundworkers, a) so you know how much they have quoted for the work and b) so you also know how and when they want to be paid. In my experience, the small groundworks companies like to be paid weekly, whereas the larger companies will tend to invoice once a month.

If you are going to be receiving your mortgage drawdowns in arrears, paying the groundworkers monthly would take a lot of cash flow pressure off you. Better still, if they invoice monthly, they normally do it at the end of one month / start of the next, so you will then have up to a month to pay it, which could give you a 2 month period where you are going ahead with the build, but don't have to pay for the work. If this happens, just make sure you have the cash ready to pay them, before the end of that 2 month period, or you could get into their bad books (*and being in the bad books of groundworkers is not normally a happy place to be!*)

You could find a similar situation with the materials. If you open a credit account at two or three builder's merchants, you can order most, or all of the materials for the work up to slab level without needing cash. The merchants also invoice at the end of the month and you don't need to pay until the end of the following month. Those two facilities

(*Groundworkers and Builder Merchants*) can help to make your financial situation a lot less stressful during the first couple of months of the build. If you don't have the luxury of the 2 months buffer, you will have to make sure you have sufficient funds of your own prior to starting work, to get you to the first stage payment point.

**Note:** During this first period, you may need to pay some deposits on things like the timber frames and possibly windows. Don't forget to build these requirements into your cash flows for this period.

So, at completion of the groundworks, you should get your first drawdown (*or your second if you received funds to buy the land*). That money can then be used to pay off anything you owe and cover your cashflow needs for the next stage of the job. Theoretically, this is how it should go with each payment for the rest of the job.

As part of your financial planning, you need keep updating your financial records regarding the build costs, so that you know if your cash flow between payments is going to be sufficient. If it looks like you might need more cash than you will be receiving at any payment stage, you will either need to top up the cash fund from somewhere else (*such as parents, bank overdraft etc*), or, if you give the funder enough notice, you may be able to borrow extra funds from the mortgage lender (*although they probably won't be too happy about having to do all the extra paperwork and they will want proof that the extra costs are genuine and don't threaten the overall project budget*).

**Banks:**

Before you start work, try to get a decent overdraft facility set up on your own bank account. If you go and talk to your Bank Manager, you can show him/her your mortgage offer and other relevant paperwork, in order to prove that the project is going ahead and that it is financially sound. As long as your credit history is sound, they may then set you up with a temporary £10,000 - £20,000, overdraft, for the duration of the project, that you can use when cash runs short.

*If you can investigate and solve the equation of cash flow for your project early on, it could make the whole process far less stressful for everyone involved, especially towards the end of the build.*


## THING 32: GET A DECENT SOLICITOR ON BOARD

When you start to plan the project, it is a good idea to get set up with a good Self-Build Mortgage Adviser, and a Solicitor who has a knowledge of the self-build market. Sounds sensible doesn't it? Two sets of people who know what they are doing? It very rarely happens!

For a long time after I started out in this business, I had a great Solicitor. He was a specialist in Construction, and it never really occurred to me how good he was. I just thought that this is how it must always be. It was only when he retired and the company gave me someone else to work with, that things started to change. Processes slowed down, communications became fewer, and I started having to chase the new guy to get results. In my naivety, I just thought I had been landed with a poor Solicitor, but over time I realised that it wasn't the person that was the problem. The real problem was that he was a standard *Conveyancing Solicitor,* and land / new build were not his specialist subjects.

I eventually left that company, and went with someone else. Before I did so, I made sure that I was going to be dealing with someone who was a construction specialist. He was ok, but nothing like as knowledgeable as my original guy. The purchase and sales processes still didn't go as smoothly as I had hoped, and again, I would end up constantly chasing him to do the things that had always been done automatically by my original Solicitor.

After a couple of years, I changed again, and finally managed to get someone who was similar to the original guy (*the funny thing was, his name was also nearly identical too!*). Since then, I haven't needed to worry that progress might be going a bit slow, or that no-one is chasing on my behalf. I *know* that he will be doing what he should be doing, and he will be pushing the other side to do what they need to do. He will also be chasing me to get things done my end, and even gets impatient with me if I don't react as quickly as *he* wants *me* to, when he wants me to, *and I am paying him*! – That, to my mind, is how it should be.

What I am really saying here, is that the process of buying a plot of land, and doing all the legal work involved, is complicated. So, if possible, try to get to a situation where you are dealing with someone who is professional, who won't let the other side get away with anything *and who also knows about the self-build industry*.

When you are ready to purchase a plot of land, don't be afraid to ask your present Solicitor if he / she has experience of land / self-build deals (*as opposed to standard house purchase deals*), and if they don't, enquire as to whether there is anyone within the company who does, and if so, could they manage *this particular* deal for you? (*Blame me if you like. Say you have just read a book by someone who said using a Solicitor who is knowledgeable about of self-build is a good idea. So, you were just wondering ............?*)

The difference between having someone who is good at doing this job and someone who isn't, could potentially be measured in months, and when you consider that Solicitors charge upwards of £175 an hour for their services, it could also be measured in the £1,000's. Add to that the stresses that things going slowly can bring, especially if someone could potentially come along and pinch the plot from under your noses, while you wait for the legal people to get their act together.

> **Note:** *This is not one of the most critical subjects that I cover in this book. It is included because as the book title says, it is a "Thing" that, as a self-builder, it is good that you know, so that you can at least give it some consideration. If you can't find a specialist*

*self-build Solicitor, it is not going to be the end of the word. It might just take longer to complete the transaction, cost a bit more and be a little bit more stressful.*

## THING 33: **THE PLANNING PROCESS CAN BE TIME CONSUMING AND EXPENSIVE**

Whenever I am making a planning application, I make sure to meet, and speak to the Planning Officer who will be looking after it. At that first meeting, I always ask the same question: *"How busy are you at the moment, and how long do you think it will take to get the approval signed off?"* The standard answer, pretty much every time, is:

*"Well the guidelines are about 8 weeks, so we aim for that sort of timescale, as long as there are no problems".*

**Don't be fooled, it is not true, at least most of the time (*and in my experience, <u>every</u> time*).**

I must have made dozens of planning applications over the years, and I have never had one that took 8 weeks. Possibly around 12 – 14 weeks would be my guess at the shortest time I have ever managed to get an application approved. On average though, by the time I receive the Planning Permission Approval documents, between 5 months and 10 months will have elapsed since I made the application.

At the risk of becoming an enemy of planners everywhere, in my personal opinion, the single biggest problem in the planning system is that being a Planning Officer is a *job for life*, even if you mess up spectacularly. Ok, there might be internal targets set for application processing times, but no-one seems to be held to account if they don't meet those targets. I have never known anyone take so much holiday time off as Planners seem to, or be off "ill" as much!

I do have to say that I have never met an unpleasant Planning Officer. Some of them get a bit defensive if you push them for something you want, that they don't want to give, but overall, they are a decent bunch of people. They just don't seem to have any drive or enthusiasm when it comes to being efficient and getting jobs done. To be fair, it may not be all their fault. The whole system associated with the planning process seems to be driven through a network of people who are all in the same positions as the planners themselves, none of them have to, or do, hurry.

When anyone make a new planning application, the application documents are sent out to numerous different departments (*most of which operate within, or in close connection with the Council*). All of those departments will have their say as to whether or not the application should be approved. There is supposed to be a maximum time allowed for the different departments to respond to enquiries, but it is rarely met.

To try to hurry things along, I always chase progress, and I will call the planner, maybe three weeks after making the application, asking for an update. By that time, it will have been registered (*taking about 2-4 days on average*), and the enquiries (*relevant questions about the application land*) are sent out to the various departments.

At three weeks into the process, the enquiries should just about all be back with the planner, complete with comments and recommendations. During the conversation I have with Planners at the three weeks stage, when I ask how progress is going, I will usually be told something like:

> *"Enquiries are ongoing, but we are still on schedule for an 8 weeks decision "*.

Only to be told 2 or 3 weeks later, something like:

> *"Well, I've had two of the enquiries back, but there are still a few to come in. I'll give them a few more days and then chase them"*

(in other words, *"Go away and leave me alone"*).

Two weeks later I'll call again and might be told:

> *"I've got most of the enquiries back now, but the guy from the Highways department is on holiday until next Monday, so I am just waiting for him to get back"*.

I won't bore you with the minutia involved in the full process, but that theme can continue for many weeks. There will be departments who ask questions, or are not happy with something, or want more information. Then, to top it all, if I then leave it for two more weeks before I call again, the Planner him or herself will either be on holiday or sick leave!

## A Recent experience:

My most recent planning application was made in **May** of one year and went to the Planning Committee for a decision in the **January** of the next year (*getting on for 9 months later*). In this case, the delay caused a major problem: During the delay, the *"Red Line"* map of where Planning Permission will be granted in that local area, was redrawn, and our land had now been moved to outside the boundary line, indicating "No new development here"!

The application was due to go before the Planning Committee the week before Christmas, with a recommendation for approval, when suddenly we received a letter saying:

> ***"Your application has been withdrawn from the Planning Committee meeting, due to the facts that it is now outside the Permitted Development boundary. We have now changed our planning decision advice to recommend rejection of the application***

> **(They forgot to add: *Thank you for your time, have a nice day!*)**

When I had scraped myself off the ceiling, I got straight on to the Head Planner, who was totally arrogant about the whole thing, basically saying "*I am sorry, but these are the rules*". I pointed out (*after finding out about what had happened and done some research*), that the boundary would not change until *late January,* and that the regulations stated that only applications made after the previous *mid-November* would be subject to the new regulations. Our application had been made in May, and had been sitting on their desks, doing absolutely nothing for the best part of six months. The Head Planner would not back down, so I requested an urgent meeting with her and the Planning Officer himself.

We had the meeting. When it started, she was very firm, and stated the law of the land, as she saw it, basically saying "*Sorry, but you'll have to put up and shut up*". I had my say and, by the end of the meeting, she was a lot quieter! I pointed out all the time that had been wasted by her department, and also noted that this was a simple application, that there was no reasonable excuse for any of the delays, and that we should have had the approval, according to their own guidelines, sometime in June, five months before the cut-off date for relevant applications, and 7 months before the boundary changes went in to practice!

The meeting ended, and I had a phone call the next day from her (*speaking in a far more pleasant manner and tone*), saying that she had referred the matter to the Welsh Government in Cardiff, and they had told her that the planning application should not have been rejected, and should be re-recommended for approval, and immediately added to the next Planning Committee meeting agenda a few weeks later.

**The lesson to be learned here is**: Do not let Planners get away lightly with tardiness. Be pleasant but also be *reasonably* firm. You need to keep them on your side, so don't fall out with them. For all their faults, they have a lot of power. If they aren't doing what they should be doing, give them just enough hassle so that they get fed up of you constantly calling or emailing to chase progress, so they will get your application processed, if for no other reason than to get rid of you!

## THING 34: DO WE NEED TO USE A PLANNING SPECIALIST?

*I think I probably need to be a bit careful; If I get too negative about the professionals who operate within the self-build industry, you will start to think I am against anyone who makes any money at all out of Self-Builders. However, just for this section, I'm afraid I going to do it again!*

Be assured, I am not against Planning Specialists; I have used them in the past, and a good one can be very helpful. All I am a bit concerned about, is the way that a lot of people tend to think that as soon as they start a self-build, the first two things they need to do are: 1) Find an Architect and 2) Find a Planning Specialist. That is not necessarily, or even usually true.

Ok, I have been doing this for a long time, and I would very rarely need either, but that doesn't mean that because you might just be starting out on your first project, that you need to think that you have to go belt and braces on everything, and you don't need to think that you automatically have to pay large sums of money to people to do jobs that you could possibly do *yourselves*.

**What will a Planning Specialist do for you?**

Planning Specialists are generally good at solving problems and giving advice on planning matters. Depending on how much experience they have in the industry, they can also often advise you on other related subjects. One thing they *can't do* is get you a Planning Approval if your application includes things that are outside the Planning Policy. However, they might be able to find loopholes, and come up with ideas that you might not think about or be aware of, but that deal with planning matters that are open to interpretation. That knowledge might just sneak you over the line on a difficult or complicated application.

Planning Specialists can also be a reassuring presence to have with you, if and when you need to go to meetings with the planner. They can usually answer technical questions that you wouldn't be able to, and they can professionally present alternative, possibly better ideas than the ones you, or the Planning Officer might have, on a range of subjects, if and when required.

**(There, see? I like them really!)**

I would always suggest to anyone who is applying for Planning Permission, especially if the application is fairly straightforward, starting the process without using specialists, and only taking them on if and when you think they are needed.

The first parts of the planning process involves getting together plans and information about your plot, getting your house designed, and completing the Planning Application forms. I am sure that **you** could usually cope with those tasks. If you don't feel confident at the moment, I am quite sure that after reading this book, and maybe one or two others, you would be confident enough to at least have a go at those kinds of tasks. If you find you are struggling, *then* get some help.

**Here is a quick example of one case where a self-builder tried the Planning Specialist option first, when going alone probably would have been a better option:**

About 10 years ago, I got a contact from a couple who owned land with Outline Planning Permission. They had been trying to get permission to build a bungalow on land they already owned. But they lost confidence in their own abilities early on in the process and wanted to make sure they went about things properly. They did what they thought they should, and took on a Planning Specialist. He then advised them on what he thought they should do.

After following his advice and getting plans drawn up, the planning application was made. The plans immediately hit a problem, and they all ended up going to a meeting with the Planner where, even though they followed the specialist's advice, they failed to make any progress. They kept following his advice, changed the application slightly, and tried again. They made two attempts at getting over the problems and both times they failed.

The couple then saw my details in a Grand Designs show brochure, and came to see me at the Excel Show in London. I asked them to give me a rundown of the history of the process so far. They told me that the Specialist had helped them to design the house and had told them what position and orientation it should take on the plot. Their own ideas differed with his, but he was very persuasive and definite about his plan, and apart from that slight disagreement, he was quite helpful.

I asked about the meetings with the planner, and they said that he had got a bit annoyed in the first meeting. He had insisted that the house should not face in the direction that the planning specialist wanted it to. They didn't fall out about it, but there ended up being a bit of an atmosphere at the meeting. The specialist said that the if the applicants were happy to make a couple of changes, that should solve the problem, but he was adamant that the house should stay facing the way he wanted it to, and that the owners should take the matter to appeal if the Planner refused permission, based on any remaining disagreement.

The couple happen to live in Wales, only about 20 miles from where I lived at the time, so I suggested that I call in sometime in the near future, to look through everything related to the application, with them.

We met, and they showed me the site, then we went back to the house and they showed me the plans of the house. On site, in one direction, the view was of a mountain, and in the other, the view was of a housing estate. Without having seen the site or location plans, I immediately assumed that the planner had wanted the view from the main windows of the house, to be towards the housing estate (*maybe to conform with some planning guidance for that particular location*), rather than towards the mountain. I said that I could see that it would be worth a bit of a fight to get the view over the mountain, and was told that in fact, the planner wanted the house to be orientated to have the view over the mountain, and it was the specialist who wanted the other option!

It turned out that the specialist had strong ideas about the entrance to the site, the parking areas, and how the sun would light the garden and house, at different times during the day. Those ideas meant facing the house towards the estate and it was that that the owners disagreed with. It wasn't the planner causing trouble, it was the specialist!

I asked the owners to make another appointment, and to tell the planner that they now had someone new involved, who wanted to see if they could work something out. I amended the drawings to show the house facing the mountain view, and we went in to see the Planner with that proposal.

The meeting started, and we showed him the new sketches of the positioning and orientation of the house, and everything changed. Within 10 minutes he was saying that, if we got new drawings in quickly, he would move the whole thing forward straight away and recommend for approval. We now had happy applicants, a happy Planner and a satisfied me!

*The moral of this tale is: Don't think that experts necessarily have better ideas than you, they might just think differently, and only one of you can be right in those circumstances. So, if you can muster up the confidence, first try to work through the planning process for yourselves, before starting to pay someone else to do the same job.*

## THING 35: ONCE YOU HAVE FOUND A SUITABLE PLOT, ARRANGE A PRE-PLANNING MEETING

The meeting I had with the Planner in the previous section is known as a Pre-Planning Meeting. It is where you and the Planner who would be dealing with your application, get together to discuss your thoughts and ideas, to see how they compare with what the Planning Department will be looking for from that development.

These meetings used to be free, but in recent years the Councils have started to realise that a) They are a good idea, and b) They could charge for them. So, nowadays you will probably find yourself paying anything from £50 to £250 for a meeting, and possibly more for follow on meetings. Whichever of those fees you have to pay, this is a very valuable meeting, and you should make the most of it by preparing thoroughly. Your aim should be to come out knowing what you need to do to give your application the best chance of being approved, first time around, and with minimum delay or fuss.

Being prepared doesn't necessarily mean that you need take a full set of drawings with you, it just means:

*"know what you want to get from the meeting and have a plan for how you could achieve that goal"* .

Your ideas might turn out to be exactly what the Planner is looking for, or they could be nothing like them. Just because you might have different ideas for the development, does not mean that you can't meet in the middle, with something that would eventually gain planning approval.

You should arrange the pre-planning meeting to take place before you formally agree to purchasing the plot. The best time for the meeting is after you have had an offer accepted, but before you instruct a Solicitor, or hire specialists to work with you. That way you will have the meeting *before* you start to pay significant sums of money out. So, if you then come out of the meeting thinking "*Well that is a complete nonstarter*", you don't need to take the plot purchase any further, and won't lose out financially by calling it a day.

As I said earlier, Planners are not a bad bunch. They are annoyingly slow, but they are usually ok to get along with. **But don't start trying to tell them what they must do.**

Approach the Pre-Planning meeting as if it is just a friendly chat, during which you can knock all your ideas back and too with them, listen to their thoughts and try to come up with jointly acceptable ideas.

**What do you need to do to prepare for the meeting?**

It is good if you can take along a visual representation of the sort of build you envisage. This could be photographs of similar houses you have seen elsewhere, or simple drawings that you have prepared yourselves (*the first option of those two is the better one*).

If you can, get hold of a scale drawing of the site, and mark on it (*again, to scale*), the outlines of where you would like to position the house. Also, if you can, add to the same drawings, anything you think might be relevant to discuss, such as trees, water courses, other building etc. Those details could be very useful during the conversation. Photos of the site are also good things to have with you.

The Planner will already know the site by the time you meet up. They will probably go and have a look at it before the meeting, to refresh their memories, so they should know what you are referring to if you go into detail about any particular aspect (*and the photos will help too*). Before you go to the meeting, make some notes about the things you think are most important to discuss, and make sure you cover everything that you want, or need to, before you leave.

The Planner might also bring up some things you didn't think of. Either way, when you come out that meeting you want to be in a position where you can decide whether or not this project is going to be a goer, or whether there are too many problems and hurdles to overcome. If that is the case, *now* would be the time to pull the plug.

# THING 36: CAN WE BUILD WITHOUT PLANNING PERMISSION?

**The quick answer is *"Yes, sometimes, but don't be surprised, if you don't get Planning Permission before you start and then end up having to pull it all down later"*.**

**To explain:**

This subject is better understood these days than it was 20 years ago. Probably due at least partly to the increase in the popularity of TV programmes such as Grand Designs. However, it is still complicated, and some people are still at risk of getting caught out by testing the system.

I have come across people who have built things like extensions, garages, garden offices etc, without Planning Permission, and have not had any problems. It may be that they were lucky, but it could also be because they didn't actually need Planning Permission but weren't aware of that fact.

Usually, if you try to take liberties with Planning Permission, your neighbours will be the ones who let the Planning Department know what you have been up to. There is always someone in the neighbourhood who will see it as their civic duty to find out if anyone has been acting illegally in *their* neighbourhood. I am not quite sure why this is. It is probably something to do with us being British!

However, there are things that you can do to your own property, without needing Planning Permission. They are all covered under a thing called *Permitted Development Rights*. I am not going go into any specific details here, due to the fact that the rights vary from area to area, and some areas have highly localised restrictions. The UK Planning Portal recommends that if you want to find out what you can do to your own property, without having to go through a planning application, that you contact your local council to discuss your thoughts and ideas. (*if you want to find out more, go to "planningportal.co.uk" and find your way to the Permitted Development Rights page*).

Putting aside Permitted Development Rights, anyone who thinks they could quietly knock themselves up a small house, log cabin or anything else that could be lived in and classed as a permanent building, without getting into trouble, needs to know that they cannot legally do so, and could be told to take the whole thing back down.

However, there are some things that you can install on your property, temporarily and possibly permanently. These include some temporary buildings.

But what is a temporary building?

If a building is on wheels, and can be rolled from one place to another, in principle it is a caravan. A caravan is usually classed as a temporary building (*unless it is used for commercial purposes*).

A static caravan (*single, or double unit*) could also be classed as temporary and if so, would not automatically need Planning Approval to site it.

If you want to find out more about the regulations covering temporary buildings, have a look at: "*The Caravan Sites and Control Act 1960*", and / or "*The Caravan Sites Act 1968*" (which seems to say that a static caravan is classed as temporary building).

*This whole subject is a minefield, and you need to stay away from it if you possibly can. You are pretty safe living in a caravan while you build your new home, getting water from a bowser, with a solar generator and a septic tank. But don't ask me to plead your case for you if you start taking liberties!*

## THING 37: SIMPLIFY THE PLANNING PROCESS

I have already talked about how slow the planning process can be very slow. It is very frustrating, but there are few things *you* can do to try to reduce the length and number of delays, in addition to acting on anything you are asked to do, as soon as you are asked.

Here are some ideas (*in no particular order of importance*):

- **Keep the design and the drawings simple:**

  Depending on the complexity of the house design, there could be anything from half a dozen to thirty or forty drawings, details and specifications included in the package you submit to the Planning Department.

  A keen designer (*or one who wants to squeeze you for as much money as they can*), will prepare not only the basic drawings required, but also significant numbers of *construction details*, explaining everything in full detail. This may be good to have when you are actually building, but is not always necessary for the application process. Not only does it cost you a lot of money to get these details drawn up, but if they are in your application package, they all have to be registered and checked by the admin department and the Planners. Also, the inclusion of lots of documents can create extra-long lists of queries that, if they were not included, would not be raised. Dealing with all those queries can delay you getting the Planning Approval and lose you weeks or months of progress on site.

  *"Hang on"* (you say), *"Are you telling us to submit an incomplete application?"*

  **No.**

  When you make the planning application, you will be requested to submit *all relevant* drawings, plus various other standard bits, and pieces. When I make an application, the *requested* documents are all I send. I will have other documents that I could send, and can prepare and provide yet more documents if they are requested, but I only ever send the bare bones of what they ask for, just what they need to consider and pass the application. (*By the way, Building Regs is a different matter, they need a lot more information*).

- **Double check that the application includes _all_ the basic information requested:** The application forms list the drawings and other documents that are required. These will include plans of each floor, elevations, site layouts, location plans and some other items. If any of these are missing or are found to be incomplete or incorrectly annotated, they will not even get through the registration process. If that happens, a couple of weeks after you make the application, you will get an email or letter, asking you to amend, or add to the information you have already submitted. That one little error could result in 2 or more weeks being lost in getting a decision. As I said above, the trick is to provide _just enough_ information, but to also make sure that what you send in is _correctly formatted_ and _includes everything that it should_. In other words, try to minimise the chances of problems being found, and giving the planners an excuse for time being wasted.

- **Respond to queries quickly and fully:** If you do get a request for more information, or are asked to correct incorrect information already submitted, act quickly. Do what you need to do and get everything back to them asap. The Planning Office registration system is slow and is used for everything that comes into the office. So, every time you have to respond to a query, it could then take a few days for it to get back in the system. The reason for the slowness of the registration could be that when the post comes in, or emails are received, they seem to be dealt with in the order in which they arrive. I find that if I take applications or any extra information requested, into the planning office by hand, they get dealt with faster. I am not sure why, perhaps it is just because when it is taken from me, it is put at the top of the _to do_ pile, so gets seen sooner than some of the items sent by email, or routed through the standard registration process.

- **Be nice:** Remember that you are only one of many applicants that the planner will be dealing with at any one time. They are human, and if someone is being (_what they see as_) unnecessarily unpleasant to them, they can start to resent that treatment, and purposely slow down an application, just to get their own back. Sounds petty but it can happen, so just be _at least_ a little bit patient, and try to be nice.

## THING 38: **WATCH OUT FOR RANSOM STRIPS / RIGHTS OF WAY / COVENANTS**

You are probably familiar with the term "Rights of Way" and possibly "Covenants", but you possibly have not heard of "Ransom Strips". You need to be aware of all three of these potential job stoppers.

**Rights of way:** The general public has the right to access some private land for walking, and for some other leisure activities. Occasionally a building plot may include a right of way within its title. If it does, whoever the landowner is, they must allow the access as described (*sometimes called Permissive Access*). I have recently encountered this regulation on a development for 3 houses. The Permissive Access Right on the property, originally agreed a long time ago, gave *one* neighbour the right to take a horse box from a field owned by him, through the land, to access a main road. The whole of our project had to be designed to take this right of way into account.

In this case, the access was just for the one person, but often it is simply for "Public Access", meaning basically *anyone*. If you like walking in the countryside, you may have come across rights of way that go straight across people's gardens *(it is a bit strange to open someone's gate and head off across their lawn, past their vegetable patch and out of another gate at the back!)*.

As far as I am aware, you cannot cancel a right of way. However, if its route is not detailed specifically, as was the case on the land I was developing, then you can usually choose you own route for it. In my case, there was no specific, pre-agreed route. The Title Deed simply recorded it as being *from the main road, to the boundary of the neighbouring land*. The way I dealt with it, was to route it along the new main driveway, which was to be shared by the 3 properties. It then went along one of the boundaries at the side of one of the houses. I included this access strip in the title for that particular plot of land, telling the buyers about it before they bought the house *(so that they had the opportunity to investigate any negative aspects of owning the land, prior to buying it)*. Do not assume that all land sellers would do the same. Many people would rely on the *"Buyer Beware"* legal term, that puts the onus on the buyer to find the problems, rather than requiring the seller to make them all known.

The main downside of a right of way is that it could restrict where you can position the house on the plot. There could be other downsides too, so make sure you keep your eyes open for this potential *pain in the backside* as you carry out your search for a plot. (Note: If you ask a landowner, *in writing* if there are any rights of way, and they tell you (*again, in writing*) that there are not, the, if there actually *are*, they could end up in legal trouble.

*So:* As soon as you are interested in any plot, ask the owner **in writing**, if there are any rights of way on the land.

**Covenants:** These are another *in-built hazard* often found on land. They are basically restrictions of one form or another, placed on the land, usually by the present or a past owner when the land is being sold. They legally restrict what can be done to, and on the land. It can cover things like what type of building you can build, what its floor level will be, how high the building can be, where it is positioned on the plot, what can be done with the land (*as in commercial activities or anything else that could affect the neighbours or a previous owner*).

Covenants are something I have regularly come across, and I have never had a particular problem absorbing them into the developments, but that may not always be the case. On our most recent project *we* included a covenant that prevented the new owners from parking large camper vans, or siting mobile homes on their driveway or garden. So, covenants do not necessarily have to have a negative effect on the land.

Again, these are just one of the things you need to be aware of and find out about. Ask the owner if there are any covenants when you ask about the rights of way.

**Ransom strips:** These can be very nasty little things, that are sometimes found on otherwise lovely plots of land.

If you are plot hunting, and you find a nice plot that seems to be very attractively priced, but has been for sale for a while, before you get carried away and make an offer, *just press the alarm button* in your mind, and ask yourself: *"Why is such a nice plot so cheap, and why wasn't it sold immediately it came on to the market?"* The answer will often be *"It has a ransom strip".*

So, what are Ransom Strips? They can be anything from tiny little slices of land, only a few inches wide, that lie across the entrance to the main plot, between a public right of way and the main area of land.

The problem they cause is that their owners can refuse access over them, from the public area to the plot. Basically, rendering the plot itself, worthless. They are owned by someone other than the person selling the plot and there will usually be a legal agreement that the owner of the ransom strip will require that it is *bought from them* before access can be legally gained onto the plot, *by anyone or anything.*

I have come across a few of these, not many, but when I have, I normally walk away. The problem is that the owner of the ransom strip knows the power they have, and often takes advantage of it. If they don't want anything to be built on the land, they can put a restrictive price on their small strip of land, knowing that no-one in their right mind would pay that much for it.

On one occasion I found a nice, large flat plot, with lovely views. The asking price was £60,000, which was about £30,000 below what it should have been worth. However, it had a 12" ransom strip across the front access, for which its owner wanted £40,000. He knew how good the plot was, and he wanted to get as much out of the deal as he could. The main landowner was peeved that the ransom strip owner was messing about with his potential profit, so he was trying to squeeze out every penny he could from his own land.

*I decided to just let them both get on with it, and as it appeared, other potential buyers had also done.*


## THING 39: WHAT IS A SECTION 106 AGREEMENT?

On the basis that any new development has an impact, one way or another, on the community, and that house builders make a profit on their developments, councils have started to require that they pay a contribution towards things that positively affect some aspect of the community and/or the general infrastructure of the area. How much you will pay is decided locally, based on any number of considerations.

Self-build has become a bit of a grey area with regards to 106 charges. A few years ago, in England, the charge was ended for self-build projects (*but was not ended in Wales, Scotland, or N. Ireland*). A year or so later, after a court case, it was reintroduced in some parts of England. Since then it all seems to have got even more complicated and, as the situation is still fluid, I am not going to comment on how things stand presently, due to the fact that, by the time you read this book it might have all changed again!

I suggest that, once you have decided to take on your own self-build project, and have found a plot of land that you are interested in, you should contact the Local Authority covering that location to find out what the latest update is, and whether or not, you would have to pay section 106 charges if you were to go ahead with the project. If so, try to get an idea of what the amount payable is likely to be? A few hundred pounds might not cause you too many problems, but a few thousand pounds might. If the requested contribution is going to be too financially onerous, you may be better looking elsewhere for your plot.

## THING 40: **WHAT IS "RIGHT TO BUILD"**

This is a scheme that was launched by the Government in 2016, with the aim of helping self-builders (in England only) to access good quality, serviced plots, at reasonable prices. It forms part of a push to find ways to solve the housing crisis, and can theoretically help first time buyers to get on to the housing ladder.

**This is how it works:**

Anyone who wants to build their own home in England, can register that fact with their Local Authority. They do this via the *"Right to Build Register"* (*you can find the information you will need to do so, by searching: righttobuildregister.co.uk*)

It is the responsibility of each Local Council around England, to make sure that there are enough plots available to cater for the demand in their own areas. The plots that are available must have had Planning Permission granted on them within the past 3 years.

In 2019, the Government requested that individual councils publish details of whether or not they had granted Planning Permissions to the people who had registered for the scheme between April and October 2016, and if so, how many of them?

Government records show that in the year from October 2016 to October 2017, **15,174** Planning Permissions were granted on plots, for either new build, or conversion projects in England, up from **11,850** the year before. So, for that year at least, it seems that the scheme worked. Hopefully, it will stay that way. (*By the way, "Planning Permission" does not necessarily equal "Build". It means "Can Build"*).

As I write this book, the scheme is only available in England, but this may change in the future (*between updates of this book*), so it may be worth readers living in Wales, Scotland and Northern Ireland checking with their own Local Authorities to see if the scheme, or anything resembling it is now available where they live.

To find the "Right to build Portal" you can go directly to: (https://nacsba.org.uk/campaigns/right-to-build-portal/) or simply do a search on "*Right to Build Portal*" and find your way to the correct page.


## THING 41: WHO DO YOU NEED ONBOARD DURING THE DESIGN PROCESS?

I get to discuss this subject a lot with guests at the shows (*and it has also been touched on earlier in the book*). It appears, from the conversations I have had over the years, that the majority of people who are taking on a self-build project, generally think that the first two things they need to do, is to go and hire a fully qualified Architect, and a Planning Specialist to, between them, look after everything related to the project. That is not the case. In fact, my message to the people I talk to has always been that the most important person to guide the process at the start is _**you**_.

There are many tasks that need to be carried out before you will be ready to start work on site. Some of them require expert involvement, but some, maybe around 30% of them, don't. The 30% tend to be made up of all the tasks that need attention right at the start of the process, and to my mind, the best people to do those particular tasks are the people who are going to be living in the house when it is complete.

So, what I want to do here is run briefly through a shopping list of the people you might need to have around, during the design and the *pre-start* period of the project:

1. **YOU.** The first person you will need is, in my opinion, you.
2. Once you have done *your* first bit, the next person would usually be a **House Designer** (*note, I did not say "Architect"*). The designer can be a Draughtsman, an Architectural Technician, an Architectural Draughtsman, A CAD Designer, or (*ok, go on*), an Architect! Any one of those people should be able to produce all the drawings and information that you will need to achieve Planning Permission, obtain the Building Regs approval, and build the house. You do not *need* someone with the letters: "RIBA" (*Royal Institute of British Architects*) after their name. If you want to hire an RIBA Architect, that is fine, but you do not need to, and a lot of people cannot afford to.

3. You *may* also need to take on a **Structural Engineer**, although this is fairly unlikely, as most house designers will have contacts with Structural Engineers who they regularly work with.
4. If you already know that the land could have some sensitive issues, you may need a **Planning Specialist.**
5. You may need a **Land Surveyor** if the land is sloping, or has complicated geographical features. They may need to do a full topographical survey.
6. **Wildlife Specialists:** I don't usually advise taking these people on unless you need to do so (*usually due to some requirement of planners*), but if you become aware that that there are going to be some major issues with any type of wildlife, it might be a good idea to find someone to look after those matters, early on, to save time later.
7. If your build is expected to cost upwards of £500,000, you *may* find it prudent to take on a **Quantity Survey** or **Estimator** to look after all the cost estimating and financial record keeping.

Over the first few weeks of planning / researching your project, and especially once you find your plot, it should soon become clear which people you are going to need, and what you will need them to do.

## THING 42: YOU DON'T USUALLY NEED A FULLY QUALIFIED ARCHITECT

*(Here we go! This is where some of you start to think: "Who is this guy, he doesn't know what he is talking about!")*

Architects (*the ones with letters RIBA after their names*), seem to have achieved some sort of God like status in the Self-Build industry (*not quite so much in the Commercial Building Industry*). When they arrive on self-build sites, they appear with a "*celestial glow*" around them. They are the all seeing eye, the fount of all knowledge, he or she who must be obeyed!

**Do I sound bitter? Don't worry I'm not, but I do find it all a bit amusing!**

I work with Architects all the time, and some of them really are *the fount of all knowledge*. However, from many conversations I have had at the shows, and from working with many different Architects over the years, it has to be said that although some of them are great, some of them are a bit of pain in the neck, with their heads so far up in the clouds, that they lose sight of what is going on down on the ground.

The problem is related to some Architects (*but nowhere near all of them*) being quite proud of their Godlike status, and because of it, they think that everyone around them should just obey and be thankful. Others can be more concerned about having another photograph of a stunning looking, top notch design to put in their marketing brochure, than they are about making sure the client gets what they want, what they need and what they can afford.

*The main complaint I have, is that I have constantly been hearing over the years, that the client is often not being allowed to have the house design that they want and that they are going to be paying for.*

If the Architect envisages something different being built on the plot to what the clients want to build, problems can start. Often the Architect will insist that he or she is right, and that the client *really must* follow their guidance, otherwise the job will be a complete failure (*Section 35 discusses a real life example of this happening, but in that case, involving a Planning Specialist*).

At the shows, I usually know if the person coming to talk to me is having *Architect troubles*. They will start talking, looking a bit sheepish, as if they are *telling tales on* someone. They will say *"We've got a bit of a problem and we don't know what to do about it"*, then go ahead and recount how the Architect has basically been bullying them to build what he or she wants, and will simply not listen to them trying to get what they want. *That sort of thing really gets my back up!*

Whenever this happens, I advise the self-builders that this is not how it should be. It is *their* project, not another Architect's vanity project. I tell them to insist on having what they want, and firmly get the message over to whoever is involved, that: *"We are the clients, we pay you, you therefore do what we say, we don't do what you say"*.

If the Architect takes the huff and walks away, they did not deserve the business in the first place. There are plenty of other people who can do the job just as well.

So, now I have got that off my chest, I will move on to the *real* subject of this item, me saying that you don't usually need a fully qualified Architect.

**Some facts:**

1. To get a stage Mortgage, you need to prove that you are capable of Project Managing the job, or if you cannot, that you will be taking on a Builder, or Project Manager who can. You won't usually have to say that you are hiring a fully qualified Architect.
2. You need a set of drawings for Planning Permission and Building Regulations. For a simple house design, this is a simple job, not needing a fully qualified Architect (*I do all my own designs and have no qualifications in the field of Architecture. All my houses are still standing!*)
3. The design process usually follows this procedure: Design sketches (*drawn to scale*), are prepared, based either on *your own* rough sketches or ideas for the layout and appearance of the house, or sometimes based on ideas and drawings that the designer may suggest. When you are happy with the initial sketches, the designer turns them into more detailed drawings that conform with planning application requirements. Once you are happy with the drawings, they then send them

*(anything between one and six copies of each drawing / specification, depending on how the Local Authority operates in that area)*, with the correct fee, to the Planning Department for processing. *That's it, - Job done!*

The charge for a house designer to do that level of work will usually be anywhere between £500 and £1500 for the basic planning application drawing package *(which can sometimes also include all the Building Regulations information)*. The cost for a fully qualified Architect could be anywhere between £1500 and £5000+ for the same thing, but probably presented in a higher quality package, maybe including a glossy, custom printed folder, with some other shiny paperwork included, creating an impressive looking document.

4. If, for any reason, you need to prepare more detailed construction details *(which is rare, unless requested by the planners)*, a basic House Designer can usually prepare all the basic drawings and associated documents. If they can't, they will almost definitely be linked to someone who can *(they pass work back and to between each other)*.

5. The Builders, and your Project Manager *(or you, when you get to that stage)* should know between them what needs doing on site and how to do it. All the information they need will be on the basic Planning Permission / Building Regulations drawings. If it isn't, they can ask you, and you can ask the house designer or Architect if necessary.

6. If you are Project Managing the job, you will need to do a bit of research before you begin each section of work, just so you don't look foolish. But, for example, if you have decent groundworkers, the best thing to do is leave everything to them, and you just keep your eyes open for anything that might not look quite right. If you miss anything important, the Building Inspector will be making sure that everything is being built correctly as it progresses.

7. Architects sometimes say that they can offer a "supervisory" role for your build. *Be careful!*

   I am not saying that they can't offer that role, but I have found that, quite often the client doesn't seem to get the level of service that they might have expected, compared to the fees they are charged for the service.

8. What would the Architect's "Supervisory" include? They will usually charge a couple of thousand pounds upwards for the basic service, then, as the works progress, either when you either specifically ask them to visit, or when they are passing *(usually on the way to somewhere else)*, they will call to site, have a look round for 10 – 15 minutes, answer any questions you have, see where progress is up to, have a chat with the subbies, asking if everything is going ok, and take some photographs. A couple of days later, they will then send you a 2 or 3 page report update, and a bill for a few hundred pounds!

   > **Note:** *This description does not apply to all Architects, but before you sign anyone up to taking a supervisory role, just make sure you find out exactly how they see their role, how they will carry that role out, and what the charges for the service*

*will be. You can then decide whether you think this is an extra you think is worth paying.*

9. To find someone who would be happy to prepare your Planning and Building Regs drawings, make a search on Yell.com, or look at the advertising pages in your local newspaper (*if it still exists*). Alternatively, do a search on the computer for *"House designers"* in *"Your Town"*. That should bring you some relevant results, even if it just sends you to more pages similar to Yell.com.

*(By the way, if you can find an RIBA qualified person for a decent price, that is fine, there is no problem doing that. I am just letting you know that any type of house designer (including Architectural Technicians) can usually do just as good a job at drawing up some house plans and will charge less than onse with letters after their name).*

### A final Note on this subject:

Feel free to ignore my minor rant here. I do have strong feelings when I see or hear about Self-builders being taken advantage of by professionals. If you want to use an Architect, just bear in mind what I have said, and remember to ask some pertinent questions (*including probably the most important one: "How much will you charge?"*) before you sign anyone up.

## THING 43: COULD WE DESIGN OUR OWN HOME?

*Possibly. Why not have a go? Even if you only do the basics, it could save you a lot of time and money.*

As I have previously mentioned, the first job a house designer will normally do, is to prepare some sketch designs. They will be sent to you and once you have looked over them, you will make comments. They will then be altered and re-altered until you are happy with them. Once you reach that stage, some designers will offer to prepare Virtual 3D renderings of the design that you can walk through on your computer screen. That process can take weeks and get quite expensive (*but is a good way for you to be able appreciate and get a feel for the overall layout and rooms sizes*).

If, instead of your designer sending you the sketches, you could send your own sketches to the designer, you could save a significant amount of time and money. So, why not have a go at drawing up some of your ideas yourselves? It is not that difficult, and if you find that you can't do it, you can just revert to the normal way of doing things.

**Here's how I would suggest you go about it:**

Have a look at some web sites, books of house plans, or go and visit some new show homes. Try to find house styles, sizes, and floor layouts that you like. It doesn't matter if you mix and match a few different styles and layouts in your sketch designs, as long as you like them. Once you have gathered your ideas together, you need to get something down either on paper, or as a computer aided design (CAD).

1) **Option 1: Draw them onto paper:**

To make a decent stab at doing this properly, you will need to kit yourself out with a bit of equipment (*you could order all of this from Amazon in one go*):

- A scale ruler.
- An adjustable set square.
- A couple of A4 or A5 pencils.
- Cheap Technical Drawings pens with 0.1, 0.3 and 0.5 nibs
- A rubber
- An A3 technical drawing board, one with a sliding bar (*you'll know what I mean when you see it*). You can get these for around £30 - £35 on Amazon
- A pad of A3 tracing paper
- A roll of Sellotape

Once you have all the equipment:

i. Set the drawing board up with the A3 tracing paper fixed to it with little bits of sellotape across the corners (*sit the paper on the sliding bar, so that it is level, before taping it down*).

ii. Using an A4 pencil, the adjustable set square, and the scale rule, have a bit of a play around, drawing rectangles and house shapes.

iii. Once you have done that for a while, use the scale rule, at a scale of 1:50, to draw some parallel lines depicting walls at 100mm and at 300mm apart (*they are the internal and external wall thicknesses*).

iv. When you feel confident enough, start to draw floor layouts, using your own sketch ideas, photos of houses you have seen, or just anything that comes to you.

v. As you get more confident, start to get the drawings a bit tidier, until you  think they could be used to show someone else what your ideas are.

vi. One slightly technical detail is this: Once you have designed the ground floor, to then design the first floor, you need to make sure that the stairs you have drawn downstairs are in  the same position on the upstairs plan. This is not difficult to do, just use the scale rule and copy the measurements from one drawing to the other.

vii. Choose your favourite floor layouts.

viii. That's it, you are done.

If you are feeling brave, you could have a go at elevations. If you do, use measurements from your own house, for windows, doors etc, to give you an idea of sizes, heights, and widths.

Once you get to the stage where you are happy with the design, take the drawings to your house designer, talk them through what you have been trying to achieve, and they should then be able to go away and draw up your first official house design in a couple of days, saving you having to pay them to produce various different options.

2) **Use a computer design package:**

A lot of the CAD house design packages are aimed at the DIY market. They don't cost much and can be easy to get the hang of (*at least easy enough to knock up a few floor layouts*). "Sketchup" seems to be popular with potential self-builders. I often get guests at the shows turning up with their own Sketchup designs, and some of them are pretty good!

Have a look at:
- https://www.smartdraw.com
- https://www.sketchup.com

I won't try to guide you through learning to use these software packages but have a look online for tutorials to get you going.

**Printer:** If you are using a 1:50 scale for your layout drawings (*which is most common*), you will probably need an A3 printer to be able to print them out on one sheet of paper.

I always use "Brother" printers. They make good, professional A3 printers quite cheap, which you can buy at PC world or online (amongst other suppliers). The ink last for ages, especially if you get the XL cartridges.

## THINGS 44: WHAT DO WE NEED TO THINK ABOUT WHEN DESIGNING A HOUSE?

### "A good house design almost designs itself".

I use a simple, 15 year old version of a CAD design package to design all my houses (*Chief Architect: chiefarchitect.com*). It is simple to learn and use but is expensive.

As I work on a new design, I usually find that as I draw, if the design is a good one, the process goes smoothly. The rooms tend to fit nicely in their logical positions, at the right sizes and in the right proportions (*not long and narrow or oddly shaped*). The overall layout flows and makes sense, and the whole thing just seems to *work*.

**So, how do you come up with a good house design for your own house? Here are a few ideas:**

**Floor plan:**

➤ Try to use well-proportioned rooms. Rooms that resemble wide corridors should be avoided.
➤ Aim for a good *flow* between the rooms (*don't have little annexes or odd rooms dotted around the place*).

- ➢ Think about where the rooms should go:
  - • The Dining room: Next to, or near the Kitchen *(so food can be taken straight in to where it is needed)*.
  - • The Kitchen: Near the hall and the front door *(so you don't have to carry shopping through the house)*.
  - • The Living room: Next to, or near to the Dining room *(so when you entertain, you can move from one room to the other without having to walk through adjacent rooms)*.
  - • The Utility room out of the way, and with the back door in it *(so visitors don't see your mess, and also for taking out laundry / coming in from gardening)*.
- ➢ Stairs not restricting light coming into the house (i.e. not being positioned where windows should sensibly be).
- ➢ Decent sized windows, so you don't have dark rooms.
- ➢ A good sized Master bedroom, with en-suite and any view that there is to be had. *(Also, If possible, with a large shower in the en-suite)*.
- ➢ Reasonably sized double bedrooms, big enough to take wardrobes, drawers etc and so you don't have to squeeze between the end of the bed and the wall.
- ➢ Reasonably sized single bedrooms that can take a single bed, bedside cabinet, wardrobe, and drawer unit.
- ➢ Good sized Family bathroom. (bath *and* shower?)
- ➢ Storage cupboards / rooms *(ideal for filling in leftover spaces on your design when you can't think what else to do with them)*.


**External appearance:**

- ➢ A balanced design where possible. Houses can look less attractive if they are lopsided *(e.g. no windows on one half of an elevation, but windows on the other half)*.
- ➢ Front doors look nice if they are in the middle of the front elevation.
- ➢ Design a bit of interest into the front elevation, but don't pepper it with features. Try to keep it simple and attractive.
- ➢ Cladding can add character *(there are some nice self-coloured plastic / wood composite claddings now that last a long time without needing maintenance)*.
- ➢ Don't oversize or undersize windows on the front elevation, try to get a balance with the other features. Sides and back don't matter as much.
- ➢ If you are building a garage, make sure it is big enough to fit a decent sized car, with enough room to open the doors, plus some space left for your clutter.
- ➢ Try to orientate and position the house to make the most of the sun and the garden.

Those are my basic thoughts on the main things to consider, but everyone will have their own additional or different ideas. If so, and you like what you come up with, go with that.

# THING 45: WHAT ARE PASSIVE AND ACTIVE HOUSE DESIGN?

You will have probably heard the term *Passive House*. It both a *product* and a *concept*. A Passive house is a house which use little or no energy and has a very low carbon footprint.

The terms *Passive Design* and *Active Design* are, in a way related to the Passive House Concept, but they are not products, they are simply terms used by house designers which refer to the method by which the house reduces the amount of energy it uses.

*Passive House Design uses the layout of a building, together with the materials it is built from and the physical form it takes, to reduce the amount of mechanical cooling, heating, ventilation and lighting that a building requires via a standard energy supply.*

*Basically, it does its job by just being there.*

A passive house uses the building's orientation to the sun, the positioning of windows, and the methods of ventilation, to reduce the energy it consumes. It also uses *Thermal Mass* to store heat within the building, and release it as required.

**Examples of thermal mass would be:**

1) **A thick concrete wall** positioned and orientated so that it absorbs energy from the sun, then releases it over an extended period.

2) **A "Trombe Wall"**, which is a solid, dense wall, possibly painted matt black, built behind glass, again orientated so that the sun's heat is magnified through the glass, and stored within the wall and then released slowly.

A popular product used in Passive house construction is Solar Panels. It might be a tossup between calling these *active* or *passive* products, but they tend to be classed as the latter, probably due to the fact that they have no built it working parts. Just pipework / wiring etc.

One of the most common material used in Passive Design, is simple, everyday insulation. Products such as Mineral Wool, Lambswool, Polystyrene, Straw, Phenolic insulation boards *(also known by the trade names of Kingspan, Cellotex and others)* and Paper, are all products that are available to every house builder, but they are used in far greater quantity in Passive Houses.

**Active House Design:** Whereas *Passive Design* uses products that *do nothing*, but still reduce energy requirements, Active Design uses products that *work* in some way, to either produce or save energy. Products such as Wind Turbines, Highly efficient boilers, Ground Source Heat Pumps (*systems that are installed below ground, to draw natural heat from the ground itself, and send it to be used for heating buildings and providing hot water*), Air Source Heating (*systems that can take heat from the air, and as with Ground source, send it to the building to provide heat and hot water*).

*(**Note:** There are sections a bit later that talk more about Ground and Air Source heating).*

Self-builders looking to reduce heating and hot water bills, will often use a mixture of both Active and Passive methods. They might include high levels of various different types of standard insulation, together with either Ground or Air Source systems.

***My view?** I would always choose passive design over active design. Some of the active systems are expensive, complicated to install and need maintenance, where insulation is relatively cheap, easy, and quick to install, and doesn't need maintenance, and solar panels are now coming down in price, whilst also improving in efficiency.*

*I would rather spend £10,000 on the best insulation throughout the house, than £15,000 to install an active energy generating system. If the prices for active systems were to come down, that stance could change, but to be honest, probably not.*

*<center>Comments welcomed.</center>*

## THING 46: IS BUILDING A PASSIVE HOUSE A SENSIBLE OPTION?

*I will need to put my environmentalist hat on for this one. I <u>am</u> into saving energy, money, and the planet, but Passive Houses are always something I have looked at and thought to myself: "Why"? (That doesn't mean my view is the correct one, and is why I need to "change hats" for this one).*

I have read about Passive Houses, a friend built one, I have spoken to plenty of people at the shows about their ideas to build passively, but I have never been convinced.

I'll run through some of the pro's and con's here, just to give you some ideas of what you should think about and look into, if this is something that interests you.

Most of the people I have spoken to about Passive Housing have seen something on the TV, or on a stand at a show. They are usually naturally conservation orientated in their thinking and their lifestyles, and a Passive House seems like a great next step up the ladder, a good way to help the environment, and a good way to invest their money (*the last one of those is my main problem with this concept*).

So, a quick bit about what a Passive House is (*yes, I know I mentioned this in the previous section, but some readers might come straight to this section, so it is worth repeating*).

A Passive House is a house that has been specifically designed and built to use either very few, or none of the planets resources, to fulfil its role as a house and a family home. Gaining *Passive House* certification is a very lofty target to try to hit, and if you want to achieve that status, you are going to have to jump through quite a few hoops to do so.

I am not going to get into the detail of all the Passive materials and methods in this book. There are books written specifically on this subject. They have the scope to discuss those details and options in depth. I just want to try to give you a *sketch impression* of what is involved in designing and building a Passive House, so that if it sounds like an interesting subject, you can carry out a lot more of your own research into it.

**So, here are some thoughts on the general subject:**

- You will need to decide that you are building a passive house *prior to starting work*. You must be registered and have taken on a *Passive House Certifier* to monitor your progress throughout the build if you want to eventually be able to use the term Passive House to describe the building.
- If you do not meet a stringent set of criteria with the build, you will not receive a certificate to confirm that your house is Passive. If you don't have the certificate, your house cannot formally be described as a Passive House.
- It is an expensive house to design and build, and will take significantly longer to complete than a standard, well insulated house.
- You will need to include some specialist equipment (*possibly a mixture of the Active design products such as wind turbines, ground source or air source heating etc*).
- Once you are living in the house, your running costs should be negligible.
- You will be helping to save the planet.
- You will benefit from having a system of mechanical ventilation throughout the house. This recirculates air around the house and gives a healthy living environment.
- You may benefit from feed in tariffs to generate income.

As I re-read that list, I admit, it is not a particularly rousing list of incentives to persuade you to build your own Passive House, but I can't really find anything else *useful* but *brief* to say on the subject at the moment! I have searched web sites, and all the benefits of Passive Housing seem to be measured in heating efficiency, healthy air and saving the planet. That is great, but I can probably get 90% of the same benefits for a fraction of the price with standard self-build methods and techniques. Sorry, but at least I gave it a shot!

*Finally: My friend who built a Passive House for his Mum, told me that she complains because it is "too cold" in the winter if she doesn't use the heating. He told her to put a cardigan on! – So, a hi-tech, highly insulated, expensive to build house, and his mum was cold. Nuff said!*

**I suppose you are either a fan or you are not.**


## THING 47: **MAKE SURE YOUR HOUSE IS SELLABLE**

Occasionally self-builders will design a home that, while it may be nice inside, either looks a bit unusual, quirky, or a bit boring on the outside.

The second house I built, now I look back at it, was boring. A huge great big lump of a house, with nothing about it really grabbing any attention. No star quality. We managed to sell it ok, but probably only because it was in a nice location, had loads of accommodation, was sturdily built, as well as being highly thermally and sound insulated (*this was in the eighties when insulation was usually an afterthought for house builders*). My design input was the weak link! (*Sorry, I don't have any photos of it and would be too embarrassed to include them if I did!*)

Since then I have tried to improve the appearance of my designs. For my latest offering, I have taken a bit of a sideways leap, to come up with the house pictured here (*it* might *look nice, but it was a swine to build*)! This design has turned out to be very sellable.

If you want to be sure that, if and when it comes time to sell the house, it gets a good price and sells quickly. To give it the best chance of doing so, here are some important points to try to incorporate into the design and build:

- A visual design that is pleasant to the eye.
- A balanced appearance, especially on the front elevation (*the house pictured above is fully symmetrical on the front elevation*).
- Attractive building materials and/or attractive, modern, but inoffensive colours, such as white, grey, cream etc (*some colours go out of fashion, but white, cream and grey seem to stick around*).
- Good sized, well-proportioned rooms.
- Light and airy design and "feel".
- Sensible, practical internal layout.
- Don't go overboard on quirky features that you may regard as giving the house *character*. You might like them, but the reason they are given the name "quirky" is because they only appeal to smaller numbers of people.
- High quality finished appearance. You don't need to spend a fortune on finishes, but just small touches can make a big difference. Nice lighting features, a modern chandelier, nice flooring, a wood burner, bi-fold doors, modern internal doors and ironmongery, nice kitchen, and bathrooms etc.

## THING 48: **MINIMISE CORRIDORS, SMALL NARROW ROOMS AND DARK AREAS**

An easy mistake to make, especially if you don't have a lot of experience in designing houses, is not remembering that the design drawings get turned in to houses. With this in mind, there are a few things that you need to keep your eyes open for, regarding the practicality of your design, whether it is you or someone else who designs your house.

Self-builders, who are not used to seeing house designs on paper can be forgiven for coming up with their own designs that could present practical or aesthetic problems or anomalies when they are built, but even professional designers can still be guilty of not noticing important, possibly problematic issues, and only finding out about them once the shell of the house has been built.

It is only when you can physically walk around a house and get the feel of each space, that you can start to decide whether the *individual rooms*, and the *overall design* has worked as you hoped it would. It is easy to put pen to paper and come up with a layout that has all the rooms you need, all looking like they have enough space within them to be able to do the job they are supposed to do. It is a bit more difficult to try to imagine each room on a drawing, as it would be in "3D", as if you are actually standing in the room, but it is important that you at least try (*"3D CAD drawing walk throughs" partly solve this problem, but are still no substitute for actually standing in a room and looking around*).

I have seen photos and drawings of either existing or potential self-build projects, that more resemble *Travel Lodges* than *Individual Executive Properties*. There was such a property on one of the developments where I was building one of my own Self-Builds. The plot was fantastic, with a river running right past the garden, trees all around it, large garden, and the outside of the house looked fine. But inside?

The entrance was ok, roughly in the middle of the front elevation, but as you walked in through the (*solid / no glass*) front door, you entered a dark narrow corridor, probably 1.5m (5ft) wide, that went from the front door, probably two thirds of the way through towards the rear of the house. The first door on the left was a small study, with a front window. As you went down the corridor, the next door on the left was the living room. It was ok, but only had a rear window to let light in, so it was a bit dark. It ignored the fact that the side of the house looked overlooked the river. Instead of installing a large, maybe Bi-fold door for this side of the room, they had built a huge, ornate brick fireplace, that protruded into the room by around 3ft, making it appear a lot smaller than it was, and also restricting the positioning of furniture. It also meant that the room was quite dark.

On the right of the entrance corridor, by the front door was a WC, with a small window. That was ok.

As you walked along the corridor it got darker and darker, not helped by the fact that the owners had painted the walls with a dark cream matt paint. You then took a right turn, onto a similar width corridor, running right through the middle of the house, all the way to the right hand side wall. The corridor had no windows, so needed to have the light on most of the time.

Off that corridor, on either side, were what could be described as simply *"a bunch of small rooms"*. I don't really know what most of them were, but one was in fact, a dining room (*which was next to the living room*). This room was just about wide enough to get a decent table in, and to squeeze some chairs around it, but would accommodate no other furniture, and there was very little circulation space.

At the end of that corridor was a door that opened on to a huge extension to the main house, which was all one room, the kitchen. It had a large open plan sitting area, which was actually a very nice space, with wide folding doors on both the rear and side walls. It had windows at the front and a nicely designed, expensive kitchen. I imagine that most time would be spent in that one room. I would be surprised if the rest of the ground floor got much use, being made up of small, dark, oddly proportioned rooms. Basically, they were just quite unpleasant, fairly useless, spaces.

So, now you have read about how *not* to do it, make sure you take all the steps you can, not to repeat these types of mistakes.

One way you can do this is to go and look at some commercial house builder's show houses. Pick up a brochure and walk round each room in each house style, looking, as you go at the measurements of each room as they are listed in the brochure. You can then make quick notes about how you would change them for your own design. Things like:

**Living room**: *make it 3ft longer and 2ft wider and more windows + bi-fold.* **Entrance hall**: *Too much like a corridor / Needs more light.* **Bathroom:** *Very poky, needs to be much bigger... and so on around the house.*

You can then use these notes as a check list when you start to work on your own design.

## THING 49: QUOINS AND WINDOW SURROUNDS

Quoins are a simple Architectural feature that can come in useful. The image below is of a house I built about 20 years ago. It has a traditional style.

When I did the original design, it did not have the corner features (*the quoins*) or the features around the windows. Before I went in for Planning, I could see from the drawings (*and had already learned from previous projects*) that when it was built, it could end up looking a bit boring. I therefore came up with the idea of adding the quoins and window surrounds. I thought it all pulled together quite nicely. My only comment on it now, would be that the traditional look is not particularly fashionable at the moment.

You can buy quoins and window surrounds from Builders Merchants, or on the internet. The most visually attractive style is reconstituted sandstone, which comes in various colours, but it can work out quite expensive.

A lower cost option is to buy the concrete versions. They can either be painted or left as a natural white concrete.

Cheaper again is to get the company who are doing the rendering to *hand form* the quoins and window surrounds in render, as part of the overall rendering work, then paint them once the render had dried. That is the option I went for on this house and 20 years later, they still look good.

**Idea:** If you are designing a modern style house, using a CAD system, and are familiar enough with the system to be able to add detailing to your design, you could insert quoins and window surrounds onto the CAD drawing, and if they don't seem to work, erase them, so you don't have to wait until the house is built to find out if they will look ok.

## THINGS 50: **FUTURE PROOF YOUR DESIGN (Lifetime Homes)**

One thing house design in the UK has never given much attention to, is how a house needs to change over time, to suit the needs of its occupants.

In 1991, a concept called *Lifetime Homes* was introduced by the *Joseph Rowntree Foundation* and the *Habinteg Housing Association*, with the intention of making new homes more adaptable, whilst incurring minimal extra cost in doing so.

It was a bit of a slow burner of an idea for a while, but in 2008 the UK government announced its intention that all new homes would be built to Lifetime Homes recommendations, by 2013. That has obviously not happened, but although the concept has taken a while to catch on, it is now gaining momentum, and is now having a lot more attention paid to it. It is about time too. This is one of the most common sense based ideas around at the moment.

The Lifetime Homes concept introduced 16 recommendations, detailing how the design and structure of new homes should take more account of the way the building interacts with its occupants, and how the design should allow it to be easily adapted at any time to take in to account changes of owner, illness, disability / mobility, and the occupants age.

None of the recommendations are particularly onerous, complicated, or would be expensive to build in at the design stage, but each one could potentially make a sensible and very useful contribution to improving the ongoing quality of life of its inhabitants for as long as they stay in occupancy.

**Here are the areas covered by the Lifetime Homes recommendations:**

1) Car Parking widths.
2) Moving from the parking space to the house.
3) The approach to the house.
4) Entrances.
5) Stairs.
6) Doorways and hallways.
7) Space to turn and move around.
8) Living space.
9) Convenient bed space.
10) Accessible WC and potential shower on the ground floor.
11) Stronger bathroom walls (*to allow for fixing rails, to assist people exiting the bath*).
12) Stairways, and allowance for a stairlift to be fitted, plus an area for a *personal lift* to potentially be fitted between floors.
13) Moving between bedroom and bathroom.
14) Bathroom layout.
15) Windows.
16) Sockets and controls.

To find out more about these criteria and / or Lifetime Homes in general, go to:

http://www.lifetimehomes.org.uk

I am a fan of this concept, so much so that all the new houses we now design and build, include at least some of the criteria, such as:

**Car parking widths:** The idea is that there should be plenty of room to be able to load and unload vehicles (*including wheelchairs*) without obstruction. The recommendation is that a parking width of 3.3m is available. This is something you can easily remember when it comes to positioning your house on the plot. Most self-builds will, almost by default, meet this recommendation. **Extra cost to us: £0**

**Stairs:** The recommendations concentrate on Communal stairs offering easy access. Our treatment of stairs is, where there is enough room, we fit wide staircases (*1000m or more, wide as opposed to the standard 800mm or 850mm width*). On a standard softwood staircase, this can cost as little as £150. We also strengthen the wall at the side of the stairs in case a stair lift is required at some point in the future. To do this, we simply plate the whole wall behind the plasterboard, with 22mm thick OSB board, which will give it enough strength to take stairlift equipment. **Extra cost to us: around £250**

**Doorways:** The recommendations suggest wide doorways. All our doorways, on *all* floors are designed to take 2'9" doors (*as opposed to Building Regs requirements, which say 2'9" doors are only required on the ground floor*). Cost? Very little extra per door, possibly £5 - £40, depending on the quality of the door. **Total extra cost: between £60 and £600 depending on door choice and the number of doors.**

**Hallways:** I like wide halls, they let more light into and around the house, and give an overall impression of space. The recommendations state that wheelchairs should have room to manoeuvre in hallways. **Extra cost? £0**

**Living room:** A simple one. The requirement is that there is a living space on the ground floor, accessible from the front door. We provide two living spaces, a family room, and a living room. **Extra cost £0**

**Accessible WC and a shower on the ground floor,** accessible by way of a 2'9" door", (*which is required anyway*). We always include a full shower room on the ground floor. I think this is a good idea to include in *any* house that has room for it. At some time in the future, a family room and a shower on the ground floor could provide full accommodation for a family member who cannot easily negotiate the stairs, and potentially removes the potential need for a stairlift. **Extra cost £0**

**Bathroom layout:** We always include a spacious family bathroom. The recommendations also ask for strengthened walls, to take grab rails and other similar fixings. **Extra cost £150**

**Entrance level bed space:** The recommendations ask for a room where temporary bed space can be provided. We include a ground floor family room. **Extra cost £0**

**Sockets and controls:** This is pretty much covered by Building Regs these days. Sockets and switches are now set at suitable heights for wheelchair user to be able to reach them comfortably. **Extra cost £0**

*I really think that Lifetime Homes is something that self-builders should seriously look in to, with a view to including as many of the recommendations as possible into the fabric of their homes. They may not be needed immediately, but none of us know when things might change.*

## THING 51: A SQUARE IS THE MOST COST EFFECTIVE DESIGN

I often cover this topic when I am presenting seminars at the shows, and I love the reaction it gets from the audience. All it is, is some basic maths, which, if used in your own designs, could potentially save you *literally* thousands, if not tens of thousands of pounds on the build costs, whilst, at the same time, making the most efficient use possible of the floor space within a building.

**Have a look at this** **image of a simple house shape:**

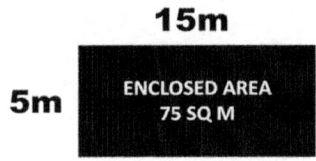

If you add up the perimeter measurements, you get a total of **40m**. That is the length of the external walls, *whatever they are made of*, that you would need to build, to enclose the internal space. In this configuration, you would be giving yourself **75sq m** of floor area per floor, to use as rooms. So, over 2 floors you would get a total of **150sq m** of living space inside your home, for the cost of **40m** of external wall wrapped around it.

**Now look at this image:**

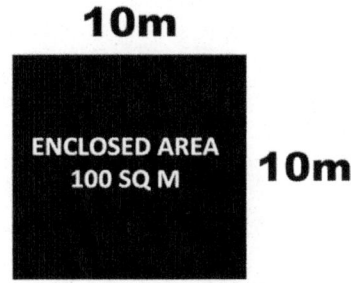

If you add up the perimeter measurements of this shape, you get the same **40m**. The difference here, is that for the same 40m of external walls, by using a square shape, you now get **100sq m** of internal space per floor. So, over 2 floors, that would give you **200sq m** of living space inside your home.

**By using the more efficient square shape, you have just given yourself 50sq m, or 25% extra living space, for what would be a fairly similar overall build cost.**

50sq m works out at roughly three extra rooms at 4m x 4m (*possibly 2 extra double bedrooms and a family room*). Having those extra rooms not only gives you a bigger living space, it also increases the value of your home significantly.

You may say *"But squares are boring"*. Below is an image of the house we are using on our next project. It is pretty much a square building but is not boring.

I am not saying *"Build square houses"*, but now you have seen this example, you are aware of the fact that a square is the most efficient shape to build, and can decide whether to use it, or not (and if not, why not *"squarish"*?)

**Note:** The longer and narrower the rectangle, the lower the relative amount of internal space will be.

If you design a house with a shape similar to this next image, you compound the effect of wasting internal space:

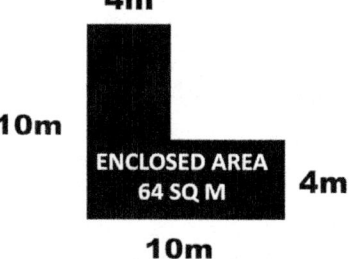

The external wall length of this shape is still 40m, but now you are only giving yourselves 64sq m of internal space per floor, 128sq m in total.

### *Food for thought?*

## THING 52: TWICE AS MUCH HOUSE DOESN'T NEED TO COST TWICE AS MUCH MONEY

You may think that if you build a house twice as big, it will cost twice as much. That is not necessarily the case. To explain why, I will use a slightly exaggerated example:

Think of a building that is 7m x 7m square x 2 floors (**98sq m**), with a living room, family room, dining room, kitchen, utility room and toilet on the ground floor, and 4 bedrooms, bathroom, en-suite and family bathroom on the second floor.

All those rooms are going to be quite small, and each one will obviously need walls, doors, door frames, door handles, skirtings, architraves, windows, lighting, sockets, switches, and the walls and doors will need decorating. The house will also need kitchen units and appliances, utility room units, bathroom equipment for the family bathroom, the en-suite, and the W.C, plus tiling for the kitchen and bathrooms.

Now imagine a house 10m x 10m x 2 floors (**200sq m**), with the same list of rooms. The individual rooms would be much larger, so, to build them, it would take *some* extra concrete for the ground floor, *some* extra timber or blockwork for the walls, three or four extra joists, a few extra floor boards, plasterboards, and some more wall and floor tiling. However, none those extra items would cost significantly more than in the previous example (*just believe me on that bit!*).

On the other hand, the larger house would only need the *same number* of door frames, doors, door handles, windows, lighting, kitchen units and appliances, utility units, bathroom equipment and it would need a little bit more tiling, compared with the first example.

So, the consequence of pretty much *doubling* the size of the floor area inside the house, may add just 30% - 40% in extra build costs, and the main reason why that happens is that most of the extra space inside the building will be made up simply of **air**.

-------------------------------------------------------------------------------------------------

**So, bringing section 51 and 52 together:**

*A square shaped house, as large as you can build it on your plot, should give you the best value for money build, <u>per floor</u>.*

-------------------------------------------------------------------------------------------------

## THING 53: **THINK ABOUT HOW YOU WILL USE EACH ROOM**

At the design stage, it is a good idea to give some thought to how you will use each room once the house is built. If you think about this as early as possible, it may save you from making design mistakes that you won't notice until the shell of the house is up, and you are taking your first proper look around.

Here are some of the things you should consider as you think your way through each room (*in no particular order*):

- Will your kitchen be the social centre of the house, or just the place you cook food? How much social space will you need in this room?
- Will the living room be the social centre?
- Is the family room mainly for the kids, so Mum and Dad can stay in the living room and get some peace? If so, is it big enough, and does it have TV and BT points?
- Would a shower in the downstairs loo be a good idea for getting people and pets cleaned up after adventuring *(and for futureproofing)*?
- What will the utility room *actually* be used for?
- Is the hallway going to make a statement about the rest of the house, or just be somewhere to take your shoes off?
- If you are having a downstairs office, what furniture will you want to get in there? How much use will it get, and by whom?
- Do you want the stairs to be a statement, or just something to walk up between floors?
- What is each bedroom going to need to provide in the way of space and amenities (*which family members need most space*)?
- Should the kids get shower rooms?
- Is the family bathroom, or the en-suite, or both (*or neither*) going to be "posh"?
- If you are going to have an attic space, what will its use be, and what will you need up there with regards to lighting, amenities, and drainage?

Once you know what you would like each room to do for you, it is a good idea for you to have a look at some existing houses, so you can visually calculate whether or not rooms in other houses would be able to offer what you will want and need from the same rooms in your own house. As I have said previously, developers Show Homes, or the house you are presently living in, are ideal for this sort of task.

Just by walking round a few show houses, knowing what you will be looking for in each room in your own house, you will probably find yourselves saying things like: *"We would need more room than this to get the TV on the wall and our big settee in"*, or *"This kitchen layout is good, maybe we could base ours on it"*, or maybe *"The recycling area in the utility room is a good idea"*, and so on around the house.

*This pleasant task should give you a much better feel for what you will want and need from your own designs.*

## THING 54: HOW HIGH SHOULD MY ROOMS BE?

This is a short, but important point to make. The most common ceiling height for new homes in the UK is 2.40m. Metric sized plasterboards measure 2.40m x 1.2m, so are designed to suit this height. The 1.2m also suits the default 600mm centres that timber studs in walls are set at, so using this sized board minimizes cutting and waste.

The metric boards also suit the centres that ceiling joists are set at, as standard (either 400mm or 600mm).

If, for any reason you need to, you should be able to find *imperial* sized plasterboards, which measure 8ft x 4ft (or 2.440m x 1.220m), but these are less common. Using these boards could present you with significant problems if you are building using a standard Timber Frame, or any other offsite manufactured product, as you would need to trim the width and height of every board to suit joist, timber stud centres and room heights.

**Bear these board sizes in mind when you are designing the house and ordering plasterboards:**

**Taller rooms:** There is nothing stopping you from making your rooms taller than the standard 2.4m, however if you do, you could find yourselves having to cut a thin strip of plasterboard to fill in the gap that the extra room height creates above the top of each standard height board, **_around the whole building_**. Not only that, you would need to fit a supporting timber horizontally across the gap where the two boards meet *(again, all round the building)*, to give the edges of the two adjoining boards extra support.

*(**This is not a good idea. I am telling you about it, so hopefully you won't think about doing it!**).*

*Also remember: Taller rooms = higher heating bills.*

## THING 55: **THINK ABOUT "RECYCLING" AT THE DESIGN STAGE**

Recycling is now an accepted way of life for everyone, but it has only started to be that way over the past 5 years or so. We are not quite there yet with it, but things are changing at a greater rate now than they have done at any time in the past and that change will continue for the foreseeable future.

House designers, both commercial and private, have been a bit slow to cotton on to the fact that recycling necessitates a fairly dramatic re-design of the way we use some of the rooms in our homes, as well as the external recycling areas *(formerly known as "The bins!")*.

The main rooms to be affected are the kitchen and utility room, but I wouldn't be surprised if the effect also creeps into other rooms, such a bathrooms and bedrooms *(I can see it now, little "recycling centres" in each bedroom and bathroom)*.

Self-builders are now incorporating these changes into their designs, which is not a particularly easy thing to do: A bin is a bin and making it out of shiny plastic and chrome doesn't change that fact, but people are doing their best.

So how do we solve the recycling problem?

## Kitchen / Utility rooms:

Most kitchen unit ranges now include recycling units, with small bins that slide out, being built into the base units, as (usually expensive) extras. These are better than nothing, but because they are small, would have to be emptied pretty much every day, if a family of four was using the kitchen. The only other commonly available kitchen based solutions are the "posh bins" (the plastic and chrome ones I mentioned previously).

## Other possible solutions to consider:

1) Fit the small recycling bins inside kitchen cupboards, and larger also create a space in the utility room for a set of large bins. This would obviously require you to design the house to incorporate a decent sized utility room, so that you can create a large space, probably under the worktop for this purpose (*this is where recycling is starting to change the way we see and use rooms*). The problem with this solution is that you would be constantly having to empty the small bins into the larger bins. Either that, or you would have to walk between the kitchen and utility room carrying small items of waste to put in the large bins, to save the small bins for the smaller items of waste. Either way, it would be a bit of a nuisance.

2) Design your kitchen to be large enough to include three or four spaces under the worktop in the kitchen, which are large enough to take the  full sized "posh" indoor bins (*choose the bins before you design the opening*). The side panels in this area could be finished with the same panels as the cabinet door fronts, and the floor finish used for the rest of the kitchen could also go into the space. This would create an area that looked like you meant it to be there (*as opposed to just appearing to be a stopgap solution*), so would not necessarily detract from the overall quality feel of the kitchen. Also try to choose a place for the bin area, that is not centrally visible in the kitchen, but is still close to where it will be most needed. You could also think about fitting a sliding screen of some type, to cover the whole area at times when you don't need to use the bins.

3) You might be aware that in America, they use under sink waste disposal systems. You can get similar systems over here (*search "InSinkErator" from TLC Electrical supplies*). This system would grind up your food waste into a slurry, which then goes into your general drainage system and not to landfill sites (*so is a more environmentally sound solution than those, ugly worktop sitting, plastic food bins*). This system won't reduce the rest of your waste, but it would free up extra worktop area and be one less bit or recycling equipment to have to put out each week. The full kit costs from about £200 (plus fitting) and you would need a suitable sink to fit it to.

4) Why not mix and match all three of those options, to provide possibly the best set up solution, whilst keeping everything relatively simple?

**Garden:** There are various, not too expensive bin stores and screen options now available for the multitude of Local Council bins that we have to find room for. You just need to think about what type to use and where is the best place to locate them.

*A bit of thought at the design stage can minimise the negative visual and practical impact of these slightly annoying, but necessary items.*

## THING 56: DO I NEED TO KEEP PIPEWORK RUNS SHORT?

It has always surprised me at the shows, when I am discussing house design, how many people quickly bring up the notion that:

*"Bathrooms need to be above kitchen and near to the boiler, so hot water has the minimum distance to travel and won't waste money by sitting in long lengths of pipes, going cold".*
*(and we weren't even talking about the plumbing!)*

The people who bring up this subject tend to be in their forties. It is something that doesn't seem to bother younger self-builders, but the people it bothers, *it really bothers*.

The reason for this worry about long pipe runs is usually based on people's personal experience from three or four decades ago. The memories of standing in a cold bathroom, with your hand under the hot tap, but getting cold water, waiting for the water to eventually arrive from the cylinder (*which can be at the opposite end of the house*), possibly thinking, as you stand there:

*"All this cold water in this pipe was hot last time this tap ran. How much am I paying for all that wasted heat, for every hot water tap in the house, after every time it is used?"*
(it is a valid point).

On the other hand:

i.     Is it worth restricting the layout and design of the house to save a bit of hot water? The enjoyment you are going to get from living in the house, as well as its market value, will partly depend on how well it is designed, *not* on how far the boiler is from the taps!
ii.    There are ways to minimise the problem without messing about with your house design.

If pipe lengths are a concern, instead of trying to bunch up all the bathrooms and toilets, try thinking along the lines of keeping ***most*** of the water usage appliances ***not too far*** from the boiler.

Let's consider the different choices of hot water systems, and how they could affect the amount of hot water pipework you will need to install:

1) **Cylinder system:** If you use a cylinder system, a small output boiler will usually be fitted in the kitchen or utility room and piped up to the cylinder, which often ends up somewhere near the centre of the building (*usually on the landing*). You will therefore have a length of hot water pipe running from the boiler to the cylinder, which won't necessarily be called in to use when you turn a tap on, unless you run it for a while. It will just be used to top up the cylinder *on demand*, when the cylinder asks for more hot water (*which will be whenever the thermostat decides that it is getting too cold*).

   Pipework then goes from the cylinder to the hot taps. One pipe coming from the cylinder, will split at appropriate points, to either drop down or go up to tap positions. Which means that wasted hot water will only be accumulated in the small section of pipe that it is drawn through, from the cylinder to each tap. In other words, not much.

2) **Combi Boiler systems:** This system only heats water up on demand. It will usually be situated downstairs in the kitchen or utility room. It keeps a small amount of hot water (*a few litres*) always ready to be drawn, in a well-insulated tank, within the boiler unit itself. It only heats water up (*almost instantly*) when it needs to , which is whenever a hot tap is turned on. The rest of the time it just sits there, very occasionally topping up the heat in the small storage unit. The hot water pipe running from the boiler to the taps will be longer than the cylinder systems equivalent pipe, but again, not by much.

**Question:** Ok, but why the wait when I used to turn the hot tap on, and is that problem fixed?

**Answer:** It is pretty much fixed.

The differences between when we used to stand waiting for hot water, and now are:

- A couple of decades ago, cylinders often weren't insulated or, if they were it would be with an almost useless insulating product (*does anyone remember the old red plastic cylinder jackets, tied round the cylinder with a piece of chord?*). All cylinders are now very well insulated, so stay hot, which means that less cool water needs to be drawn up through the cylinder, before the hot water gets into the pipework and starts to reach to the taps.

- Where possible the plumber will design and fit the pipework to keep the individual runs as short as possible.

- Houses are now much better insulated generally, so stay warmer, which means that pipework doesn't go cold as quickly, and therefore takes less time to start to feel warm when you turn the tap on.

- Because combi boilers only heat the water up when it is needed, very little heat is wasted, sitting in either a cylinder or the pipework.

*So, the days of standing, waiting for the tap water to warm up, should now be behind us and we can design our houses without giving the subject too much thought.*

## THING 57: **STAIRS**

Stairs don't really get a lot of thought or attention in commercially built housing. A standard set of plywood stairs, softwood handrail, cheap spindles, and posts (*correctly known as newels*), painted white, is generally the way they go.

Self-builders tend to approach the subject very differently. The staircases are often seen as being something that makes a statement about the house, saying to the world: "*I am special*", and sometimes large amounts of money are spent on designing and installing high spec stairs that help to make that statement a come to life.

**A few facts on stairs:**

- A standard set of softwood stairs can be bought for less than £200 at Builders Merchants.
- With the handrails, spindles (*the posts that go all the way up the stairs*), newels (*the thick posts at the top and bottom*) and all the other bits and pieces, including labour to fit them and 3 coats of paint or stain, a standard staircase could cost from around £1,000 - £1,200 (*depending on whether the handrail turns and runs along the landing*).
- The most recent custom stair installation that I installed for a client, was made up mainly of oak, with glass panels, running up two straight sets, one from ground to first floor and one from first floor to attic, with handrails, turning and running along the first and second floor landings. All the oak was given 3 coats of a clear oil stain. The materials cost was just over £8,000 (including the glass panels), the labour cost was around £1,000 and the staining around another £1,000. Total £10,000 (or £5,000 / set).

For that money, the clients created a visual centre piece, a grand statement for the entrance hall, which probably increased the value of the house by approaching the amount that it cost.

If you, as a self-builder really want to *go for it* with your staircases, it wouldn't be particularly difficult to spend north of £8,000 *per flight*.

The amount that you will actually spend will obviously depend on your budget. I have never been big on stairs. I appreciate that they can look very nice in the entrance hall, but personally, I would rather spend the money on a better kitchen, really nice en-suite, a decent built in sound and cinema system, decking and garden design. The sorts of things I can get enjoyment from, and that make my life easier. Having said that, depending on my budget, I would go for an, attractive, but not too expensive set of stairs. The image below is from a recent house we built. The handrails are white oak. The newels and the stairs themselves are softwood, with a clear semi-gloss stained finish. The spindles have been painted with an off white colour. When the job was finished and the flooring laid, it looked really nice, in quite a large hall, with oak doors (*again clear stained*). Cost? Around £1500 per flight, including fitting and decorating (*the spindles could have been swapped for glass for a few hundred pounds more*).

*By the way: For our next development, I have positioned the stairs between 2 walls, so all we will need is a standard set of stairs and one handrail. No spindles, newels, minimal labour, and no decorating! The job will probably cost £600 all in!*

## THING 58: USING THE ROOF SPACE

Previous sections have looked at how the efficiency of the design can give you extra living space within the building, without increasing the build cost significantly. Depending on the shape of your house, you can sometimes take that process one step further by going up into the roof space.

Most modern commercially built houses use standard roof trusses. Readers familiar with house building will probably have heard of attic trusses. These look pretty much the same as standard trusses, but instead of having lots of thin bracing timbers at angles across the trusses, attic trusses are manufactured to be a lot stronger, whilst also creating a large open space in their centre.

The images shown are of a self-build I completed in 2005, using a very simple squarish design and attic trusses, to give me a spacious 4 bedroom house. It took about 16 weeks to build, and the area within the roof was surprisingly spacious. The bedroom was at the rear of the property, and I installed French doors, plus a Juliet balcony on the rear wall of this bedroom, which gave me open views over one of the Welsh valleys. From the bed, the view was through the rooflights, which was also pleasant. As a personal opinion, I think that sloping ceilings in a bedroom add extra character to the room.

(This photo is of the master bedroom).

One thing to be aware of when using attic trusses, is that to maximise their benefit, you need to keep the house design as simple and square as possible, and the roof pitch fairly steep. The narrower the house and the lower the roof angle, the less living space it will provide. I suggest a roof pitch of around 45 degrees.

## THING 59: COULD WE PROJECT MANAGE THE BUILD?

It is a fact that, to a greater or lesser extent, the majority of self-build projects are self project managed. After all, the term *"Building your own home"* should do what it says on the tin shouldn't it? (*Well, to an extent*).

When considering whether or not to Project manage your own build, you need to ask yourselves some questions:

- What are you like at taking pressure, organising, accounting, learning, and understanding new things, solving problems, and taking measurements from drawings (*for ordering materials*)?
- What is your knowledge of safety like? Could you inspect a scaffold, or make sure the whole site is safe?
- Are you prepared to take at least a couple of courses, to get the safety certificates that you need to officially manage a building site? The most important ones would be: **First Aid** and **SMSTS** (*Site Management Safety Training Scheme*).
- Could you do the paperwork involved in running an active building site? Would you be able to check over a foundation dig to see if it is ready for inspection, or notice construction errors around the site that could cause problems later?
- Are you a *people person*? As a Project Manager you should be able to communicate and negotiate in a friendly, clear, but firm manner. If you can't do that, when the pressure is on, you could be found wanting.

If you are happy that you tick the boxes for those things, you would be perhaps 20% of the way to being a good Project Manager!

Now, before you throw this book against the wall, shouting *"Well, stuff it, I didn't want to be a Project Manager anyway"* just hang on, it's not as bad as it sounds!

Yes, a good Project Manager is able to do all those things, and a lot more besides. It is a complicated job, but a Self-Build is not a factory, a hospital, or a housing estate. It is a small scale, usually fairly slow moving, and quite simple, personal project, that you will probably spend a lot of time preparing for before you launch yourself into it.

The reason a lot of Self-Builders sign up an Architect to supervise their project *(see section 43),* is often that they are nervous about taking on what, to them, is a massive task, related to a subject that they are not familiar with. However, because of the nature of the self-build process, if you are reasonably intelligent, diligent and observant, with a good level of common sense, you may be able to negotiate your way through a fairly simple project successfully, without having to resort to taking on and paying someone else to take over the role.

Just reading books like this, investigating other avenues of knowledge, and maybe taking a short course in Project Management, would help to turbo boost your ability to successfully manage the wonderful adventure on which you could be just about to embark.

So, my conclusion on this subject is this:

*There have been hundreds of thousands of Self-Build project run successfully by amateur Project Managers over the past 40 years. There have also been some that failed because of the amateur Project Manager. It is totally your call as to whether you think you can do the job, or whether you decide that you need some help. If you are reasonably confident, but would like to know there is backup when you need it, think about taking on a builder who has a few different trades on their books. Someone who regularly builds houses, and who would probably be able to solve any problems that you can't. If you then struggle with something during the build, you can, at least turn to them first, before you need to find and pay anyone else.*

*My gut feeling on this matter is that successfully running your own build would be something you would be very proud of yourself for doing. It would be a shame to pass up the chance, simply because of nervousness.*

*But if you go for it, just make sure you are* <u>*properly prepared*</u>*.*


## THING 60: **INTEGRAL GARAGES v SEPARATE GARAGES**

**Pros and Cons of each:**

**Integral garages:**
- Are cheaper and (*obviously*) easy to build. They are cheaper because they form part of the main shell of the house, and are in effect, just another room (*although they do need a few additions, such as fireproofing to the walls, and also have a lower floor level*).
- Can have a door leading directly into the house. Useful in bad weather, especially if you have a remote controlled opening garage door, which allows you to stay in the

car until you are out of the rain (*remote control systems are not particularly expensive, starting at about £500*).

- Are a good place for the boiler to be fitted, so you don't have it constantly clicking on and off in one of the habitable rooms.
- Can dramatically *negatively* affect the ground floor space (*especially if it is a double garage*), so can make the living accommodation feel lop-sided, with lots of space upstairs, but limited space downstairs.
- Are a handy place to have, where you can *put stuff for now,* without having to go outside.
- Can be converted into an extra living room in the future, if required.

**Separate garages:**
- More expensive to build.
- Take longer to build.
- Need a larger plot and usually a larger driveway area.
- Can restrict, or determine the driveway shape, size, and location on the plot.
- Can restrict the house size and its location on the plot.
- It is not sensible, or practical to fit a boiler in an external garage, so if the main house does not have a utility room, the boiler might have to go in the kitchen (*possibly noisy*).
- Leaves more ground floor area to be used as rooms.
- Will require electrical cables to be run from the house for lighting, power points, heating etc. Underground cables will need to run inside *armoured cable* (for safety), which is expensive.
- Because you will already have the maximum ground floor space possible, you won't need to think about doing a conversion sometime in the future.
- Might require you to walk in the rain to the house after parking the car (*unless you add a canopy to and external door on the house*).

**Half and half garages:**

I have used both previous alternatives, and this option. I am calling it a *half and half* garage because it does not sit fully within the main shell of the house but gives some of the advantages of doing so. This one protruded out from the front of the house by around 5'. That was a good distance to allow the roof to extend across to provide a canopy for the front  door, which I think looks quite attractive. It also allowed me to situate a family room and a utility room behind it, adjacent to the kitchen.

Sharped eyed readers may make the comment; "*I thought you said that we should keep the designs squarish. What about the "sticky out" front bit of the house?*" Yes, you are correct, I did go away from the idea of keeping it squarish for the house design, however this plot was fairly compact, so there was no room for a separate garage. This design allowed me to extend the dining room forward (*on the left side of the house*), whilst achieving a well-proportioned, large living room to the rear of the dining room. It also included a large kitchen, a family room and good sized utility room, plus the double garage, all on a *fairly* efficiently shaped footprint. The main extra build cost was for the bit of the roof that is over the front extension.

**As an aside:** From a layout point of view, this is probably the design I am most pleased with from all my house designs. There was plenty of space downstairs, the design "*flowed*" well, and upstairs was huge, with 5 bedrooms and 3 bathrooms. I also like the simple arched window on the landing, which adds a nice bit of character to the front elevation. Unfortunately, I didn't take any internal photos.

*By the way: The chimney on this house was false. There was no fireplace, but the planners insisted on it, to be in keeping with the general nature of housing in the local area. The chimney stack is constructed out of 4" x 2" timber and plywood, with mesh fitted around it, and then rendered, to match the rest of the house.*
*The marks on the roof are from where it rained soon after it was painted, and the paint hadn't quite dried! I ended up building a scaffold and going up to clean it off some months later before I sold it!*

## THING 61: **ARE BUNGALOWS A GOOD IDEA?**

Over the past few years, bungalows seem to have all but disappeared from commercial housing developments, apart from where planning regulations stipulate that they must be included as part of a development. In Wales, there are still a few being built, but not many.

**Why is this?**

One of the main reasons for their diminishing popularity is the cost of land. By default, a bungalow is going to need a significantly larger plot than a two storey house offering the same amount of accommodation. Other factors responsible for their reduced numbers are related to their build cost:

- Bungalows require twice as much foundation and ground floor, to give the same amount of accommodation as a two storey house. Foundations are where unexpected costs are most likely to occur and concrete floors are a lot more expensive to construct than joisted floors.
- They require twice as much roof as an equivalently sized two storey house.

- They also require larger (longer) drainage systems, for both foul and surface water (*extra cost*).
- They can be harder to design efficiently, usually needing more corridors to access the more spread out rooms (*corridors reduce the amount of space available that can be used as rooms and are often quite dark*).

It is worth bearing these points in mind, especially if, due to the higher price of the larger plot, plus the higher build costs, the total development cost ends up being higher than the resale value of the completed property.

Due to fact that larger plots are needed (*which are harder to find and more expensive*) and the increased build costs, the idea of building a bungalow would be a non- starter to a lot of self-builders. However, if your main reason for self-building is *specifically* to be able to live on one floor, then *cost v value* equation loses its importance.

**You could think about "cheating":**

Where you really want, or need to build a bungalow, you could cheat. Instead of accepting the fact that a bungalow is, by default, a one storey building, you could design a bungalow, with everything you need on one floor, but also with an attic trussed roof. The roof area could then be kitted out as one large single room (*maybe with a bathroom*). This area would not add a lot to the total build cost but could be used as a multifunctional space (*office / guest suite / social area for Christmas or family get togethers, etc*). It would also increase the value of the property and make the *cost v space* equation a bit less painful.

I personally think bungalows are on their way out, not just because of the cost aspect, but also because there are now ways to design a two storey house, so that it can effectively cater for all the same needs and wishes that only bungalows used to be able to satisfy.

One product that has started to appear more and more in two storey houses, could be the thing that makes the difference as we move into the future: *Personal lifts*.

Lifetime Homes recommendations (*see section 51*) suggest that *all* new two storey dwellings should consider designing an area of the house that at some time in the future could be easily adapted to allow a personal lift to be installed.

*As part of the initial the build, this would simply require strengthening an area within the intermediate floor, to allow for a lift to be fitted in the future.*

*However, there is nothing stopping you from installing the lift at the outset, providing permanent access to both floors for everyone.*

This type of lift can presently be bought from around £8,000 but that price will probably come down as they get more popular.

*If we can build two storey houses that will be fully adaptable for anyone to be able to use throughout their lifetimes, and if land continues to increase in cost and decrease in availability, then I don't really see the need for building many new bungalows in the future.*

**Comments welcomed**


## THING 62: UTILITY ROOM OR BIGGER KITCHEN?

I have noticed that a lot of the new commercial house builders are now rarely including utility rooms in their new homes. This may be because they are trying to cram so many houses on to each development, and shrinking the living space inside the houses, that if they want the kitchen to look at least reasonably spacious, there simply isn't enough room to also have a utility room.

I often go and look at the show houses of the commercial builders, just to see what they are up to. I visited one recently and asked the salesperson *"Why don't the larger 4 / 5 bed properties have utility rooms?"* I was told that *"They have gone out of fashion"* (and with that a pig flew past the window!).

So, should you include a utility room, or opt for a larger kitchen with everything in it? I would go for the utility room option every time. Why?

- As a room, these days, the utility room does a different job to the kitchen. The kitchen can be the social centre of the house. Having a utility room, can therefore allow the kitchen to be (*theoretically*) kept in a reasonable state of cleanliness, while the messy stuff is kept in the utility room. So, if you have unexpected guests, it is easy just to close the door on the messy area.
- Who wants a noisy washing machine or tumble drier banging away in the background in the kitchen, while *you* have friends' round for coffee?
- The utility room is a good place to locate the boiler. They are not pretty things, and have unsightly pipes sticking out of them. They can also be quite noisy when they are working at full power.
- A tall larder cupboard in the utility room gives you an idea place to store the vacuum cleaner and ironing board when they are not being used, and your washing basket can be kept on the worktop in the same room.
- The utility room doesn't need to be large to be able to do its job. A worktop is 600mm wide and you need sensibly at least 900mm of floor to walk on between the worktop and the opposite wall, in order to be able to get to the back door (*which is also usually 900mm wide*). So a room width anything upwards of 1.5m (5ft) will be ok. The room can also be as little as around 8' (2400mm) long, and still get the following layout along one wall:

- A 600mm wide, tall larder unit
- A washing machine (600mm)
- A drier (600mm)
- A sink over a 600mm wide base cupboard (for your cleaning materials)

- The utility room can be a good place to keep your recycling bins.

  **Note:** *A lot of developers put the downstairs w.c within the utility room, which means you have to go into the utility room to get to it. This is not a good idea if you want to impress your visitors!*

## THING 63: BUILDING REGULATIONS

**Most readers will know what Building Regulations are, but may not be aware of their importance as part of the Self-Build process.**

*They are of critical importance.*

The term *Building Regulations* is self-explanatory, but as a self-builder, you need to be fully aware of how they will they relate to your own individual project. Once you know what your responsibilities are as a house builder, you can then decide whether or not you will be able to cope with administering their requirements, or whether you will need to get some practical and/or technical back-up, to make sure that they are being fully and correctly adhered to.

**Let's start with what the Building Regs are:**

Builders in most countries around the world are required to build to certain standards. In the UK, making sure those standards are achieved, is the job of the Local Building Regulations Department, whose representatives are the Building Inspectors.

The inspectors are responsible for ensuring that the quality of all new build, renovation and refurbishment projects in their area are built according to the Nationally accepted levels.

The Regs are basically the *minimum standard* that will be accepted for the creation or modification of any building.

**How does the system work?**

*I am only going to deal with the subject of self-build here, but the process works pretty much along the same lines on renovation and refurbishment projects.*

When you are getting ready to start work on your own project, you will need two sets of information:

1) **Construction drawings:** These are the drawings you will have submitted for Planning Permission, plus any technical details that may be required.
2) **Building Regulations drawings and documents,** which will include the same plans, elevations as the Planning drawings, but they will also include all the information about how you intend to physically construct the building, to ensure that it complies with all the construction regulations related to housing.

In reality, as the drawings are the same for both sets of information, you only need the Building regs package. You should make multiple copies of the drawings and the build specs, so you can give a full set to each sub-contractor (*which they should ideally, sign for*).

**Note:** in case you are not sure why there are two sets of information in the first place, I explain It like this:

**PLANNING PERMISSION IS: *"WHAT DOES IT LOOK LIKE?"***

**BUILDING REGULATIONS IS: *"WILL IT STAND UP?"***

They do different jobs, and that is why they are dealt with by different departments in the Local Authority

## Who prepares the Building Regs drawings and documents?

This work would usually be carried out by whoever prepares the planning application drawings.

The building regs are a standard set of information. Their basics don't vary from house to house, or any building to any building, they are simply intended to make sure that whatever is built, wherever it is built, meets a certain *minimum quality standard.*

So, if a house designer has access to a *standard set* of Building Regulation documents, all he/she needs to do, is to copy the relevant details for each new house, from the Building Regs documents, to the drawings or documents relevant to that project. There is nothing complicated about the process.

The builder then has to make sure that the work on site complies with everything that is shown on the approved drawings, and written in the approved documents.

The local Building Inspector (*or an inspector from a commercial company that has been approved to carry out the inspections*) will call out to check the work at certain stages, as the build progresses. The builder (*or Project Manager*) will normally book an inspection *the day before* it is required.

**The stages for the inspections are:**

1. Foundation trenches, prior to pouring concrete.

2. Slab formation, prior to pouring concrete (*or, for a suspended slab, prior to screeding*).
3. Prior to covering the roof trusses with roofing felt.
4. Prior to plaster boarding.
5. When the drainage has been fully installed, but not backfilled.
6. At completion.

Once the final inspection has been carried out and the building has passed, a Certificate of Completion will be issued to the builder, which can then be forwarded to the buyer / client, as proof to the lenders that the building has been completed to the required standards.

If, at any stage during the build, the inspector finds problems, he/she has the authority to halt progress on construction until they are satisfied that the problems have been resolved.

## THING 64: STANDARD ASSESSMENT PROCEEDURES (SAP'S)

A Standard Assessment Procedure (SAP) is a tool used by the government to assess the energy efficiency of buildings. The SAP rating of a building is based on the level of thermal performance that can be expected from the building, as a whole entity.

Building Regulations require that a SAP calculation is submitted for new dwellings, prior to the commencement of work. It must prove that the building will conform to the present SAP requirements (*which may change over time*).

### How does it work?

The SAP calculation gives a score, ranging anywhere from 1 to 100+ for the estimated annual energy cost (*gas and electricity*) of running a building, based on:

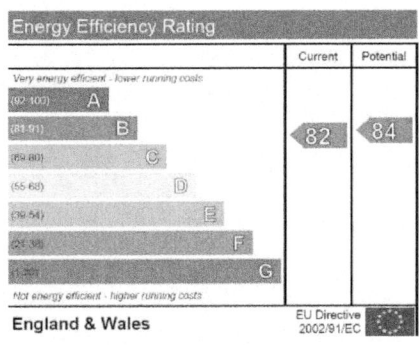

i. The elements of structure (*what materials are used in the build*)
ii. The heating and hot water system (*what sort of system is being used, how efficiently does it operate, how much energy does it consume?*)
iii. The internal lighting system (for example: A*re all the lights low energy, including spotlights? Are the lights dimmable?*)
iv. Renewable technologies that are used in the home (*is there a high efficiency condensing boiler? Is there a wind turbine, an air source, or a ground source system?*)

The higher the SAP score, the lower the running costs. A score of 100 would indicate that the building should, theoretically have a zero energy cost.

Getting a SAP calculation is not expensive. It is a simple desktop exercise, based on the Building Regulations drawings, plans and specifications of the building. It is done before the building work starts, so that if amendments to the build spec need to be made to achieve a satisfactory SAP result, they can be done without having to alter any work that has already been completed.

The higher the SAP rating of a property, the more attractive it will be to future buyers, should you ever decided to sell the house (*which as a self-builder, you have a good chance of doing, as soon as you get over the first one, and get the urge to do it again!*)

As I write this, the average SAP score for the UK is 62, this is an improvement from 45 in 1996, and should continue to increase, as insulation requirements in new buildings also continue to do the same.

A quick on-line search for *"SAPS Calculations"* or *"Energy Assessors* in *"where you live"* should find you someone suitable to carry out your SAP calculation.

*SAPS normally go hand in hand with EPC's*

## THING 65: **ENERGY PERFORMANCE CERTIFICATES (EPC'S)**

An EPC report gives a snapshot of how a building performs with regards to energy consumption, and makes recommendations of how to improve that performance. Every building needs an EPC if it is going to be sold, let, or changed in a way that could affect its rating. It is valid for 10 years if there are such no changes made.

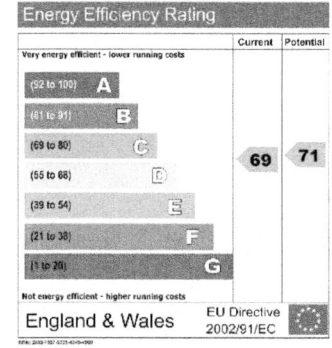

EPC's are usually calculated and provided commercially, by Energy Assessors (*the same people who prepare the SAP's reports*) and generally cost about £35 - £45. A set of both the SAP and EPC should cost around £65 - £75.

**High EPC ratings = lower running costs**. As energy price continually increase over the coming years, that will become more and more important to house buyers.

*As Self-Builders, you should be aiming for at least a B rating on both your SAP's and EPC's. Good ratings could increase the value and saleability of your home.*

## THING 66: COMMUNITY INFRASTRUCTURE LEVY (CIL)

CIL is a charge levied by the Government on new build homes. The money charged goes towards funding community project such as schools, roads, and flood defences.

When it was introduced, it potentially added up to tens of thousands of pounds to the cost of a self-build project. However, in 2014 the Self-Builders were made exempt from the charge if, prior to starting their projects they claim exemption, by going to the Government Planning Portal (*planningportal.co.uk*) and filing a "*Self-Build Exemption form*".

**IMPORTANT NOTE 1:** If you don't register your self-build project for CIL exemption prior to commencing it, using the exemption form, you could find yourselves receiving a demand to pay the full levy.
Once a demand has been issued, you may not be able to get it cancelled.

**IMPORTANT NOTE 2:** The exemption is in place as this book is being written, however, as with most Government related matters, things could change. I strongly suggest that you check that the exemption is still in place before you start planning and costing your own build, as a bill for many thousands of pounds could have a dramatic effect on the overall viability of your project.

## THING 67: AIR SOURCE HEATING

One of the big changes in the self-build industry over the past decade or so, is the increase in the importance, availability and use of renewable energy equipment.

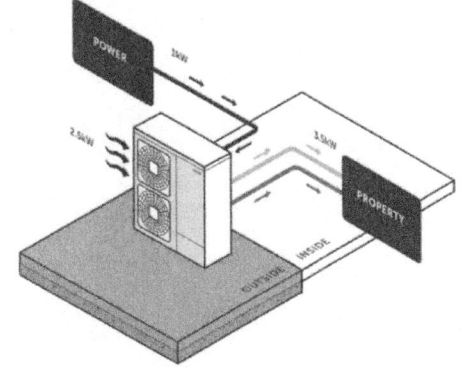

One of the options for providing heating and hot water to a building, is Air Source Heating. As the name suggests, it is a system that pulls heat out of the air *outside* the building and sends it to be used *inside* the building.

The system is simple in concept: An air source heat pump is installed outside the building and connected to another system inside. One or more fans in the heat pump will draw air into the pump, which then goes through a heat exchanger (*a simple device which takes heat from the air, then sends it to the building, whilst the cold air is expelled from the building*). The heat from the warm air passes the heat into a liquid refrigerant. That warm liquid is then fed to the central heating system, where the heat it contains is used to provide heating and hot water for the house.

The first question I asked when I first heard about this system, many years ago was: *"What about in the winter, when the air is freezing?"* At that time, I was assured by salespeople that the heat pump could take heat out of the air at incredibly low temperatures, and it was not a problem. I wasn't convinced.

There seems to be a bit more common sense at play now. The advertising literature and fact finding materials do tend to say that, in the winter, the system will need some sort of back up (*in other words, a more standard method of providing heat and hot water*). That statement highlights an important aspect of using this system, which is:

*If you install an air source heat pump for a few thousand pounds, you will still probably need to install a normal boiler that gives you somewhere near the same sort of level of performance that you would need if you didn't have the air source heating system in the first place. The pump itself costs a little bit of money to run and will need maintaining regularly.*

*So, where are the benefits that make paying a lot of money out for the system, worthwhile?*

I have mixed thoughts on this system. It is good that, by installing the system, you are doing you bit to be extra energy efficient, but is that enough to justify all the research and the initial installation work and cost? Are there better ways to use your money, so you spend less, whilst achieving higher levels of energy efficiency?

**Comments welcomed**

## THING 68: GROUND SOURCE HEATING

Another product to that has slowly made inroads into the self-build market is Ground Source Heating. This system has been around for a long time, but I didn't hear about it until about 10 years ago. Today, like Air Source Heating, it still remains a niche product within the industry.

If you don't know about this system, or how it works, it might surprise you to know that, not far under the ground surface (about 8ft or 2.4m), the temperature remains fairly constant all year round, and is warm enough to be drawn off and used to heat homes. Installing a ground source heat pump allows this to happen.

**What is it, how does it work?**

The main constituent of the system is pipework, laid in trenches that are excavated to the correct depth (*which may vary depending on where you are situated geographically*). This pipework is filled with liquid (*usually anti-freeze, but sometimes biodegradable products are used*). The length of the pipe installed will depend on your heating requirements. The heavier the demand, the longer the pipe.

Cold liquid is pumped into the pipe from the heat pump and, as it travels through the full buried length of pipe, back to the heat pump, it absorbs heat from the ground. This heat is then transferred, via heat exchanger, to the plumbing / heating system inside the house, where it is used to heat radiators, water, and other heating elements (*such as underfloor heating*).

Although this system is expensive (*a friend of mine installed it for around £16,000 inclusive of everything*), I prefer it to air source heating. I like the fact that the ground temperature stays the pretty much the same all the time, so should be able to provide your heat and hot water throughout the winter months.

One thing to bear in mind before you get too far with researching this system, is that you need a **long** *length of trench* to allow the pipework to absorb the heat it requires, so the system will only really be suitable for houses with reasonably large gardens. There is the option to drill downwards into the ground and install the pipework into a shaft rather than a trench, but this can get very expensive.

## THING 69: **WIND TURBINES**

We are now all familiar with these . Like them or not, they are popping up like mushrooms all over the place. As they become more common, the price of installing them has come down significantly, and will continue to do so for a while yet.

They work simply by harnessing the power of the wind and converting it into electricity, which can then be either stored in batteries for use in a building, or fed into the national grid, to create income for the owner via the Governments *Feed In tariffs*. They provide clean energy, create zero $CO_2$ emissions and no waste. The higher they are, the more energy they tend to produce (*wind tends to be stronger at higher levels*).

If you are considering buying a domestic wind turbine, in order to generate enough electricity for an average sized 4 bed house, you need to be looking at something like 10kw model or higher (*the 10kw refers to the maximum amount of electricity it can produce at full power*).

If you want to ensure that you have a constant electricity supply, no matter what model of turbine you choose, you will still need to be connected to the national grid (*in case there is no wind for a while, and you use all your storage energy*).

If you are planning on going completely off grid for your electricity needs, you should contact the turbine suppliers, to discuss your plans and requirements and to get their advice, before committing yourself.

Residential wind turbines can be either roof mounted or installed on to a base at ground level (*these are called* mast mounted *turbines*). At the time of writing, prices start at around £2000 for a roof mounted turbine (*plus installation costs*) or around £20,000+ for mast mounted model, however these prices vary greatly depending on a number of factors (*you will find relevant information on the manufacturers websites*).

At the time of writing, you need to get Planning Permission approval before siting a wind turbine.

My thoughts in wind turbines?

*Nice idea, but is a domestic wind turbine a good investment for the future?*

I think the large commercial wind farms are fantastic. Once those turbines are in place, apart from maintenance, we can get free energy indefinitely, without raiding the earths scarce resources. However, is a domestic wind turbine as good an idea. Possibly not.

If you think about it. In a few years, wind and solar power will account for a large percentage of our energy requirements, which means that the power you use in your home, could well be being generated by a wind turbine (*or solar panels*). If that is the case, do you really need to spend up to £30,000 of your build budget, to get your own "mini" turbine in your garden? – Would things like better insulation and high efficiency boilers be a better investment?


## THING 70: COULD WE GO COMPLETELY "OFF GRID"?

Theoretically yes. Practically, that may prove to be too big an ask, and too expensive.

**Why?**

I'll break down the different parts of the equation:

1) **Water:** Below the ground surface is a thing called a water table. Its depth can vary hugely, from less than a metre, to hundreds of metres, depending on its location, and other geographical and topographical factors. If the water table is classed as being in an aquifer (*an area of a certain geographical structure which filters out impurities*), it can usually be consumed safely by human beings.

   If you like the idea of your new home having its own water supply, you will need to research the nature of the underground water in your area, to find out about its quality, and at what depth it is likely to be found. You could start by going to the relevant Environment Agency website for your local area.

   To bring a supply from the water table to the surface and then to the house, you would need to drill a borehole to *below* the top of the water table (*however deep that is, and allowing for seasonal fluctuation in levels*), then feed pipework down to below its lowest projected annual level, and connect it to a pumping system. The pump will draw the water up to the surface and in to the building, or to a storage tank, or both.

The cost of a shallow well could be reasonable, and potentially within your build budget, however accessing deep water table could be impractical from a financial point of view.

An alternative way to stay off grid for your water would be to get water delivered to a storage tank on your land, however, for the real *"off gridders"* that might feel like a bit of a cheat (*carbon footprints for delivery and all that!*)

2) **Electricity:** The previous section looked at wind turbines. Solar panels are also now commonplace and reasonably priced. They do need to be orientated correctly to make the most of the suns energy, but if your house is not facing in the right direction, you could consider mounting the panels in a frame at ground level (*as you see in the large solar farms springing up all over the country*). These days, solar panels are a good system to use for heating, hot water, and electricity, and they are continually improving and coming down in price. These are one of the *"must have's"* for off grid living.

3) **Gas:** This is not really a viable option for off grid living unless you go for an LPG Gas tank. The tank would be situated outside the building and would be refilled by tanker delivery, as required. Again, this could be seen as a bit of a cheat by true off gridders.

4) **Drainage:** You will most likely either have heard of septic tanks or might use one for your own drainage. They are not uncommon, and there are good systems available. They work simply by installing a large, specially designed tank underground, in a suitable location, within your boundaries. The foul drainage pipework from the house is then connected to the tank.

The inside of the tank is usually spilt into separate treatment areas, where the waste settles, and the solids are separated from the liquids. The liquid waste is fed through the tank and out into a system of irrigated pipework called a "drainage field", where naturally occurring bacteria break down the remaining waste and dissipate it into the surrounding ground. The length of the system of pipework will depend on the amount of foul drainage waste expected to be created from the property. Calculations will have to be submitted for Building Regulations approval prior to work starting.

The solids in the tank slowly accumulate and the tank will need emptying every few months. This job is carried out by waste management companies, using a mobile tanker with a hose, pumps and fittings which connect to the tank and suck out the sediment.

5) **Telecoms:** This is probably the least of your problems if you want to go off grid. The only thing you may need to bear in mind is getting a satisfactory broadband service if you are not connected to BT. Mobile broadband is improving all the time, but is still quite expensive and still a bit slow, but this should improve rapidly over the coming months and years.

# THING 71: HOW IMPORTANT IS AIR TIGHTNESS?

This is something that now seems to be very important to the *"men in the tall towers"* who make the rules, and also to the Building Regulation people. To my mind, it is getting *too* important.

Call me an old timer, but I remember when we could live in a house, open windows, and doors, and leave them open, without worrying about letting heat out of the building. If that cost us 50p in extra electricity over a month, so be it! We were not daft enough to leave everything open in the winter, but it was nice to just be able to give the house a blow through every now and then. And why not?  It clears damp air, makes the whole place smell fresher and be a more pleasant place to live.

Nowadays, to get the *blow through* experience, we are being persuaded by the Government to keep the windows and doors closed, and instead install a Mechanical Ventilation System. These systems take stale air out of the house and feed it to a heat exchanger, which then takes the heat out of the stale air, and transfers that heat across to a separate source of clean air. That clean air then gets pumped into the house. The system provides a continual (*but slightly convoluted*) supply of clean, fresh air within the building, whilst not wasting the heat that was in the stale air. *Great!*

But how much does the system cost? A couple of thousand pounds upwards, depending on the size of the house and the type of system installed.

So, what's wrong with that? Well nothing major, but how long is it going to take to reclaim the cost of the heat exchanger and the other installation costs, especially when it has its own running and maintenance costs? Also, from my own experience of living in a house that had the system installed, we just tended to ignore it, and open the windows and doors anyway. If the sun comes out and you want the fresh, warm air in your house, you will also probably prefer to open the doors and windows straight away, rather than waiting for the system to do its job. It is only common sense.

As a Housing Developer, I do have to say that the drive for airtightness seems to be getting a bit out of hand. The biggest practical problem I have with it is that I now have to consider it *from day one* of each project, from before the house is even designed, or the build method chosen.

**Fact 1:** Traditional Build (*brick and block*) is not a very airtight way to build. If you build this way, you will have more problems getting the building airtight.

**Fact 2:** Timber Frame is a better bet when it comes to airtightness. It simply has less ways for the air to get out.

**Fact 3:** As part of getting Building Regulations Approval on the finished property, you now need to carry out an airtightness test. If you fail this, you will not get your Completion Certificate until you remedy whatever the problem is. That could be a simple or difficult thing to do, and could cost you next to nothing, or cost you a lot, in both time and money.

So, if I want to make my life easier with regards to airtightness, traditional build might not be the best idea, so that is one build choice gone (*I would have to say that I am not particularly unhappy about that*).

**Fact 4:** ICF (*Insulated Concrete formwork*) is generally a better bet for airtightness than Timber Frame. So, does that mean I now need to consider using ICF instead of Timber Frame? (*you could do*).

**Fact 5:** Passive houses are **VERY** airtight, so maybe I need to think about that option?

**Comment**: *I am pleased that we are building more environmentally friendly buildings now, but when do we say, "Enough is enough"? I would be interested to see some calculations that tell me how much more energy a building costs to run over a year if the airtightness test were to fail by 5% or 10%. I really don't think it would be much.*

Anyway, moan as much as I like, you will still have to pass the air test at the end of your build, so when you are talking to your designer, make sure you ask for advice on the how you can make sure that the building will pass first time.

Here are a few pointers to get your started:

- Do not build in brick / blockwork.
- Make sure that any potential leakage points around the external walls are filled, especially around window and door frames (*tiny little cracks and gaps can let a lot of air out*).
- Make sure the plastering does not leave any escape routes for air, in the walls, ceilings or around openings.
- Mastic seal around sockets, switches light fittings, door frames etc (*if air escapes into a hollow wall in the middle of the building it can quickly find its way to the outside*).
- Fill gaps around water and gas pipes where they go through walls, and also electrical cable where they come in or go out through the external walls.
- Do the same for drainage pipes and anything else that goes through the external walls (*including ventilation pipes*).
- Ditto for light fittings (*especially downlights, which often don't fit tightly to the ceiling*).
- Seal skirtings (*top and bottom*) and architraves with "painters caulk".
- Before you think you have finished the job, walk round the whole building looking for weak spots that you might have missed.

*I have not had a house fail an air test yet, but I spend a lot of time making sure that they don't.*

# THING 72: STRUCTURAL WARRANTIES / ARCHITECTS CERTIFICATES

You need to obtain either a Structural Warranty, or an Architects Certificate on any new home, prior to it being inhabited. Whichever you choose, it will go hand in hand with the Building Regulations Certificate, but is needed for a different purpose.

Where Building Regulations make sure the building is completed to a minimum standard in order to make sure it is safe, warm and suitable for habitation, Structural Warranties and Architects Certificates are more geared to reassuring lenders that the money they lend is being used properly, and that the building will be sellable in the future, allowing them to recoup their money from the borrower.

Structural Warranty and Architects Certificates both have the same inspection regime, with the either an Inspector, or the Architect normally calling at the following stages:

1) Foundation excavations complete, but prior to pouring concrete.
2) Slab prepared for concrete, but concrete not poured.
3) Roof structure completed, but not covered.
4) First fixes complete, but not plaster boarded.
5) Completion.

Architects Certificate and Structural Warranty inspections can sometimes be a bit more informal than Building Regs inspections:

**Architects** tend to live fairly close to works, and may call in while passing, so may not need to make a specific appointment for (*for example*) the morning when the concrete is going to be poured for the foundations, if they have already visited the job a day or so earlier and were happy then that everything was ok. The Building Inspector will be doing a final check, just before pouring.

**Warranty Inspectors** can sometimes live at the other side of the country and may have to travel three or four hours for a single inspection. In some cases, if they can't make it to site on the right day, they will ask you to take photographs of the job, and email them over to them. They will then include these in their *stage report*.

This may sound like a bit of an amateur way to run the things, but, as mentioned above, they operate in a slightly different way to Building Regs, in as much as they view the inspections and certificate issuing process as setting up an insurance policy on the house. In other words, they are carrying out a risk evaluation when they do an inspection, not a technical investigation. For a complicated job, they may want to make all the visits, and spend a lot of time on site, but for a simple house, they sometimes don't worry too much if they have to use photos for one or two of the reports. (*It also saves the companies money, by them not having to pay inspectors to travel long distances, sometimes even staying overnight for just one inspection*).

**Note:** There is nothing to stop either inspector asking for additional inspections, if they think they are necessary.

Where the Structural Warranty normally covers the building for 10 years, Architects Certificates don't tend to have an official time limit attached to them. They are usually backed by the Architects own Professional Indemnity policy. This concerns me a little: It is rare for a claim to be made on a Structural Warranty or an Architects Certificate, but what if you did need to make one and the Architect had either died, or lapsed the policy? Would you still be covered? This is not a question I have ever had to consider as more than as a passing thought, but it is a bit of a grey area. So, before you think about using an Architect's Certificate for your own project, it might be a good idea if you ask the question.

## THING 73: **DISABILITY REQUIREMENTS FOR DRIVEWAYS**

I'll just mention this one quickly. It nearly caught me out many years ago, so I just want to make sure it doesn't trip you up in the same way:

When you are designing your new home, you will need to decide on a ground floor level (*correctly called the "Finished Floor Level", abbreviated to "FFL"*). It is normally 150mm (6") above the ground level.

That is one of two important factors that you need to consider when designing your driveway. The other is the level at the entrance to the site. In the section on drainage I was talking about how the drainage needs to have a minimum fall from the house, to where it connects with the public drainage system. The same idea comes in to play for the driveway levels and falls, this time related to Disability Regulations. There are rules that govern the maximum falls for the driveway in certain areas (*generally adjacent to the front door*), but depending on the geography of the site, they may also affect the whole of the driveway area. What the regulations expect the builder to achieve, is a driveway that is generally suitable for people in wheelchairs, or with other mobility problems.

I am not going to quote any figures for allowable gradients here (*just in case they change over time*), but the idea is that at least part of the driveway needs to be constructed as a solid, smooth surface, and at a gentle slope, so wheelchair users can navigate it comfortably. Additionally, the area of driveway which will form the access into the house, will need to be raised, by means of a gentle increase of the gradient, up to the finished floor level of the house, across the width of the door. (*Note: Everywhere else around the building there, a 150mm step up from the drive to the finished floor level is still required*).

Bear those couple of things in mind:
1) When you are deciding on the ground floor level of the house and
2) When you are deciding which door into the house is going to be the main designated disabled access.

# SECTION 3:

# BUILDING METHODS

## THING 74: TRADITIONAL BRICK AND BLOCK

Traditional cavity brickwork has been around for decades (*not centuries, as some people may think*). The term does not just cover a brickwork house with a blockwork internal skin, it also covers houses built in two skins of blockwork, with a render finish on the outside.

Generally, this method of building has done its job, mainly because it creates a reasonably strong finished product. (notice that I say "*reasonably*", not "*very*"), we all understand and accept it, and it doesn't take too long to build.

For the first ten or so years of my housebuilding career, I would only build houses using traditional build, and scoffed at the new ideas that were starting to be introduced. (*building a house using timber instead of concrete blocks? No, never, don't even suggest it!*)

*Traditional build is still the most common form of house building. But that is now changing, and the rate of change is picking up speed.*

Over the past 10 – 15 years commercial housing estates have slowly started to dip their toes in to testing the timber build options, and they are now starting to come to terms with the fact that traditional build might not be the *be all and end all* of house building after all, especially as we start to become more environmentally aware as a society.

**Why the change?**

You will most likely have already picked up on the fact that I am no longer a fan of traditional build. Here is a list of facts that explain why a lot of builders (*commercial and private*) are now starting to understand that, good as it was in its day, it may now be time to move away from this method of building. Here are some of the reasons:

- **It is slow:** An average shell of a standard 4 bed house, from ground to completion can take anything from 3 weeks to 4 months, depending on several factors.
- **It is weather dependant:** If it rains, you cannot lay brick facework. The mortar will run, and it will look terrible. So, when it rains, you stop work.
- **Scaffolding goes up in stages:** When the walls reach certain heights (*based on the comfortable height to which an average height bricklayer can lay bricks and blocks, called "lifts"*), work stops and the scaffolders are booked to come and erect a lift of scaffolding, which then has to be loaded out with all the bricks and blocks needed for the next lift.

Depending on the house design, this can happen 5 or 6 times during the build. The delays to building work during this process depends on how quickly the scaffolders can get to site, how much work is involved in erecting the next lift, and the weather. The bricklaying work may only need to be stopped for a day, based on the amount of scaffolding to be done, but if for some reason, the scaffolders don't turn up for 3 or 4 days, or if brickies go on to another job while they wait for the work to be done, it can be many days before they return to carry on laying bricks. This reduces the efficiency of the build process significantly.

- **Work also stops for the joists:** Once the walls reach joist level, brickwork has to stop while the joists are fitted. More days may be lost if the brickies head off to another job while this work is done, especially if they can't get back as soon as the joisting work is complete.

- **Plant hire costs increase:** During these delays, any plant that is on hire will be costing money (*usually a large cement mixer, and maybe a hoist will be on site while building of the shell of the house*). A few hundred pounds can be lost on wasted hire charges, over the duration of a complicated house build.

- **Loading out:** Once each lift of scaffolding is completed, it has to be loaded out with all the bricks and block needed for the next lift. This can take a day or so to complete, at each lift stage, so can be responsible for the loss of a week's bricklaying over a full house build.

- **There is a lot of waste:** Many brick and blocks need to be cut to size. This takes time, especially with the blocks. The offcuts are then thrown away.

- **Walls are only as "plumb" (vertical) as the bricklayer's spirit level.** Believe it or not, using an old spirit level can result in a wall that is up to two or three inches out of plumb in its overall height. If the level is reading a couple of millimetres incorrectly over a 2ft length, over the full height of a building you can potentially end up with any number of walls being significantly out of plumb.

- **Window and door openings can be out of plumb or the wrong size:** Again, a faulty spirit level, or just poor workmanship can result in openings being 10mm – 20mm out of plumb. The slip of the tape measure can also result in openings being built to the wrong size. If these sorts of errors are not caught quickly, they can compound and become a major problem in numerous ways, especially when it comes to fitting windows and doors.

- **Bricks and blocks are poor insulators.** To attain the high levels of insulation that new homes now need, in traditionally built houses, the external wall widths are getting wider and wider to allow for the required amount of insulation to be incorporated into their construction. Fixing the insulation to, and/or within the wall can be slow work, and products used all need to be weatherproof, so are expensive. Also, the wider the walls, the less room there is inside the building (*this is more noticeable on the small commercially built houses than it is on self-builds, but it still has an effect*).

- **It is not very recyclable:** Bricks and blocks don't grow on trees. Timber does!

- **You can't do any other jobs on the house until the brick / blockwork are complete:** A house does not start to become weathertight until the roof is on and covered. When you build using bricks and blocks, work cannot start inside the building until the shell of the house is complete, the roof installed and, at least the felt and battening fitted. Therefore, as well as it naturally being a slow process, any delay to the progress of the brick / blockwork holds up progress on the whole house. (*Other build methods don't have this problem, see next few sections*)
- **Airtightness is sometimes hard to achieve:** The nature of traditional build, where there are literally *thousands* of joints around the house, makes achieving good levels of airtightness quite difficult. The problem with that is that you won't know how well you did on getting the building airtight, until the *completed house* is tested, then you might have to try to find the weak areas that it failed on.
- **Lenders are still happy to lend on traditionally built houses.** Because they are a tried and trusted method of building, you shouldn't have a problem getting a mortgage on a traditionally built house, although that could change in the future, as running costs become more important when making decisions on build methods.
- **Many buyers still prefer traditional build:** Although timber frame is becoming a lot more popular (*now accounting for 30% - 40% of all new house builds*) and is very popular with self-builders, traditional build is also still popular, especially with older self-builders.

*I will stop there. I could go on, but I think you'll get the idea of what I am trying to say. In this modern world of innovations and new ways to do thing, I just think that traditional build has now pretty much had its day. You will obviously make up your own mind on this subject, but my hope is that you will at least consider what I have written here before you make any decisions on the subject.*


## THING 75: TIMBER FRAMES

*As you are already aware, I am a fan of timber frames (but you might be surprised to hear that they are now not at the top of my list of preferred build methods. – See later sections for why that is).*

As I have already said, I started my house building career building traditional brick and block houses and was a *full on* fan of the system. However, over time I noticed that these "new-fangled" timber frames had started to gain in popularity.

Being interested in new ideas, despite the fact that one of the major house builders had managed to give the product a bad name already, by building very cheap, inferior versions of it, I decided to do *just one* timber frame, as a self-build for myself. That way, if it did turn out to be rubbish, I wouldn't get lawsuits from clients, and could stick with what I already knew.

*I completed my first timber framed house in 10 weeks, and after I completed it, I decided that I would never build a Traditional Brick and Block house again, either for me, or for anyone else.*

As I am keeping the sections of this book fairly short, I won't be going into a lot of the detail about why I made that decision. Instead, as I have just done with traditional build, I will run through a list of the facts about Timber Frames:

- **It makes <u>your</u> job easier, especially if you are a first time self-builder:** Once your drawings are completed, instead of having to investigate everything you will need for the shell of the house, you simply send the drawings out to Timber Frame companies, who will give you prices for providing and erecting everything related to the *internal* skin of the *external* wall, plus the internal walls, the floors and the roof structure. Your job is then simply to compare the prices, like for like between the different quotes, do your due diligence, maybe go and visit two or three of the most professional sounding, cost competitive companies, and make a choice which you think offers the best package for your project.
  Your quotation will normally include cost of all labour to fully erect the frame and roof, ready for felt and battening (weatherproofing), and also crane hire.
- **The whole thing comes on large trailers, usually including the roof materials:** Once you decide on a supplier, and pay the deposit, you then simply coordinate with the supplier on delivery dates, and can get on with constructing the foundations and slab, concentrating on making sure that you will be ready for the delivery on the agreed date. A frame for a standard 4 bed house will normally come to site on anything from 2 to 5 trailers. When the first delivery is due, if you are going to need a crane (*which you may not for the ground floor panels*), you will also have to make sure that it can drive onto the site, position itself where it needs to be, and then can turn round to exit the site. Again, you will coordinate with the supplier on this, who will send someone out to check those sorts of details with you, prior to delivery. These people do this every day or the week, so will know what they are doing.
- **The shell goes up quickly:** Once it gets to site, the frame usually goes up quickly. Depending on the complication or simplicity of the house design, the shell of the house could be built, <u>and</u> the trusses fitted, ready for felt and batten, in anything from a week, to two or three months. An average frame and roof for a simple 4 bedroom house would normally be up in around two to three weeks, after which, once the felt and battening is complete (*usually a couple of days work at the most*), you can consider starting the internal works, before the roof tiling starts.
- **Scaffolding is normally mostly erected prior to framing work starting:** With a timber frame construction, prior to the frame arriving on site, the scaffold is normally erected on 3 sides (*back and two sides*), leaving just the front open for getting the ground floor panels in to the building area. Once the ground floor panels (*or sometimes the ground and first floor panels*) are built, the scaffold erection is completed across the fourth side. This reduces the number of visits for the

scaffolders compared to the traditional brick and block method, and should result in lower quotes for the work.

- **The weather rarely stops progress:** Framers normally work in the rain, which is not damaged by getting wet (*it is made of trees!*). Even ice and snow do not necessarily need to hold up work (*although a decision on a health and safety grounds may make this appropriate*).

- **There is little waste:** Because the frames are made complete, in a factory and come to site ready to simply be place and fixed wherever they need to go, site waste is minimised (*saving on skip hire charges and leading to less work keeping the site clean*).

- **They are built and installed within tight size tolerances:** Because the frames are factory made, it is much easier to achieve tight manufacturing tolerances, on both the overall sizes, and the verticality of the walls and openings. If a frame is not manufactured to these tight tolerances, it simply does not fit together properly, so errors soon become obvious as the erection proceeds.

- **It is warm:** Although the timber of the frame itself is not a particularly good insulator, because it forms a hollow shell, the specified insulation can usually be installed *within* the frame itself, keeping wall widths to a minimum. The insulation is also normally fitted *internally* once the roof is on, so has no effect on the speed of erection of the frame. The type and thickness of the insulation will dictate the overall insulation values of the wall (*"U" values*), but can reach passive levels if required. Insulation can also normally be installed by an amateur (i.e. the self-builder), thus offering a chance to save money.

- **It is recyclable:** Unlike bricks and blocks, timber frames are nearly 100% recyclable.

- **It is cost effective:** Notice, I don't say *"Cheaper than traditional build"* (this is a grey area), but the efficiency of the way the building goes up usually saves a significant amount of money in other areas of the build (*such as scaffolding, insulation costs, lost time, interest costs on borrowing, to name but a few*).

- **It is strong:** Despite what some builders say (*usually brickies, who don't get as much work out of a timber frame*), timber frames are very strong. They are designed to be so and must pass checks on all strength calculations and materials choices. They are actually better on lateral impacts (*impact from the side*) than traditional build.

*I once saw a house that a car had run in to and badly damaged the front corner of the ground floor. It was built in brick and block, and the damage caused by the sudden shock of the car hitting the blockwork cavity wall, had cracked the whole lengths of the front and side walls (which were rendered, so the damage was visible). The damage caused the whole structure to be unsafe, so the owners had to move out for a few months, whilst the insurance was sorted, a scaffold erected, and the walls re-built.*

*If that had been a timber framed house, the blockwork outer skin would have been demolished, but most likely, because all the panels are separate, and nailed together, only the 2 timber frame panels making up the corner would have been damaged. The timber structure above and to the sides would have been fine. The repair would have involved the damaged panels simply being removed and replaced as quickly as possible (maybe without even needing scaffolding). This would mean that the owners could stay in the house while work was carried out. The damage to, and cracking of the blockwork skin would have still been a difficult job to put right, but the overall cost, time and interference with the lifestyle of the owners would have been a fraction of what it ended up being.*

- **Airtightness is easier to achieve:** Due to fact the that the panels are accurately manufactured in factories, and also due to there being far fewer joints in the building overall, airtightness is much easier to achieve than it is with brick and block construction.
- **Mortgage companies are happy to lend on Timber Frames:** This was not always the case a decade or so ago, but that has now changed. I have not heard of anyone having a problem getting a mortgage on a timber frame build, for quite a few years.

*One slightly amusing thing I am finding (as a housing developer) recently, is that I am now being asked by potential buyers "It is timber Frame"? But where that used to be a defensive question, by people who preferred traditional construction, it is now the other way around. They are asking to make sure that it IS timber frame!*

## THING 76: HOW FIREPROOF ARE TIMBER FRAMES?

This may sound a bit glib, but the answer is: *As fireproof as you want them to be.* Let's just look back to what we call a *traditionally built* house for a minute. Assuming that by "traditionally built", we mean the part that is built of either brick or blockwork, we are only talking about the outside skin of the external walls. *That's it!*

Here are the timber items that are used in timber framed houses, that are also used in traditionally built houses:

➢ Floor slabs can be concrete or timber (*there are hundreds of thousands of existing houses in the UK with suspended timber ground floors (often houses built on slopes, or with cellars).*
➢ Floor joists.
➢ Floorboards.
➢ Either just the upstairs internal walls, or sometime the upstairs and some of the downstairs internal walls are constructed in timber.
➢ The roof trusses and bracing.
➢ Window cills.
➢ Door frames.
➢ Doors.

- Windows (sometimes).
- Patio and bi-fold doors (sometimes).
- Boxing in of pipework.
- Built in cupboards.
- Kitchen & utility room units and worktops.
- Tables.
- Wardrobes.
- Bedroom furniture.
- Etc.

*So, bearing that in mind, whether we build traditionally, timber frame, or anything else, the fire risk is significant, and we need to take sensible measures to make sure that the occupants are safe.*

**How do we do that?** More often than not, simply by using plasterboard.

Plasterboard is fire resistant. The thicker the board, or the more layers of board that are fitted, the more fire resistance they provide. A half inch thick plasterboard usually gives half an hour fire resistance, two board thickness can give 1 hour protection.

So, as an example, if you have any steelwork on the job, it needs to have at least 1 hour fire protection for it to pass Building Regulation, so it should have a minimum thickness of 2 x ½" sheets of half hour rated plasterboard fitted around it.

Likewise, half inch plasterboard on timber stud walls gives half an hour fire protection to that wall. If you insulate the wall with Rockwool (*or a similar fire retardant material*), that half hour will increase slightly. If you want to go *belt and braces*, you could double up on 12.7mm boards, staggering the joints, to get a full one hour fire resistance.

*If you are still in any building one hour after a fire has started, you have probably got bigger problems than the fire potentially getting through a plasterboard!*

So, if we compare build methods in details, there is not a lot of difference between **traditional** and **timber frame** build when it comes to fireproofing, and both can be upgraded as much as the builder wishes.

*Note: There are a number of other issues which relate to fire protection in new housing. I am not looking at those here. The only point I am making in this section, is that the myth that timber frame is a fire hazard, is not factually based. As with everything else related to the build, it depends on what you use, and how and where you use it.*

# THING 77: SINGLE SKIN CONSTRUCTION

If there is one change that I would like to see in the UK house building industry, it would be that we started to build more houses using *single skin* construction.

Some people are surprised to hear that the outside skin of a cavity wall is not usually doing any of the load bearing work. It is mainly cosmetic. It also forms one side of the cavity, which helps to protect the inner skin from rain and damp penetration. The outer skin usually simply *stops,* just above the soffit board at the eaves (*in other words: at roof level*). *Nothing sits on it*, either there or anywhere else.

It is the *inside skin* of the wall that does all the work. It carries all the weight of the roof and shares the weight of a lot of the other constituent parts of the house.

If you consider the amount of work, time and cost involved in building this mainly cosmetic outside skin of the wall (*which, using a nice facing brick, could account for up to 70% of the overall cost and time of the whole shell of the building*), and then consider the possibility of getting rid of it altogether, I would think that most sensible people would be at least interested in looking into that alternative.

That is exactly what a lot of other countries have done. It is called (not surprisingly) *single skin construction.*

So, why hasn't the UK adopted this method? I really don't know. Building Regulations don't seem to have a problem with it. There are already many single skin buildings in the UK, such as log cabins, steel clad factory units, garages, garden rooms, blocks of flats and some houses. So why not more houses?

From the information that I have gathered from various sources, it appears to be that it is the UK mortgage lenders that are nervous about the product. That old British reluctance to try anything new, until they know it works. It happened with timber frames, and now it appears to be happening with single skin construction.

You may ask: *"If a wall only has one skin, how does it get the weatherproofing it needs?"* There are numerous answers to that question, for example:

- For either a *timber frame* or a *single skin* building, the standard weatherproof breather membrane is fitted around the whole of the building (*the green, blue, or silver wrapping that you will see on timber framed houses under construction*).
- In single skin construction, treated timber battens (*usually 50mm x 50mm*) are usually then fitted to the wall, vertically, at 600mm centres.
- For timber framed single skin buildings, those battens are fixed through the outer layer of the frame itself, into the strong timber studs on the inside.
- For blockwork single skin buildings, the batten is fixed to the blockwork, usually with a damp proof membrane between the batten and the block.
- In both cases, the batten creates a 50mm cavity, just the same as the cavity brick and blockwork normally has.

- The construction is then usually completed using either:
  1. A cladding system fixed to the battens.
  2. A waterproof cement board, then a specially designed mesh, fixed to the board, followed by a rendered finish (*so the building ends up looking just like any traditionally built building*).
  3. A cement board and "brick slips" (*thin slices of brick that are glued to the board and jointed with cement to look like a traditional brick wall*). The joints are then pointed with normal mortar. (See: https://brickslips.co.uk/)

**If this system became more widely available and acceptable in the UK, it could provide a major boost to our Self-Build industry, making the build quicker, simpler and more cost effective for people who would benefit from the simplicity it offers.**

## THING 78: MODULAR BUILD / CLOSED PANEL CONSTRUCTION

This system *is* a real step forward for house building. It is the system I now prefer over Timber Frame. And it is just starting to get a foothold in the UK.

If you have watched some of the Grand Designs TV programmes, you have probably seen the beautiful (and expensive) flat pack kit houses, that are brought over from Europe, for Self-Build projects over here. They arrive on the right day, on the back of smartly presented, clean, modern trailers. The erection team arrive in sign written vans, are all smartly attired, with matching *clean* overalls, and all the proper safety gear.

The house kits themselves (*which are usually based on a standard timber frame panel system*), come with insulation already fitted in to the frames, sometimes the electrical wiring and plumbing pipes. They are plaster boarded at the factory, have light switches and sockets built in, and some kits have even had pre-glazed & pre-finished windows and doors fitted at the factory.

The kits go together first time, they are built in next to no time, and just by looking at them and walking round the building once it has been completed, you can clearly see, and even *feel* that they are a high quality product.

Well, the good news is that the system is, at long last, starting to be manufactured as a *standard* frame option, in the UK. The not so good news is that, as with everything we do, it is presently generally not quite as good, or comprehensive as our European neighbours' products, and it is a bit overpriced. – But I am sure we will get there eventually.

If you are not familiar with Closed Panel / Modular Construction, an easy way to describe it, is that it starts off as a timber frame, built in the factory, but instead of being sent out to site, the frame stays in the factory and has more work done to it.

The amount of work varies from company to company. It can be that it just has the insulation, the vapour barrier and an OSB board (*Orientated Strand Board*) fitted to it (*to close the panel up and make it weatherproof*). The next upgrade would be having things like cables, pipework and plasterboard fitted, and the top of the range kit could also include the windows and doors.

The obvious main advantage of these products is that they make the self-builder's life much simpler, and speed up job significantly (*compared to traditional build and even to standard timber frame*). However, there are also other benefits:

Because they are built in the factory, they tend to be made to extremely tight tolerances (*great for airtightness*), and rarely leave the factory with many (*if any*) faults. The reason for this is that a lot of the cutting and sizing work is done automatically by computer controlled machinery, based on the project drawings, which the computer can read.

The kits are erected very quickly, they create much less waste than traditional build, and (*I think, importantly in a high quality house*), they can give a solid "*feel*" to the building once it has been fully erected.

The whole process is environmentally friendly, and the fact that they are fully manufactured in a factory, and that their use significantly reduces the number of follow on trades and further materials deliveries, they can significantly reduce the *construction carbon footprint* of the completed building.

Price wise, as I mentioned, they are expensive. However when you look at the price of these system, and compare them with the basic timber frame, then you add on the cost of all the work that still needs doing on site once a standard frame has been erected (*along with the interest charges on your borrowing over a longer time*), the price difference may not be as great as you might imagine.

What you usually find, is that the bigger modular build companies go for the mid to top end of the market, providing high spec products. They do a lot of marketing, appear at all the shows, have professional teams of salespeople, and their selling prices reflect all of that. If you like the idea of the system, do a search on *Timber Frame Modular Build* and add your general location, to see if there are any companies locally who provide this product (*there are also a few companies listed in the Self-Build Trade List at the back of the book*).

Something else to try, would be to look for the smaller, more local companies who may be starting to offer the product as an option to standard Timber Frames. These companies may not include all the bells and whistles that the *big shiny* products offer, but you will often find them better to work with, more flexible and cheaper, due to being more local to your site and having lower overheads.

We have a local Timber Frame company near where I live, who have just expanded and started to manufacture Modular Build Systems. I am thinking of comparing prices for their standard timber frame against their Modular Build product prices for our next project, so may be able to update the book with some *hands on reviews,* once we get our next development started. *(Have a look at SO Modular:* https://somodular.co.uk. *I don't know how far they deliver from the factory, but it their web site might be worth looking at anyway).*

## THING 79: STRUCTURALLY INSULATED PANELLING SYSTEM (SIPS)

This is a system I have not personally used. I can remember it being around in the UK for at least a couple decades, but it has not yet managed to gain enough popularity to be classed alongside standard timber frames in the kit house marketplace.

From what I have heard, there doesn't seem to be any major drawback to using it, costs seem to be a bit higher than timber frames, but it does have a unique benefit, which might make it worth considering for your build.

**What is SIPS and how does it work?**

Basically, it is made up like a sandwich, with 1 sheet of OSB (*Orientated Strand Board*) either side of a slab of solid insulating foam. The three constituent parts are bonded together under pressure, using a special adhesive. This creates a structurally strong unit, which does the same job as a timber frame panel, but with the insulation already installed (*saving time, materials, and labour, later in the project*).

The panels usually come at 1.2m x 2.4m. They are designed and cut to suit your design drawings and are fitted together on site.

One of their advantages is that they don't use *poorly insulating* timber studs as part of their construction in the way standard timber frames do. They therefore offer a better insulating performance like for like, than standard timber frames.

Just as with timber frames, they form the inside skin of the external cavity wall, however they differ from timber frame in how they deal with services (*electrics, plumbing etc*).

Because the unit is solid, there is nowhere for cables and pipes to be

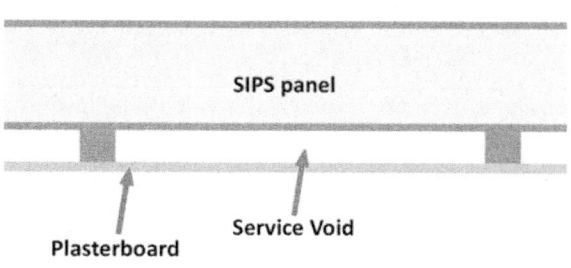

fitted *within* the panel, so a service void is created on the inside (*the room side*), to allow for all first fix cables and equipment to be fitted.

Forming the service void is quite simple. It consists of 2" x 2" timber battens, fitted vertically and spaced at 600mm centres, to suit plaster board sizes. Forming the void will use a lot of batten and cost a few hundred pounds or more in labour (*although it is a job that an enthusiastic and careful amateur should be able to manage*).

**The big benefit:**

The major benefit of using a SIPS system is that, due to the way it is manufactured and put together, you can potentially get a completely clear space inside your roof.

Instead of using standard roof trusses, SIP's houses normally use SIP's panels to form the slopes of the roof itself. This means that if you know at the design stage that you are going to use the SIPS's system for your build, you can make the most of that fact by designing the roof space to be an extra living space, simply adding an extra set of stairs to get access to it.

**Conclusion on SIP's:**

A good system. You either like it a lot, or you won't be interested, there doesn't seem to be a middle ground with the people I have spoken to about it. It goes up quickly, it can save you money in some areas and cost you more money in others. It will need SIP's trained erectors to put the kit up, so finding the right people might be a bit difficult, depending where you live. However, the suppliers usually have their own erecting teams, and include that service in their quote.

And, of course, it has to get a good few browny points for providing that free roof space.

Here is a link that you may find useful: https://www.sips.org

# THING 80: **INSULATED CONCRETE FORMWORK (ICF)**

This product fits into a sector of the self-build marketplace alongside SIPS's panels, as *"A good, niche product"*, but like SIPS, it has never gained the sales momentum that timber frames have achieved, or that modular build is likely to achieve. *It is also a product that gives you a single skin external wall (see section 78).*

Again, I have never used this product, and probably won't, but, as with SIPS's, the people who like it, *really* like it!

ICF has been available since before I first ventured into the world of self-build, in the 1980's. I remember talking to the guy who was running (*I think*) the first company offering ICF in the UK. I met him and discussed the product at the *Alexander Palace Self-Build* show at around that time.

If that fact says one thing (*apart from telling me that I am getting old*), it is that the product / package must be of a good enough quality and a competitive enough in price, to still be attracting new buyers after lasting thirty+ years in the self-build market place.

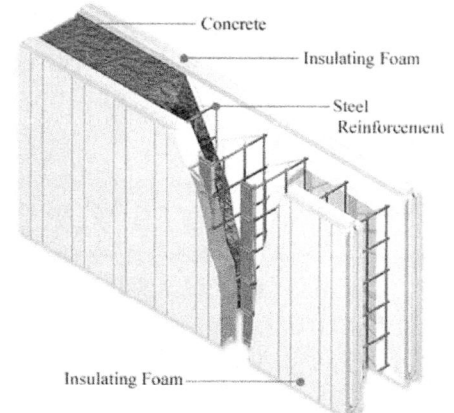

I think one of the attractions of this system for self-builders, is that it is a bit like building Lego. First, interlocking, lightweight, hollow, polystyrene blocks are built up to form "lifts" of the external walls, similar to the way traditional blockwork is built (*the polystyrene blocks also act as the insulation*). Steel rods are then inserted and fixed, to reinforce the completed structure. Once that work has been completed to the recommended height, the voids created in the wall by the hollow blocks, are filled with concrete, forming a solid insulated, reinforced concrete wall.

The thought that you, as a self-builder could be able to actually, physically build your own home is an attractive one, especially if your plan is to be as *hands on* as possible, but you don't have any bricklaying or joinery skills.

As this is a product that, compared to a lot of the other build systems, is a bit *"left field"*, I would suggest that before you commit yourselves to using it, you try and get to see at least one house that is presently being built with the system. The ICF companies you may get quotes from, should have projects progressing all the time, so should be happy to arrange a visit for you to see one of them. That way you can get a proper feel for the product, and ask any questions you may have, to the people who are actually using it.

Here is the web site for the company I talked to at the Self-Build show (*there are also a number of other companies offering the system*): https://becowallform.co.uk/


## THING 81: STEEL FRAMES

It is rare to see a steel framed self-build. Steel is a product that is widely used in the commercial building sector and is ideal for factory units, high rise buildings and lots of other larger structures. It comes in to its own on a self-build project, when a design requires larger than average open floor areas, special structural architectural design features, or openings such as wide bi-fold doors.

The way to think about steel frames is that they form the skeleton of a building. Once the steel frame is built (*often including the roof structure*), you still need to build the walls, the floors and all the other infill components that will create a weathertight building, and provide the levels of insulation that you will need for Building Regs, and that will also make the building visually attractive, both inside and out.

If your house design is a fairly standard, simple 4 or 5 bed property, with average to reasonably large sized rooms, you will usually find that you don't need to think about using a steel frame. However, you may need some individual steel beams to take specific load points, to span a large bi-fold door, or to split a wider than average room in to 2 halves, so that standard timber joists can then be used to form the shorter spans. The image

here is of our most recent project, where steel was used to support attic trusses, in order to allow us to achieve an open attic space, which could then be used as accommodation.

If the house design requires only small amounts of steelwork, any house designer will normally be able to deal with specifying it, without involving specialist designers, however if you do get to the stage where you need to think about a major steelwork design, you will probably need to take on someone more qualified and experienced, who can deal with all the complicated design details.

Things to bear in mind when considering the use of steel in a residential building include:

1) Using steel in a building is not environmentally friendly.
2) It is a poor insulator.
3) It has to be designed separately from the rest of the house but needs to take in to account the rest of the structure of the building. This can result in the design phase of a house becoming a slow and costly process.
4) Once it has been installed, you will then need to fireproof and insulate it.

*As an overall comment, I would suggest staying away from steel where possible, for small to medium sized self-builds. Use it where you need to bridge wide spans for bi-folds, to reduce joist sizes, or as I have done in the image above, to sit trusses on (the steels beams in the image above cost under £200 each, delivered). However, steel would not be in my top 5 as a standard house building material or method. I suggest you investigate other alternatives before choosing it.*

# THING 82: **STRAW BALES**

Ok, I have to admit, I am not personally very knowledgeable on the subject of straw bale housing. I have had to do some research to learn enough about it to be able to (*hopefully*) present a reasonably informed view on the subject, for this book.

Whenever I have heard the term *Straw Bale house construction* in the past, I have envisaged bales being thrown down from a cart, piled up and tied together (*as shown in the image*), then probably covered with *some sort* of mesh, to which *some sort* of plaster can be daubed (*I think I got that idea from a TV programme I saw many years ago, where I remember the finished plastered walls being, shall we say characterful, with a very rough, uneven texture, almost (literally) a hand applied look. It was not unpleasant, but not what I am used to*).

I am not going to go into too much detail about this particular type of build. I think if you want to build that way, you will just get on and do it. But if you do, you should probably be prepared to live in it for a long time, as the selling market for the product is likely to extremely niche.

However, having said that, whilst researching, I came across a method of straw bale building which is not quite as *back to basics* as I had imagined (*I'll put a website address at the end of this section and in the Self-Build Trade List at the back of the book*).

In some ways, the system I found is a bit of a cheat, but in a good way. It copies the principles of standard timber frame by, well, - *being a timber frame!* The frame, however, is a lot wider than normal, and is open on *both* sides.

With this system, the straw bales simply act as the insulation, they don't do any other job. The bales are not perhaps as you might expect them to be, they are specially made to fit neatly in to the timber frames, which come in a choice of widths from 235mm to 400mm wide (*depending on the level of insulation you want to achieve*). Both sides of the frame are then sealed in with OSB board, to make a weathertight unit, ready to be lifted by crane and positioned to form the walls. The inside can then receive battening to form a service void, and plasterboard to finish. The overall result is a bit of a cross between Modular Build and SIPS, with the solid foam insulation being swapped for straw.

The system _only_ forms the external walls. The rest of the house is constructed in the same manner as a standard timber frame.

**A few points to consider:**

1. The walls are very thick, compared to other construction methods, so your internal space will be reduced.
2. The insulation values are high and can apparently reach passive house levels.
3. If straw gets wet, it can rot, so you will need to take care during the construction. A rainy day for this build method could cause more problems for this system than it does for other build methods.
4. You can get a mortgage for a straw bale build, from the Ecology Building Society, but I have not heard of any other providers, so there is probably no competition on interest rates. I don't know how someone buying from you would fare in getting a mortgage, but at least it is a possibility.
5. The research says that straw bale homes can last up to 600 years. That may be so, but I am not sure I would want to be living in one that old! If you build with the more up to date system that I talk about above, you could probably look at equivalent lifespans to a standard timber frame, unless the straw somehow got damp, in which case you could potentially have major problems.
6. Stated costs to build this type of home are considerably lower than the standard industry self-build costs.
7. This system is for more adventurous people. If you choose it, you will be going out on a limb to a certain extent, but as a project, it embodies all that is good about the self-build concept.

**Note:** At the time of writing, I could not find a company who would warranty the straw bale build system. That may have changed by the time you are reading this.

Here is the web address for the company providing the straw bale kits:
https://modcell.com

# SECTION 4

# BUILDING THE HOUSE

## Introduction:

This is the section where we get down to the nitty gritty of the build. Before we start though, I need to say that everything you read in this section is based on *my opinion, experience, and knowledge*. If you disagree with anything I write, go with your own ideas, just make sure you always check things out before you commit yourselves.

### *As I often say to potential self-builders:*

*"When you are choosing between different ideas, products, systems and methods, there is not necessarily one* **right** *way of doing it. There are, however, definitely lots of* **wrong** *ways to do it.*

*What you think is right for you, your family, and your situation, <u>probably</u> is. Just check out your choices first. There may be something better that you haven't heard of. It would be a shame if you missed something good.*

## THING 83: WHERE WILL WE LIVE WHILE WE BUILD?

This is one of the most important *none building* decisions you will make when planning your project. There are many factors to be considered, and whatever decision you make could have a significant impact on many aspects of your life, including:

- Your stress levels.
- Your kids.
- Schooling
- Your relationships.
- Hobbies & interests.
- The build.
- The cost of site security.
- Travel costs.
- Your working lives (*your proper jobs*).
- Your living costs.
- ...... and more.

I have completed five self-build projects of my own. The first one was when I was in my twenties. I had not long been married and was keen, eager, full of energy and willing to rough it if necessary. We lived in a caravan on site while we built. We did not have running water, and only had electricity from an old generator. *We loved every minute of it*!

We built the house in about 6 months (*traditional build*) and didn't have to go through a winter in the caravan. – So not a problem.

For our second project second project two or three years later, we had sold the house we built, banked the profit, and bought a three bed semi to live in while we looked for our next plot. We got the maximum mortgage that we were allowed to have on the semi, so we could keep as much cash as possible available for a deposit on the plot.

When we found a plot, we managed to get a bridging loan which, without going in to detail, allowed us to stay in the semi, while we built. The plot was about half an hour away from where we lived, so it was nice to come back after a day working on the new house, to a warm, tidy house, a cooker, a bath, and a comfy bed.

I was single again when I took on my next project. I think I had become accustomed to a few home comforts, and stayed in the house I was living in while I built the new one. I built this one (*a five bed detached*), in traditional build, quite quickly over one summer, so again, no problem there.

My fourth build was where the decision making process backfired a bit! I was with a new partner and she had a daughter, 10 years old (*Verity*). At the time we lived in the North West but had decided to move to South Wales. I came up with the brainwave of me moving down to the area where we wanted to live, in January / February, while my partner and her daughter stayed in the North West, leaving Verity in school until the summer. I would try and get some work and an income sorted, and look for suitable plots.

Great idea on paper, but I ended up driving up country to the North West every Friday and back down to South Wales on the Sunday. I spent the weekdays looking at plots of land and, as an aside, soon managed to buy a dilapidated terraced house, which I set about doing up on my own, to try to make some money. I also bought a static caravan at a holiday park in Porthcawl (*near Swansea*) and lived in that. This was a very busy and stressful period for me, but I don't mind a bit of stress (*or at least didn't in those days!*)

We eventually found and bought a lovely plot up the Swansea Valley, with a river running behind it. It was about an hour drive from the static caravan. The plan was that my partner and her daughter would come down straight after the school term finished for the summer holiday, so she could get used to the area before starting a new school. We decided to keep the static caravan, as it had 2 bedrooms, heating, hot running water and was cheap to run. The holiday park was also ideal to keep a 10 year old girl entertained for a couple of months, while we also organised getting the drawings done and the project planned.

We decided that we would also get a large German Caravan for the site, so that once Verity started school, her mum and I could work on the house during the day, pick her up from school, go to Porthcawl (*1 hour drive*), have showers and food, then drive back (*another hour*) to the house, and sleep in the caravan. Then Verity could go to school from there in the mornings! – **IT WAS AN ABSOLUTE NIGHTMARE!**

**Conclusions:**

- Living on site and roughing it is ok for the younger self-builders, but if you like your creature comforts, doing without them for an extended period can be stressful.
- A fully equipped static caravan on site, with running water and a flushable loo (*preferably connected to the mains drainage system*), can work fine for up to 3 people for a few months, but will probably get a bit claustrophobic after that.
- Renting a property for the duration of the build is, to my mind the best all round option. Renting somewhere near to the site is even better.

If you want to keep your sanity and relationships intact, I *really* would not recommend mixing the following: *Young children, moving to a new area, taking them away from their friends, introducing them to a new school, lots of daily travelling, building a new house seven days a week, whilst trying to carry on doing another full time job, with no relaxation time or social life.*

Here is the completed house:

## THING 84: **SELF MANAGE OR HIRE A PROJECT MANAGER?**

*I touched on this subject earlier in the book, now the decision needs to be made.*

**Consider this scenario:**

**Someone Project Managing a simple, standard 4 bed detached house build, on a nice flat plot, with all services close by, plenty of local tradespeople and a decent Builders Merchant who can deliver to the site.**

Would that be a fairly manageable task for an intelligent, organised logical person, who can be decisive when needed, can quickly pick up new ways of doing things, who is a problem solver, can keep accurate records and can free up 5 – 6 hours a day to work on the project?

**Is that person you?**

I'll break that down a bit to help you think through it:

How many ticks would you give *yourself* (or *you and whoever else* would share the management of the project), and *your project,* from this list:

- Simple design?
- Simple build?
- Flat plot?
- All services close by?
- Plenty of local tradespeople available?
- A decent Builders Merchant who can deliver, within a couple of miles of the site?
- Intelligent?
- Organised?
- Logical?
- Decisive?
- Determined?
- Can quickly pick up new ways of doing things?
- Not easily panicked?
- Problem solver?
- A good communicator?
- Able to keep accurate records?
- 5 – 6 free hours a day available to work on managing the project for at least 6 months?

Every one of those items is important. If you (*or you and whoever you would be managing the job with*) cannot genuinely tick most of the items on that list, with regards to your proposed build, and your own attributes / skills, as you are getting near to the time to start building, you probably need to think about getting at least *some* professional back up, just in case you need it.

If you can only tick a couple of the items, you need to try to get either a Builder, or a Site Manager to look after the lion's share of the organisational work, with you acting as "Trainee Site Manager".

> **Note:** *that would not be admitting defeat, that would be being sensible!*

### How would you find someone suitable to manage the job?

There are a few Self-Build Project Managers dotted around the country *(I was one for a while, many years ago)*, but unfortunately not many. However, you don't necessarily need to find a *self-build* specialist. A Construction Site Manager who can competently turn his / her hand to building a house should be able to do the job just fine.

### Here is what I would do:

I.    I don't use social media *(yes, yes, dinosaur, I know!)*, but most of you do. I would first put the feelers out for anyone who knows a Construction Project Manager, fairly locally to you, who might want some extra work / income *(preferably part time)*. You might find your way to someone who is semi-retired, or who doesn't *need* to work, but does so occasionally, just to keep themselves busy, who could help you out *as little* or *as much* as you need, and take the pressure of you, without costing you too much.

II.   Search the internet for job finding websites *(agencies)* that provide *Construction trades people, including Site Managers*. Register your details, explain what you are going to be doing, and say that you are looking for someone suitable who can help you with the management side of things, on a part time basis, paid by the hour.
      You might get bona fide Site Manager, and you might also get ex Site Formen, ex-joiners, ex-brickies, or other people who know their way around building sites. It would be up to you to arrange to meet them, to decide whether they look and sound like they know what they are talking about, and are also *(very importantly)*,the sort of people you could work and get along with.
      Hourly rates to hire these sorts of people vary, depending on where you are situated geographically, but you will probably be paying the agency between £20 - £30 / hour, with a minimum hire of half a day *(possibly a minimum of a full day)*. That might sound a lot, but if you try to the job yourself and make a pigs ear of it, the cost to the job and to you, to put right the mistakes, could be significant.

III.  Another option, as I mentioned earlier, if you didn't tick enough of the bullet points listed above, is to equip yourself with the skills you need, by booking yourself onto a Self-Build Project Management course.

> *How you will set up the management of the site is a very important decision for you to make. It can mean the difference between a project that is completed in 6 – 12 months, on (or at least near to) budget, and not too stressful for you and your family, or one that drags on for 2 years, goes over significantly over budget, and the stress knocks years off your life expectancy!*

*By the way, if you do hire a Site Manager, make sure they are up to date on their safety certificates and training (they should have an SMSTS card and a First Aid card at the minimum)*

*And if you decide to run the job yourself, prepare well, get stuck in and do your best, but don't be afraid to say "I am struggling with this" at any stage and if you are, go out and find some help (see above).*


## THING 85: DRAW UP A CONSTRUCTION PROGRAMME

Construction Programmes are a valuable tool to keep with you every day, both while you are planning the project and when you are building. They help professional contractors to keep track of *what should have been done, what is being done and what will need to be done,* on contracts, small and large.

Using a construction programme as it should be used, will help you to accurately plan and monitor overall progress (*or lack of*) on your own project, and also to hit your target completion date.

Drawing up a programme is not particularly difficult, but to ensure that it gives you accurate guidance, you will need to do some homework on each of the activities that will be included in the build (*When does each activity need to start? How long will it take? How does it affect everything else? etc*).

I have included a sample programme at the end of this section, to give you a visual prompt for how to create something similar for your own project. This one includes most of the activities that will be included in an average self-build project, however, your own project may include more, or different activities, or you may wish to create your own format for how it looks and works, to suit your own project and/or the way you want to set it up. That is not a problem. Go with your own ideas.

Some activities are easy to allocate time periods to. For example, the first item: "*Set up site*". This involves getting cabins, containers, portaloo's, water supply (*or bowser*), temporary electricity supply (*or you might use generators instead*), fencing, gates, security systems, health and safety & security signage, and any other items that may be uniquely relevant to your own project. I have allocated a week for getting all that done, but actually, most of it could be done in two or three days if you are well organised. Or it might be that you decide to allow 2 weeks if this is your first project.

To be able to estimate and allocate accurate timescales to the individual items, ideally you need to speak to the people who will be carrying them out, to get *their* estimated timescales. Or, if you have not yet confirmed who is going to be doing the work, do some reading about other peoples completed self-build projects, to see how long the different tasks took them to complete (*searching "How long does it take to build a house?" should pull up relevant information on this subject*).

The sample programme is a fairly realistic timescale for a reasonably quick build of a simple, rectangular, 4 bedroom, timber framed house, on a flat plot, with a simple strip footing, trussed roof, and no notable complications. The 28 week programme is just an example timescale, but could be achieved on a first self-build, if everything went reasonably smoothly, and if the job is well organised. However, if you think that time scale is a bit optimistic for your own situation, just add some more weeks. There is no right or wrong length of time that it should take to build a house, as long as it eventually gets finished *and stays standing up*!

Once you have worked out a target time period for *each activity,* you need to format them all in to a *"what needs doing first, what needs doing second, third, fourth, fifth......."* order. That is where the sample programme should come in useful. Use it as a basic framework, into and around which you can add any other relevant activities. Just slot them in wherever you think they should go, thinking as logically as you can, through the build process, each time you do so.

Try to overlap the activities where appropriate. You need to do this to keep the overall build time to a minimum, but, to do so, you will need to look at what else is going on at the same time, and try to take into account how those activities will affect the one you are considering. Thinking about each activity, related to what else could be going on at the same time, is very important, and is how all programmes should be created.

### Simple examples:

*You need to strip the topsoil / vegetation off the land before you excavate foundations.*
*You need to set everything out before you excavate.*
*Foundations are normally followed by blockwork to DPC (damp proof course).*
*Blockwork to DPC is normally followed by slab formation.*
*Slab formation is normally followed by the timber frame, or brickwork and blockwork.*
*(Note what I have said about when and how scaffolding goes up, in other sections)*
*You can't start the roof structure until the house is built up to roof level.*
*Windows can go in as the shell is built, or after, but before plaster boarding.*
*First fixes can usually start once the roof is on, but you need to get the house sealed asap.*
*Plaster boarding comes after first fixes*
*Skimming, or taping and jointing comes after boarding.*
*Second fixes come after skimming*
*You can't decorate until you have plastered the walls.*
*Bathrooms go in with second fixes.*
*Kitchens go in about the same time as second fixes, but have a bit of flexibility. You don't want damage to be done to kitchens, so wait until the heavy work has been mostly done.*
*You can do the drainage and the foundation blockwork at the same time*

*You can decorate and fit kitchens at the same time (but working in different rooms).
etc.*

**You should be able to sensibly slot all the other constituent activities for your project in around those listed above.**

Before you start work on your own programme, I suggest copying the basic information from the programme below, onto a spreadsheet. Save it as "**Construction Programme**", change it to suit your own ideas on formatting, and have a few practice runs at drawing up your own programme. Then just keep adjusting it until you are at least *reasonably* happy with it.

*I draw up my programmes using an excel spreadsheet, using one column to denote each week, and shading the boxes to indicate time periods. This is quite an easy method to get the idea of, and is easily adjusted. If you can use spreadsheets, you could adopt this method.*

It is a good idea to draw a vertical line down the chart, at least every week, estimating how far you are through each item. As you update it, put a small "dot" on each activity to indicate where you think you are up to with that particular item, then using a ruler, join up all the dots. Doing this will give you a quick, visual guide to how the overall build is doing, compared with how you originally hoped.

Items that you are ahead of programme on, or on time, or behind time, can also easily be seen, by looking at how the line you have drawn moves backwards and forwards as it goes down the chart. Using this information, you can see where actions are either looking ok, or might need attention in order to get them back on track.

**Once you have completed your own programme, keep it around at all times while you plan and build, preferably laminated, on a wall and on A3 sized paper. Check it every day and mark it up every week.**

**It is not usually the end of the world if you fall behind. Just try your best not to. If you do, see if you can work out why that is, and try to fix the problem. If you can't, then get advice from professionals, either on site or elsewhere.**

## And don't panic.

The sample programme is on the next page.

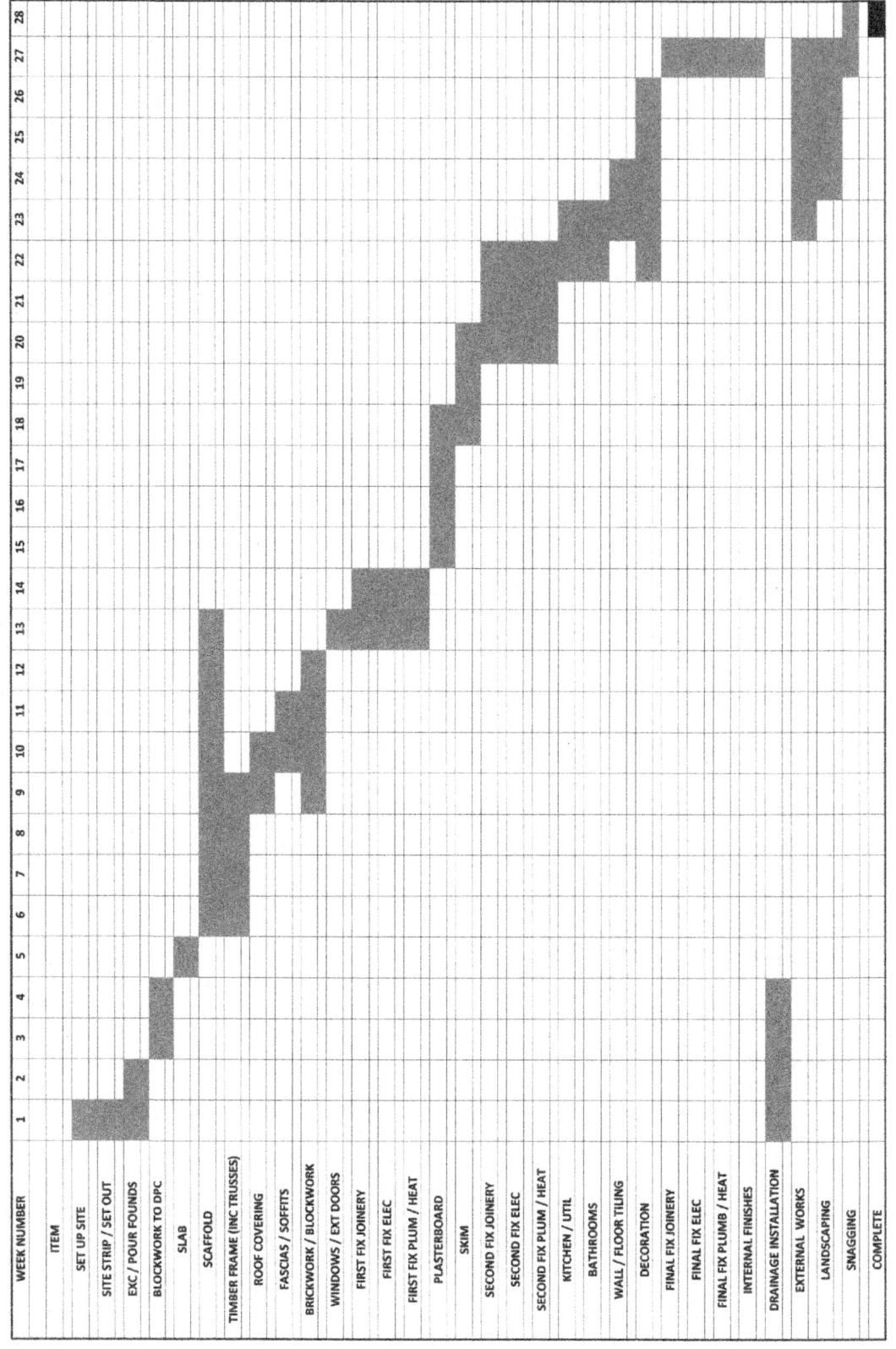

# THING 86: SET THE SITE UP SAFELY:

In these days of increased awareness of health and safety matters in the workplace, and with the potential repercussions of not giving the subject suitable attention, it is more important than ever to make sure that your building site is safe and secure.

This is not a complicated subject. Any intelligent person could walk on to a building site and immediately pick up most of the potential hazards. However, walking on to someone else's site and noticing the problems is one thing, but when you start your own project, it is _you_ who will ultimately be responsible for _everything_. Not the subbies, not the Building Inspector, or the warranty companies. **YOU!**

Laws on site safety have changed significantly over the past decade or so, and now, if there is an accident on a site, the Site Manager can be held _personally_ responsible for it, whether or not he / she even knew anything about the circumstances surrounding it. The thinking here is that, if the person running the site knows that his / her ass is on the line if anything goes wrong, they will be more likely to treat the subject seriously.

If something does go wrong on a building site, the safety inspectors will be looking for the _intent_ of the person in charge. If that person can be seen to have been taking all reasonable and necessary steps to keep the site safe, they may not get in to trouble. However, if they are deemed to have been negligent, they could be in for a rough ride.

**So, setting up your site safely:**

1. **Think logically:** What could potentially be dangerous to workers, or visitors to site?
2. **Make sure the whole area is fenced adequately:** Heras fencing is the most common type of fencing for building sites. It is cheap, fairly secure and shows that you intend for people to stay off the site.
3. **Fit lockable gates:** Often two Heras fence panels are used for this job, secured with a decent padlock and chain.
4. **Fix health and safety and warning signs** to the fences, so that they can be clearly seen, on all sides of the site that open to the public. Think about the surrounding area, and who could be likely to come into the general area of the site. If there is a school close by, you will need special signage to warn the children and site staff / visitors, deliveries etc, of the potential dangers that the site could present.
5. **Hire a welfare cabin** of a suitable size to cater for the likely workforce. It needs to have hot running water, heater, light, somewhere to dry clothes, a table, chairs, and copies of all the health and safety details for the site, fixed to the cabin walls, so that everyone can see them. The access to the cabin should also be safe. _Fully equipped cabins can be hired with built in generators and water storage._
6. **Hire Wc's:** If there are only males working on the site, depending on how many people are expected to be working at any one time, for a self-build project, just one unit will usually do. If there are going to be both sexes working, then a minimum of 2 units will be needs, clearly marked up with "Male" and "Female" signage. Again, you

can hire these units with water storage for flushing toilets and male and female rooms already designated.

7. **Create safe parking / transit areas:** Workers and visitors should be able to drive onto site, park, then turn the vehicle round an exit the site safely, in a forward gear. Once parked on the site, they should be able to walk safely to the office / cabins / toilets etc. Creating a gravelled area is usually the way this matter is dealt with. If you locate this area where the driveway for the house will eventually be constructed, the stone can later form part of the drive formation, so it won't be a wasted expense.

8. **Set up a "Site induction" system:** This simply means that anyone who comes to work on the site receives a briefing on how the site works, what the health and safety aspects are, and what their own responsibilities are. They are also told about the welfare facilities. This information should be given to them in writing, and they should sign another copy, which you will keep.

9. **Set up an onsite traffic transit system:** If possible, you should try to take deliveries off a roadway and onto the site before they unload. They then (*as with cars*) need to be able to exit the site in a forward gear if possible. This means that you need to try to provide a turning area *within* the site, and also try to locate your storage area adjacent to the route that deliveries will take. If this is not possible, you will need to set up a traffic management system, where delivery vehicles are guided both in and out of the site, by someone qualified to do so.

10. **Make sure everyone on site is legally allowed to be there:**
    All site workers should have gained a safety qualification before they can work on any building site. Before you allow them to start, you should ask them to show you proof of their *relevant* qualification (*look online at "site health and safety certificates" for information*)

11. **Get a safety qualification for yourselves:** Before you start work on site, you should be qualified to be on site, managing the health and safety aspects. *I can only guide you on this subject.* There are lots of different qualifications available, depending on what you are going to be doing. A Site Manager will normally have an **SMSTS** (*Site Manager Safety Training Scheme*) card, and the workforce will generally have **CSCS** (*Construction Skills Certification Scheme*) cards. If you search either of these abbreviations, you should find all the information you need to make sure that everyone on your site is legally covered to be there.

12. **First aid Cards:** This is another card that everyone on building sites should carry. **You** need to have one and <u>you</u> need to make sure that everyone working on site has one. There are plenty of one day, or two days courses regularly held all over the country, that you can attend to get your card. Search "*Construction First Aid courses*". (*Also have a look at "CDM regulations" to see how they apply to your development*).

13. **Think about site security:** Will you need an alarm system? Would you need to hire a security firm to monitor the site? Will you be living on site (*if so, could you look after the site security yourselves?*) Could kids get in, and hurt themselves (*even if they*

*break in, you may be held responsible for their injuries if your security is not adequate).*

14. **Do some research on Health and Safety for Construction sites:** The above points are only a *brief guideline* to your duties on site. You will find all the information you need by doing an internet search on *"Health and Safety for Self-build sites"*.

**TAKE THIS SUBJECT SERIOUSLY**

## THING 87: **KEEP WASTE TO A MINIMUM**

The cost of disposing of waste skips have increased drastically in the past 3 – 4 years. On top of that, restrictions on what you can put into the skips have also increased. Here are some examples of items that building sites generate, that you now either cannot put into standard waste skips, or you are only allowed to put a small amount:

Asbestos
Chemicals (bleach, cleaning detergents, etc.)
Oil (motor, cooking, hydraulic, etc.)
Paint Tins (unless empty)
Plasterboard
Solvents (paint, glue, etc.)

If you hire a *mixed skip* and think you may get away with sneaking large quantities of (*for example*) plasterboards in, by putting them all at the bottom of the skip, you could find that you suddenly receive a hefty invoice a couple of weeks after you have had it picked up. The skip companies now have to deal with waste meticulously, and they are required to keep accurate records of a lot of what they are disposing of, what they did with it, and where the remnants went.

Here are some ideas to help you keep your waste disposal costs down:

- **Being careful when you are ordering materials.** Check the quantities and don't round up *too much* for waste. Unless the product is not available to buy in small quantities, you can normally get *a bit* more of it from the merchants, without paying too much of a premium on the cost. So just order what you need, as and when you need it.
- **Separate the materials out that you can't put in the mixed skip, and deal with them responsibly.** It is better to pay to dispose of the items listed above legally, than to find yourselves being fined for not doing so.
- **Collect timber waste together in one place:** A lot of timber is wasted on building sites. If you can burn wood in your area, keep a pile of unwanted offcuts somewhere on the site, ready to burn on a suitable, dry, calm day. This can save a lot of skip

space and cost (*check with the Local Authority on where you stand with burning timber, before you do so*).

- **Order the largest skips that your site can efficiently cope with:** If you are not used to ordering skips, you might be tempted to get 2 or 3 small ones and spread them around the site. As a practical idea, that is fine, but from a financial perspective it is not a good idea. When you are building a house, you are usually going to generate a lot of waste, but you may not be aware that a large portion of the cost of a skip is in the delivery and pickup. Small skips therefore work out to be a lot more expensive, like for like, than large skips.
- **Shop around for skips:** I have found a significant variance in the cost of skips between different companies, in different parts of the same area. That may be related to where they dispose of the waste, the distance from their yard to the location of the site, or their general running costs. Whatever the reason, it is worth making a few phone calls to get the best price. Don't worry about bartering a bit with them, the odd tenner per skip adds up over a full build.

## THING 88: IS THERE A BEST TIME OF YEAR TO BUILD?

*I have a fairly unconventional view on this subject. I always get raised eyebrows at the shows if I either talk to potential self-builder or present seminars discussing the best time of year to start new build projects. You can make up your own mind:*

I have been involved in the Self-Build Industry around forty years. I have also completed five of my own self-builds. I have been involved commercial and housing projects, from the small to the very large. Three things I have learned during that time are:

1. It can be difficult to maintain progress on smaller projects during the summer months, due to people disappearing to go on holiday. Large companies have a system for dealing with staff holidays, small companies basically *shut up shop* for two to three weeks, during the summer months.
2. The times of year when there is least rain, are the summer and the winter. There tends to be more rain in the Spring and Autumn. Building work is more affected by rain than by snow or sun.
3. Building with timber frame (*as opposed to Traditional build*), allows more flexibility in the construction programme. (*"What has that got to do with times of year"*, I hear you say. Read on).

**Bearing those facts in mind:**

**My preferred time of year to start building, is November.**

In November, labour is generally widely available, and workers are looking for extra hours to pay for the upcoming Christmas period. The weather is starting to get colder, there is generally less rain in November than in September / October (*although that is not always the case*), and there is more chance of ground frost. That means that the ground is often drier and harder, so poorer quality ground is less likely to collapse when the foundation trenches are being dug. In Winter the ground can be too hard to work, with, and you are restricted from pouring concrete until the temperature is *"4 degrees and rising"* on any particular day, which during a bad winter can cause significant delays. There tends to be more rain in spring, so the ground can be very soggy, making it more likely that your trenches could collapse while you wait for the concrete to be delivered. It can also make a heck of a mess of the site, which can result in the groundworks process becoming less efficient, and more wasteful of time and materials.

*And in the Summer, every b\*\*ger you need is in Spain!*

## Here is how a late Autumn start on site can speed up progress:

### Trenches:

A clean, tidy, solid foundation trench can save you hundreds of pounds in machine and labour time (*less clearing muck and mud out prior to concreting, and a reduced chance of having to use more concrete to fill in the extra areas where the collapses occur*).

It may also save further time and money by you not having to dig as deep to get to a solid trench base, which is entirely possible if, what was generally decent ground at the outset, is turning into gravy as you dig. An extra foot of depth in an excavation can double the amount of concrete required for the job, potentially adding up to a couple of thousand pounds to the cost. Just because of some heavy rain.

### Foundation Blockwork:

Unless it is literally freezing cold (*which is a less common occurrence in November than it is in January or February*), the foundation blockwork can usually go ahead, even if it rains a bit. The underground blockwork won't be seen once the ground is backfilled, so it is not critical to keep it clean and free of a few mortar smudges. This means work is less likely to be stopped due to inclement weather.

### Ground Floor Construction:

The same applies to the ground floor construction. If you are planning to construct a standard concrete slab (which will receive a screed later), it does not matter if the top surface of the concrete gets rained on while it is being poured. In fact, a bit of water on the surface can actually help concrete to cure (*set*) faster (*concrete doesn't just set by drying out, it is also a chemical reaction between the all materials used. Concrete can actually set under water*).

The only time you need dry weather for pouring a concrete slab is when you plan to power float it, rather than screeding it (*power floating simply polishes the top of the concrete to a shine, so you don't need to apply a screed later, saving a lot of money. To powerfloat a slab, you need dry and "none freezing" weather. Search "Videos of power floating" to see how it works).*

**Timber Frame:** The timber frame can usually be erected in most weather conditions, so building in winter should not hold it up too much. The frame erection normally includes the roof trusses. Once the trusses are on, you can fit the felt and battening to the roof. Once that has been done, the house becomes acceptably weathertight, enough for you to start first fixes. Also fitting plastic sheeting over the window openings can give you a pretty much dry house to work in, whatever the weather is like outside. So, within 2 – 4 weeks after you construct the ground floor slab, you can potentially be working on the first fixes inside a dry building. (*Note, this is definitely not the case for a traditionally built house*).

From that point forwards, the weather only tends to affect the brickwork / blockwork outer skin of the building, the drainage, and the external works. Potential delays to building the outer skin are almost inevitable, unless you dry clad the outside of the building, or if you build using single skin construction (see section 78).

*Note: I am fully aware that most people don't choose the season to start work on their self-build projects, however, many self-builds are planned months, or even years in advance, in which case, there may be more flexibility with the start date. The reason I think that this is something you should at least be aware of, is that although I have started building houses at all times of year, in terms of speed, ease, practicality and cost, for me, a late autumn / early winter start simply works best.*

## THING 89: HOW LONG WILL IT TAKE TO BUILD?

### (Alternative title: How Long is a piece of string?)

*Unfortunately, the question of how long it will take you to build your new home is almost impossible to answer.* All I can do is give you a very rough general rule on timescales, and some ideas that you can use to potentially increase the build speed.

An average self-build project takes anywhere between 6 months and 2 years to complete. A simple, well run project could potentially be completed in 4 – 5 months. I will run through the scenarios for the differing timescales:

**To potentially achieve a 6 month build, your project needs to include some, if not most of these factors:**

- "Squarish" shaped 4 sided design.
- 2 storeys.
- Good ground conditions.
- A simple strip foundation.
- A power floated slab.

- Timber frame construction (or closed panel), with "easi joists" (or similar), which help to make the plumbing and wiring installation simpler and faster.
- External skin in either brickwork or blockwork and render.
- Trussed roof.
- Large concrete roof tiles.
- Self-coloured plastic windows and doors.
- Simple electrical and plumbing layouts.
- Either solid foam or mineral wool insulation *("spray foam" is also an option. However, I have never used it, so am slightly hesitant to suggest it)*.
- Standard plaster boarding (tapered edge boards).
- Taped and jointed walls and ceiling (*as opposed to skimming or wet plastering*), using the mechanical option for tape application (see section 129).
- Spray painted walls and ceilings.
- Prefinished skirtings & architraves.
- Pre-primed internal doors.
- Straight stairs with a handrail on one side.
- Simple bathroom suites, showers, vanity units.
- Simple wall and floor tiling.
- Wherever possible, using wide kitchen units (1000mm or 1200mm) where possible, and avoid lots of fine or fancy design detail. (*Simple kitchen designs often look best and cost a lot less anyway!*)
- Carpet or vinyl / vinyl tile floors, rather than ceramic tiling.
- Getting the service connections organised and completed as early as possible.
- Form the permanent driveway as soon as the scaffold is down.
- A successful air tightness test <u>first time</u> (*as work proceeds, eliminating gaps and cracks where air could escape from the building, such as around spotlights, at floor levels, behind skirtings etc).*
- Arrange your airtightness test asap as soon as the building is fully sealed and is nearly complete.

**The difference between a 6 month and 12 months build timescale can come down to:**
- A Complicated design
- Design errors
- Poor organisation.
- Poor ground.
- Bad weather.
- Mistakes.
- Incorrect or late deliveries.
- Labour, materials, or plant shortages.
- Trying to do more of the work yourselves.
- Not giving the project 100% of your attention.

**To potentially shorten the 6 month build period:**

- Think about using Modular Build instead of Timber Frame.
- Factor in most or <u>all</u> of the suggestions on the first list (above).
- Don't do any of the work yourselves.
- Get as many of the trades working concurrently as you can (*e.g. get joiners, electricians, and plumbers in doing the first fixes, all at the same time*).
- Draw up a short build programme. Look at it and update it every 3 or 4 days and do everything you can to stick to it. Whenever you fall behind it, try to find out why, and quickly fix the issues.
- Stay well organised and jump straight on to fixing problems as soon as they appear.

**Conclusion:**

The build times for any new home are significantly governed by the design and build choices, made early during in the planning stage. Most building projects can be completed rapidly, if the people organising them are determined that they will be and take sensible and practical measures to achieve that goal.

A house that takes two years to build can turn in to a bit of a never ending, stressful saga, rather than something that gives you pleasure.

**Set yourselves reasonable targets at the project planning stage and try to stick to them.**

## THING 90: MAIN CONTRACTOR v BUILDING CONTRACTOR v SUB-CONTRACTORS

If you are not comfortable with the thought of Project Managing your build, you have a few other options. These boil down to whether you hire a Main Contractor or a Building Contractor (*or, of course, a Project Manager, but we have already talked about that option*).

In this situation, where you would not be assuming the role of Project Manager, we can rule out setting up the job using all sub-contract labour. When you hire a sub-contractor, they expect to be given a set of drawings, told what to do, have the job explained to them in writing and / or in print and then to be monitored throughout their time on site, with them going to the Site Manager (*or Project Manager in this case*), if they have any queries.

So, concentrating on the other 2 options:

**What is a Main Contractor?**

The name sounds a bit more important than it needs to. You can have a Main Contractor on a multi-million pound contract, or on a simple self-build.

On a self-build project, they are basically companies that supply either most or all of the labour you will need for the job. Sometimes they can also get involved in supplying the materials and plant, depending how much of the project you want to give out. They will usually either have a foreman, their own Site Manager, or a Project Manager (*who will organise all their contracts, and run around between them, making sure everything is going as it should*). These people tend to simply report their progress to you, rather than expect you to tell them what to do, and when to do it. In some cases, they could take the place of you as Project Manager, but to do so, they would need to be in charge of most of the work going on (*they can't order people about who they are not responsible for*).

Using a Main Contractor will usually cost you more than using individual Sub-Contractors, due to the fact that they also have to employ people at the supervisory level, give them vans, travelling expenses etc. The extra cost could be between 15% and 25% extra, like for like, compared with what is would cost if you managed the job yourselves. The extra cost would be on the labour and maybe the plant. If the builder buys the materials, you need to make sure that, one way or the other, you get the benefit of the VAT refund, so it is usually best if either you take on that task yourselves, or at least let them use your trade account to order what is needed (*only do that if you think you can trust them*).

**What is A Building Contractor?**

These are companies who can take on the whole project, providing labour, materials, and plant, charging a fixed price, based on a quotation for the whole project. Their quote will be based on the information that you give them at the outset. If you miss anything in that information, their price will increase once it is included, and if the job changes in any way, due to any reason, their price will change further. The changes are very rarely in a downwards direction.

This option can take pretty much all the pressure away from you during the build, but it will also take away some of the pleasure of being involved. And will cost you a lot more, probably between an **additional** 15% to 25% <u>on top</u> of the extra cost that hiring a Project Manager would add.

*If you go down either of these routes, make sure you properly vet the people you are thinking of using. They will be spending a lot of your money, so you need to know that they will do a decent job for you.*
*Ask to see references, other jobs and speak to previous clients if possible. If they get defensive when you ask for these things, look for someone else.*

*To make decisions on whether to self-manage, or take on a Main Contractor, or a Building Contractor, it is a case of deciding how much you want to be, or can sensibly be involved in the project yourselves, and probably just as importantly, how much money you have available to pay them!*

## THING 91: **INSURANCE**

Before you start work on site, make sure you have adequate insurance to cover you, all your site workers, and the general public, while you build. Construction sites are dangerous place, not only for the workforce, but they also tend to attract a lot of unwanted attention, including from children who see sites as a great playground.

When I was studying Construction Law at college, I was surprised to learn that even if someone breaks into the site and injures themselves while they are there, the Builder / Contractor who is in charge of the site, *can* be held legally responsible for their injuries. Also, the Supervisor in charge of the site itself is usually the one who is most likely take most of the blame (*that would be YOU if you take on that role*).

Apart from kids and thieves breaking in, there are the quite a few other areas you need legal cover for when you are personally responsible for a building site: Accidents, fire, damage of materials or plant, damage to other people's property, Act of God etc.

**All Risks Insurance:**

For self-builders, there is a simple way to get covered for *all the risks* that exist on building sites. Strangely enough, it is called *All Risks Insurance*. It is not too expensive (usually less than £500 / annum, which you can pay monthly). You will find plenty of suitable companies on-line, and you can set it up in no time. Just do a search on *Contractors All Risks Insurance*.

**Note:** A couple of the questions on the insurance application forms may catch you out. One question normally asks: *"What are the re-build costs?"* In other words. If the whole thing got damaged beyond repair (*fire etc*) how much would it cost to clear away the debris and re-build the whole thing? The figures they expect as answers have always shocked me, for example, an £80,000 build could have a £250,000 re-build cost. I don't know the formulas they use to work the figures out, but if you are not sure how to answer that question, call the insurance agent for guidance.

*Remember that accidents can happen at any time on a building site. If you start working without having suitable insurance and something goes wrong, you could potentially find yourselves in big trouble, even in prison. So, get it sorted early, and make sure it is up and running as a policy before you start work.*

# THING 92: LEARN A BIT OF THE LANGUAGE

Here is a quick tale I tell when I present seminars at the shows. It recounts something that happened on the first job I ever took on as a Self-Build Project Manager:

I had a call from a highly stressed self-builder. He said he had tried to start his project, but quickly realised he didn't know what he was doing. He had sold his own house and had to be out in 10 weeks, *and* he was getting married that same week! – He had a building plot, had cleared the site, but was only just starting to excavate for the foundations. The house was to be built in traditional brick and blockwork. He asked if I could help.

I wasn't busy when he rang, so said I would jump in the car and meet him on site the same day, which I did. As I drove on to the site, he was standing talking to someone who looked like a groundworker, and there was a half excavated foundation trench, with two men digging with shovels, in the trench.

As I walked over to him, I could hear him talking to the groundworker. He was saying:

*"How much would you charge me to throw some pebbles in there (pointing to the trench) and stamp on them"*

I could see the look on the groundworkers face, thinking: *"I've got a right one here"*, as he sub-consciously added a zero to the end of his quote!

The building industry is a great industry to be part of, but it is full of people who want to make as much money as they can. If they see an opportunity to make more profit on a job, they will take it. This self-builder was ripe for plucking!

If, instead of saying what he did, he had said *"What would your day rates be for an excavator & driver to finish excavating that foundation and pour the nine inch concrete footing?"* He would have created a completely different builder / client relationship from the very first conversation they had. The groundworker would still look for ways to make extra money, but would know that *"This guy seems to know what he is talking about"* and would be less likely to try to pull the wool.

*So, what I am saying is that the more you appear to know on a building site, the less likely you are to be taken advantage of.*

One good way to appear more savvy is to talk the talk. If, while you research the subject prior to starting work, you consciously try to remember some of the technical terms for the processes and materials, and then purposely use those terms in your conversations with anyone you come across in relation to the job, you will automatically get more street cred with them.

So, for example:

- *The foundation holes are: "**trenches**".*
- *The concrete going into the trench would be: "**the footings**".*

- *Lots of concrete going in* would be: *"**mass filling**"*
- *How much for digging the holes* is: *"**Daywork rates or hourly rates for an excavator and driver**"*
- *Brickwork up to the ground level* is: *"**Blockwork below DPC**"*
- *The floor is:* *"**The ground floor slab**", or "**The suspended slab**"*
- *The frame builders are:* *"**The timber frame erectors**"*

And so on through the job.

I am purposely using a lot of site terms in this book. Try to remember them if you can.

*Also, don't think you have to swear a lot to be seen as an experienced Site Manager. I have worked on all types of sites for 40+ years and very rarely swear. I find it far more effective if the workers don't expect it, then if and when they hear it, they tend to listen!*

## THING 93: LISTEN TO EVERYONE, BUT DON'T AUTOMATICALLY DO WHAT THEY SAY.

Following on neatly from the previous section, it is also important that you quickly learn to listen to what people tell you on site, but do not just take everyone at their word.

The fact is that: *"Everyone on site knows everything"*. Or at least they think they do. Also, there is always more than one way to do any job on a building site. How you do it comes down to your experience / how you were trained / what the circumstances are on this occasion / how quick it needs doing (etc).

You will learn a lot from the people you work with on site. Some of them have gathered decades of very good experience from working on dozens of other jobs. But part of what you quickly need to learn on site, is to *sort the wheat from the chaff*, so:

i. **Listen to everything, but then check out what you heard before you do anything about it.**
ii. **The people on site who talk *most*, are often the ones who know *least*.**

**Additional:**

- Always listen to the Building Regs and Warranty Inspectors and act on what they say. Do not argue with them.
- DON'T always do everything Architects tell you to do. They are clever people, but often have their own strong views, which might not be your automatic choice, or even the right choice. Take on board whatever they say, go away and think about it, and if you disagree, tell them. If you are sure of your argument after you have discussed it with them, go with *your* idea unless it could be risky to the project. If

that is the case, get further advice from someone else, before making your final decision.

## THING 94: **KEEP A GRIP ON SPENDING FROM DAY ONE**

*At the start of your project, you will have a big pot of money, an empty piece of land, and high levels of excitement.*

*By the time you are heading towards completion, if you are not careful, you could have a big stack of bills, an empty bank account and, high levels of sleep deprivation!*

OK, hands up, I am just as guilty as everyone else of wanting to fly out of the traps at 100mph at the start of the job:

*"Let's get everything ordered, everyone lined up, let's get the job going, and up and finished as soon as possible!"*

However, unfortunately what nearly always happens next, is that things start to happen that you didn't expect:

- The foundations could go deeper than you had thought and cost a lot more than expected.
- You could have a few weeks of lousy weather, losing you a lot of time getting up to slab level. As a result of that, you could end up having to pay for non-productive labour time and charges for groundworker's plant standing idle.
- Maybe your first choice of brick is not available and your second choice costs £100 / 1000 more (*you might need 12,000 of them, if so, there's £1,200 gone in the blink of an eye*).

These types of delays and problems (*along with many more*) are all just sitting in the background, waiting to pounce, and, sure as *eggs is eggs,* some of them will jump out and slap you in the face, just when you are not expecting it.

Unfortunately, there is nothing you can do to foresee, or plan for unexpected problems during the job. You just need to be ready for them and react quickly when they happen.

Don't get depressed if you start to feel that you are constantly dealing with things that seem determined to go pear shaped. When you look back on the build, it will all have been part of the challenge, and the fun of building your own home! You will be regaling your friends with the stories for years to come!

To try to minimise the impact of problems that may appear out of the blue, here are three things you can do to help you prepare:

1. Make sure you allow a decent contingency allowance in your initial build figures (10% - 15% of the net build cost).
2. Try to keep as much of *your* money in *your* pocket as possible. Only spend *what* you need to *when* you need to. Cash flow is critical on a job like this, and there could be times when you are waiting for payments to arrive from your funders, but need to

pay some big bills. Pay minimum deposits on things you need to order, open as many trade accounts as possible, try to pay subbies at the end of each section of work, rather than every week.

3. Shop around: It is easy when you are ordering (*for example*) your perimeter fencing, to simply call the Builders Merchant you use regularly, and order, say 20 fencing panels. I just went online for 5 minutes and found a variety of prices for *"Heras Fencing Panels" (lightweight steel panels for perimeter fencing)*, ranging from £21 to £38 each. So:

20 panels at £21 = £420
20 panels at £38 = £760
**Difference: £340**
*(and well worth spending a few minutes online to find).*

**Builders Merchant prices:**

The Builders Merchants pricing system really annoys me. They have dozens of different pricing structures for different ranges, depending on who you are, how much you buy, and how long you have been buying from them. You never know whether you are getting the correct rates when you go to the counter to buy anything on your account. You specifically have to ask whoever is serving you to check the price against your rates (*if you don't, they will often charge you standard builder's prices, which could be up to 20% higher than your correct rates*), and when you go from one branch to another, maybe because your usual branch is out of stock of something, the same thing is even more likely to happen.

You need to bear in mind, throughout the project, that although when your start work on your project, you will possibly have more money in your bank account than you have ever had before, that pot of cash will very quickly disappear.

Try to mentally approach *every* transaction with this thought:

*"These people will want to get as much money from me as they can.*
*But I will pay them as little as possible".*

If you do that, you will stand a better chance of getting through to the end of the project with enough money to pay all the bills, and who knows, maybe even have enough left for a quiet weekend in Southend!

## THING 95: **DELIVERY NOTES AND INVOICES**

You are going to receive literally hundreds of delivery notes and invoices over the course of the project. One thing you can guarantee is that some of them will be wrong. The strange thing is, they very rarely seem to wrong in your favour.

To avoid losing potentially large sums of money, it is important that you set up an administration system to keep track of everything you purchase. So that: a) you can make sure you get it, b) make sure it is the thing you actually ordered, c) make sure you are paying the right price for it, and d) Make sure any returns, or missing items from deliveries don't just get forgotten about by the supplier, and you ending up paying for them *(a common occurrence)*.

Some of the items you will be buying will cost hundreds, or even thousands of pounds, however the value of the order does not necessarily mean that there is less chance of it being charged incorrectly. For example:

Say I order 5 packs of 55 plasterboards at £5.00 per board *(not an accurate figure)*. That is £275 per pack. The branch of the Builders Merchant that I order them from only has 4 packs, so they call another branch and leave a message for someone at that branch to send the missing pack over. That message, for whatever reason doesn't get to the right person, and the last pack of boards is not delivered.

If I have a good admin system set up, the delivery note will get to me quickly, and I will see that only 4 packs have actually been delivered, so I get an automatic prompt to think *"Where is the last pack?"*. I can then follow that through, by chasing the supplier for the missing item. If I don't have a decent system set up, I might not find out about the missing boards until the lads on site run out before the end of the job. – OK, that *should* then prompt me to check why that is, but in some cases *(for example, bags of cement)*, it is hard to accurately guess how many bags you should be using, and it is sometimes just as hard to work out how many *have been* used.

A simple way to set the system set up is to have a *delivery note box* in the cabin, or somewhere in the house itself, so if you are not there, everyone who takes in a delivery knows to put the delivery note in the box. You can then pick them all up and check them against the invoices.

This is not a difficult system to set up and, even if it only catches a few occasions where there are discrepancies, if one of those occasions involves a £275 pack of plasterboards, it will have been worth the effort.


## THING 96: GET MULTIPLE QUOTES

A few years ago, I saw a graph comparing the *average price quoted for a job*, with the *number of people who quoted*. It showed that the more quotes requested and received, the lower the price went. This might sound logical, and indeed it is something that has in my experience, proved itself to be true.

Preparing the information to go out for, say the plumbing package, can be quite an involved process. You will need drawings, specifications, a programme of the works, a list of the work you want including in the tender, details of how payments will be made, a cover letter and possibly a number of other items ancillary items.

When the tender packages are being physically put together, ready to go off, it doesn't take a lot more effort for you send it out to 6 companies, than it does to send it out to 3.

The benefits of sending the tender packages out to multiple companies are:

1) If you contact just one company, they may not be interested, and you won't get any response, so you will then have to repeat the process.

2) If a company is busy with other work, they will often increase their price to a stupidly high level, just to make sure they don't get the job, but showing you that they have made the effort. If you only approach them and no-one else, you could end up paying significantly over the odds.

3) If you go out to 6 companies, the chances are that you will get 3 or 4 responses, and between those companies, you will stand a reasonable chance of finding at least one that: i) gives you a decent price, ii) is suitable, and iii) will be available when you need them. That same principle applies for all types of tenders (*supply and fix / labour only / materials only*).

**One thing to be aware of:** When you go out for prices to some of the smaller companies, such as Groundworkers / Roofers / Joiners / Electrical / Plumbing / plastering or decorating, they may want to give you a *Supply and fix* quote. In other words, they will provide all the materials, based on the drawings you send them.

If this happens, you may be happy to go ahead with the proposal, thinking to yourself: *"That's fine, it will save me time in ordering everything, and they'll probably get better rates because they buy the materials all the time"*. Not necessarily:

1)   You going to a merchant and offering them the chance to sell you a lot of the materials that you will need to build a **full new house**, is very good business for them. You will often get pretty much their lowest *Commercial Builder prices* (*which are only beaten by the large construction companies*). In most cases, the small companies you ask to price the job will be buying nowhere near the amount of product that you will be buying, so will be nowhere near you on spending power.
2)   The people tendering for the individual packages might not be VAT registered, so they will pay, and charge you full price for what they buy. If *you* order and pay for the materials, you will get the VAT back, as part of your *Self-Build VAT refund* at the end of the job.


## THING 97: **LET PEOPLE DO THEIR JOBS**

Have you ever had someone at work who will stand and watch you working, not particularly saying anything, just standing there? Annoying isn't it? It is just as annoying for the lads on site!

On many of the self-build projects I have worked on, I will be on site, doing whatever I am doing, while the client simply stands and watches one of the tradespeople. Not just for a minute, but for 10, 15 or 20 minutes! There is then a good chance that they will *casually* wander over and start to ask questions about what they are doing, or the way they are doing it.

That is ok, once, maybe twice, but after the third or fourth time, the worker can start to get a bit miffed, especially if the client starts suggesting a better way of doing it, or asking them questions like *"Is this right?"*, pointing to something they have just done. Worse still is when the client asks, *"Could I just have a quick go at that?"*, stopping them from working (*and thus usually costing them money*).

For all self-builders this is an exciting experience, and they naturally want to learn as much as they can as it progresses, so there is a tendency to want to watch how things are done and to learn from experts. And what is the best to learn something? Watch it being done and then try it yourself! (*Makes perfect sense doesn't it? - **NO, it doesn't**)*

I feel I owe it to the workers to mention this to any prospective self-builder:

Yes, you can learn a heck of a lot from watching experts doing their jobs, but if you want to do so, at least try to do it subtly! Don't stand right next to them, stand, and view them from a distance, without making it obvious.

Unless there is a problem, or you need to tell them anything, don't interrupt them when they are working. Wait until they have stopped for a break, and then talk to them about things that aren't directly related to the progress of the job they are doing. You'll have a happier workforce if you do so.

There are people on site you can talk to as much as you like: Labourers (*who will usually love an excuse to stop working*), or the boss of a company (*who will want more work, or references from you, or from people you know*), Site Foremen (*who are generally supervising and not working, so are always up for a chat*), or your Warranty Inspector, who may have driven for hours to get to you, and fancies a break before getting back in the car.

*This is not one of the most important sections in this book, I just wanted to mention it!*

------------------------------------------------------------------------

## OK, now we are going to start building:

------------------------------------------------------------------------

## THING 98: FIND A DECENT GROUNDWORKER

*It is unfortunate that the groundworks and foundations are one of the first jobs that have to be completed when we build a house. They can be one of the most difficult, unpredictable, and potentially budget busting parts of the of the whole job, so it would be much better if we could get some simple jobs under our belts first, just to ease us gently into the build. Maybe something a bit less threatening, like decorating or tiling? Then do the foundations later? (Well I can dream, can't I?)*

In reality, the fact is that we are stuck with having to do the foundations first, we just have to grit our teeth, cross our fingers, and hope it all goes ok.

One of the best insurance policies against this part of the job going pear shaped, especially if you are new to building, is to get someone on site who knows what they are doing. Someone who will be able to find solutions to any and all problems that you might come across. An experienced, professional groundworker is just the person for such a job.

As well as sending them all the information they will need, I also recommend meeting representatives from at least one or two  groundworkers on site, before you hire anyone. Just by meeting them and spending twenty minutes or so talking to them, you should be able to get a feel for their knowledge, attitude, and competence. I always do this with any new sub-contractor, but I think it is *very* important that this is done with groundworkers.

Think about it, the weight of you *whole house* is going to sit on whatever these people construct. If they mess up the concrete footings, or if they don't put the drainage in properly, you could have major problems in the future. You therefore need to be as sure as possible, that their work is going to be completed to a high standard, before giving them the job.

When you meet with groundworkers on site, as well as getting to know them a bit, have some technical questions ready to ask them (*these can be a great way to sort out the wheat from the chaff*). Ask them things like:

- Do they know what the ground is like in this area?
- Do they prefer power floated slabs to screeded slab, or solid floor to suspended floors?
- Do they prefer plastic or clay drainage and why?
- Ask them how they would man the job, and what plant they would plan to use?
- Have they done this type of job before, and if so, how many times, and where?

Those sorts of probing questions will either get an immediate intelligent, professional response, or they may seem to be *winging* it, and blustering their way through an unconvincing answer. You can decide at the end of that meeting how you feel about their knowledge and competence, and then make your decision.

**I cannot emphasise enough how important the groundworks are to any project. If you make a mistake underground and don't discover it, the chances are that its negative effect on the overall job will grow *exponentially* as you proceed. Here is a simple example to make the point:**

*Sample scenario: My groundworkers are pouring the foundations. They run out of concrete before finishing the job, and the concrete batching plant is now closed for the day. They will have to wait until morning to complete the job. They leave the end of the poured concrete tidy, with a nice vertical joint, ready to pour up to with fresh concrete, first thing in the morning.*

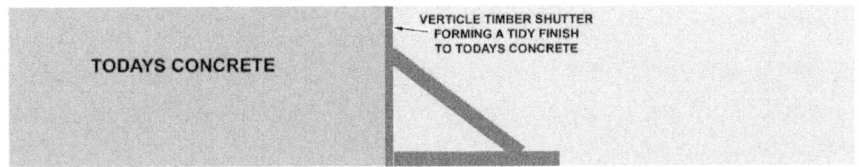

### Spot the problem?

The vertical joint is the problem: If the ground on one side of the joint is weaker than on the other side, there is the potential for settlement at one side of the joint at some time in the future, with the vertical concrete face creating a "slip plane", allowing one side to drop, following the ground settlement. This would then give the opportunity for the brickwork / blockwork above that area, to also drop. If this were to happen, you could end up with a large insurance claim, or a very big bill to put it right.

### How to fix it?

1) Before you go home on the first day of concrete pouring, wait until the concrete is dry enough to form a "step" at the end where the concrete ran out (*rather than a vertical face*), giving around 6" of flat surface.
2) Get some steel bar (*steel setting out pins will do the job*) and push two or three of them about halfway into the end of the wet concrete.
3) Leave the concrete to set (*hopefully looking something like this*):

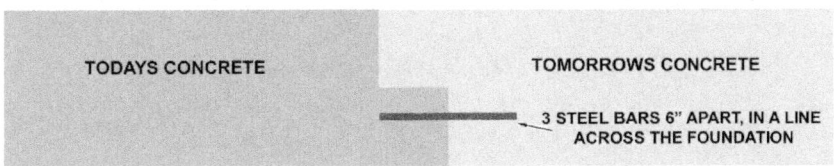

**Note:** Of course, the better alternative is to make sure you don't run out of concrete in the first place. I always order between 0.2 cu.m and 0.5 cu.m more concrete than I think I will need on the last load. It may cost £20 to £50 quid extra, but it is worth it.

## THING 99: **DOUBLE CHECK THE SETTING OUT**

Just as it is important to get the foundations right, it is also critical that the setting out is *spot on* - *first time*!

Imagine if you had a restriction on the height of the ridge of your house, imposed at the planning stage (*to make sure that a neighbour's view is not spoilt*). Or you might have a Building Line on your site (*a building line is an imaginary line that you cannot build in front of. It is normally the line of the front of existing adjacent buildings*).

Now imagine that while setting the house out, a small error is made in the calculations, which results in the ground floor level being 8" too high. That would automatically have the knock-on effect of pushing the ridge line up by 8", landing you in big trouble with the planners. Just as easy a mistake to make would be to get the building line a few inches out, in the wrong direction, resulting in just as big a problem.

In both those examples, believe it or not, the Planning Department would be within their rights to make you take the building back down once it was completed. Ok, there would probably be court cases, but the fact is that they would probably win. So:

### DOUBLE and even TRIPLE CHECK THE SETTING OUT!

The chances are that a Site Engineer will do the setting out on your site, so, if there are any important planning restrictions, make sure they are fully aware of them. I suggest that it would also be a good idea to actually *ask them* to double check the setting out. Tell them you have been really worried about this, and just want to make 100% sure that there are no errors. Knowing it has all been done properly will be worth the dirty looks they give you! (**Hint**: *When I was a Site Engineer, I always I doubled checked the setting out by starting the process from a different point on the site to the one I used first time. That way I was more likely to avoid repetitive errors*).

## THING 100: **TYPES OF FOUNDATIONS**

Various types of foundations are used for house building. Here are examples of the most common ones:

**Strip Footings:** This is the most common type of foundation for residential housing. It involves excavating a trench (*normally 600mm wide x 900mm deep*). The groundworker makes sure that the bottom of the trench is suitable to build on (*solid and clean*).

The correct level of the top of the concrete is usually set in one of two ways:

1) By hammering steel rods (pins) into the bottom of the trench, so that the top of the pins are at the correct level.
2) If a laser level is being used, waiting until the concrete is poured, then the Engineer works with the labourer, using the measuring staff to take readings on the top of the concrete to make sure it is at the correct level.

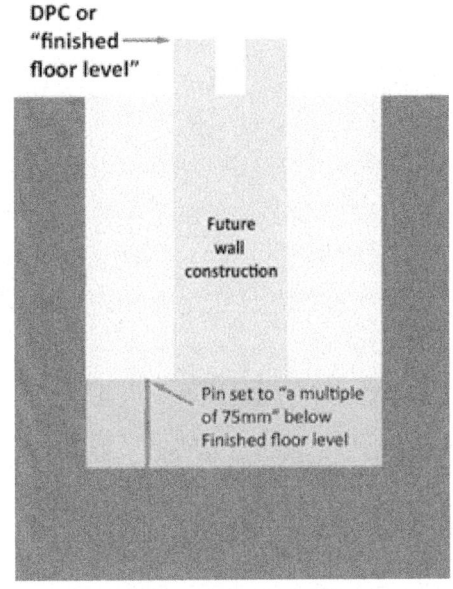

DPC or "finished floor level"

Future wall construction

Pin set to "a multiple of 75mm" below Finished floor level

Ideally, the top of the concrete needs to be accurate to within around 5mm – 10mm all the way round the trench. This is important because the concrete will form the surface on to which the trench blockwork is built, from which the finished floor level is set.

The trench is then inspected by the Warranty Company and the Building Inspector before concrete is poured (*making sure that the concrete ordered is to the correct specification, as detailed on the drawings. Normally a C30 or C35 mix*).

The minimum depth and width of the foundation concrete needed to take a standard cavity wall is 225mm x 600mm. However, the reality is, that the trench is very rarely 600mm wide and the concrete very rarely ends up at 225mm deep. It always ends up at least *a bit* (or a lot) deeper and *a bit* (or a lot) wider. The important thing is that the concrete sits on good ground and is at least 225mm deep. More than 225mm is fine, it just costs you more.

Once the concrete has set, the exact shape and size of the house can be marked out on its surface, this is normally done by an Engineer, but sometimes the brickies can do this job. As with the level of the concrete, the setting out of the blockwork should be to an accuracy of within 5mm to 10mm over the whole building and should be double checked for the same reasons as I mentioned previously.

The two walls (*or "skins"*) of blockwork that will form the cavity wall are then built up to finished floor level (*also called "DPC", or Damp Proof Course level*), ensuring that the cavity width is set to the measurement specified on the drawings (*usually 50mm these days*).

Openings need to be built into these walls underground, to allow access for the various services to pass into the building from the trench, and also to allow the drainage pipes to come *out of* the building (*the positions of the openings should be shown on the construction drawings*). The bricklayers should know what to do here, you just make sure they have the drawings with the information they need. Your job will be to make sure that all the materials they need are on site, and to double check that they build the right number of openings in the correct locations.

Once the wall has been built up to DPC, it is filled with cavity fill concrete (*a special semi-dry mix that is often mixed on site and shovelled into the cavity by hand*). This creates a solid wall underground, which is strong enough to resist the pressure exerted on it by the earth and topsoil backfill that will then be placed against it.

*Note: As an alternative to cavity fill, the wall up to DPC can be built in solid blockwork, using Trench Blocks. These are lightweight concrete blocks made to the overall width of the wall (normally 300mm). Using them saves building two skins of wall and negates the need for the cavity fill.*

### Mass fill foundations:

As the name suggests, this type of foundation is similar to the trench footing, but instead of pouring a 225mm strip of concrete, the trench is fully filled with concrete, to a level that suits the required finished level of the slab.

That level is worked out as a **multiple** of the height of a standard brick with a 10mm joint (*which totals 75mm), below* the top of slab level. (*So, with a mass fill foundation, the distance to the top of the concrete from the finished floor level could be set at 75mm, 150mm, 225mm and so on*).

This method of foundation construction has advantages over the strip foundation method:

1) It is a lot quicker.
2) You don't need to order and store all the blocks, sand, and cement etc, or the mixer
3) It avoids bricklaying time being lost due to bad weather.
3) It can work out cheaper if the trench is fairly near to the 600mm x 900mm target width and depth, however, if the trench goes wider and/or deeper, the amount of concrete needed to fill the trench can increase significantly, along with its cost.

*Comment: The problem here is that you can't really plan for which option between strip and mass fill footings is going to be best, until you have dug the trench. However, you will need to organise materials and brickies before you start digging the trenches. So it is a tricky one!*

### Reinforced Strip Concrete foundations:

Again, this is a similar construction to strip footings. The difference this time is that steel reinforcing is installed within the strip of concrete, in order to increase its strength. It is used where the ground does not have sufficient load bearing capacity to carry the weight of the building. It may be needed in some areas of the trench and not others.

The reinforcing can be in the form of a steel mesh (*if the ground is reasonably loadbearing, but not quite good enough*), or a framework of steel bars tied together (*where either the ground is poor, or the building is very heavy*).

Sometimes the need for reinforced foundations will not be apparent until the trench has been excavated and the condition of the ground becomes clearly visible. It will often be the Groundworker or Site Manager who highlights a problem, or if they don't sometimes the Building Regs Inspector (*who might not be happy with something when they come to inspect*). It is better if the problem is discovered before the Building Inspector sees it, as he / she expects it to be finished and ready to pour when they are called to inspect, and can get a bit irritated if it is not *ready and right*.

There are numerous other types of foundations, but the chances are that your build will use one of the three mentioned her. For very poor ground, a system called *a raft foundation* can be used. If you think your ground could be classed as poor to very poor, it may be worth you discussing the subject with your designer.

*Note: I realise that explaining how foundations are built, in writing is not the best way to give you a clear picture of the process. Have a look on You tube at videos of UK house foundations being built, or videos of raft foundations, to get a better visual understanding of the subject.*

## THING 101: SOLID GROUND FLOORS

### Screeded Concrete Slab:

The standard ground floor for new homes in the UK tends to be concrete, with insulation laid on top, followed by a sand / cement screeded top layer.

The floor makeup is as usually as follows (from top down):

- 65mm – 75mm sand and cement floor screed.
- 150mm of solid foam insulation (Cellotex / Kingspan)
- 150mm concrete slab
- Damp proof membrane
- 50mm sand / cement blinding
- Hardcore

This is a good, strong floor construction method, which can be paired up with underfloor heating (*with the heating pipes being buried in the screed, about 15mm to 25mm under the surface*).

There are a few minor points to be aware of with this system:

1. Being made up of two structural layers, it included two lots of expense, and two physical jobs that have to be completed. This obviously has an impact on the build time and cost.
2. The screed takes a few Days to set, so internal work halts during that time (more time loss).
3. As the screed dries out, it can form small shrinkage cracks. If these go right through the screed, they can affect its overall strength and stability. However, I have not heard of them causing any major problems.
4. The screed can be a bit dusty. There can sometimes be small areas across the surface of the screed where the sand /cement mix hasn't been perfect, where the sand can, over time, come loose. This can create a slightly rough, open surface, with dusty patches. This is not a problem if you are carpeting or tiling the floor, but if you lay the modern thin hard vinyl tiles, using adhesive, there is the possibility that some areas could become unstuck.

**Power floated concrete slabs:**

A less common floor construction than the screeded concrete slab, is the power floated concrete slab. I use this system wherever I can.

This construction is usually made up as follows (*again, from top down*):

- 150mm power floated concrete.
- Damp proof membrane.
- 150mm solid foam insulation.
- 50mm sand blinding.
- Hardcore

This is a simpler, faster construction system, compared to the screeded concrete slab and can save £2,000 to £3,000 on the overall cost of the slab, but is not compatible with underfloor heating.

With this system, the screeding layer is replaced by a power floated concrete slab, to create a shiny, smooth, very hard surface, which is stronger than a screed, and shouldn't crack to the same extent. The surface doesn't tend to suffer the dust problem (*mentioned previously*), so is better for the hard vinyl tile types of flooring.

Not all builders offer this system, there is a skill to using the power float which not all groundworkers have mastered (*it uses a similar technique to the floor polishers in supermarkets*).

To lay a power floated concrete floor, the concrete is laid first, as normal, and finished to a reasonably smooth, flat surface, using lengths of timber or a *screeding rail (see: speedyservices.com/screeding-tools)*. The slab is then left for a few hours to set. When it is possible to walk on, without leaving heavy footprints, the power floating can start.

As the image shows, the powerfloat basically polishes the drying surface of the concrete until it has set hard enough so that a *shine* starts to appear, and to the point when walking on it doesn't leave any marks. The slab is then left overnight to fully set, and in reasonably warm weather, can usually be walked and worked on the following day (*so very little productive time is lost*).

## THING 102: **SUSPENDED GROUND FLOORS**

This system is used where the ground is either sloping, or doesn't have suitable strength to take the load of a solid, ground bearing concrete slab.

The image to the right shows our most recent project, where the ground was both sloping *and* of poor quality.

The finished floor level on this house will eventually be just below the level of the driveway that can be seen to the right of the building, however, the whole of the plot area was made up of up to 3m of fill (*loosely compacted, weak ground*) that had at been deposited at some time in the past.

We had to move the fill to another part of the site and continue to excavate until we got down to the original ground level over the whole building area, so the strip footings could be constructed on a solid base (*you can see from the image, that the level of good ground varied by over a metre, from the right side of the building, to the left*).

Once the foundation had been poured, using a stepped foundation method (*search: videos of stepped foundations*), we could then build up the blockwork to the required ground floor level.

Neither Common sense, nor Building Regulations would allow us to refill the centre of the building with the loose fill, and then construct a solid slab on it, so we had to use a suspended floor construction.

The most common suspended floor for new housing is the *precast beam and block floor*, which is my preferred option. The image below shows the system being installed.

**How it works:**

1) Reinforced concrete beams are placed onto load bearing walls, which have been built up in blockwork from the foundations.
2) The space between the beams is accurately set, to take a standard concrete block, laid flat. Once the whole area has been filled in with blocks, it creates a strong *suspended shutter* across the building.
3) Later in the build, once the shell of the house has been constructed, the floor insulation is fitted and a standard sand and cement screed is laid over the top, to give the final finished floor of the house. If you don't want to use a screed, as a cheaper option, you can lay standard floorboards over the insulation. However, before you do, check with your designer to make sure that this type of finish will satisfy Building Regs.

## THING 103: UNDERFLOOR HEATING

I am a big fan of underfloor heating. I first installed it in one of my own self-builds about 15 years ago. I also recently installed an interesting *new* system in a house, where we had already built the shell by the time the house was sold, but the buyer then asked if it was possible to have it installed.

The problem we had, was that I had used a power floated solid slab for the ground floor, which meant it was already at the correct finished floor level, so there was no additional height available to add a 65mm screed, without having to shorten the internal doors and reducing the distance between the top of the floor and the ceiling (*shortening the doors by 65mm would not be acceptable to Building Regs, neither would it be practical*).

I did some research, and found a product made by "Nu-Heat", which was designed to be retro fitted in to existing houses. It wasn't designed *exactly* for the use I needed it for, but it worked fine, apart from a couple of minor hiccups. It uses a very thin but strong chemical screed, mixed as a liquid in large buckets, then literally *poured* over the floor surface and the underfloor heating pipework, finding its own level, in the same way as water does. It is then given a trowelled finish, to make sure there are no lumps and bumps in the surface. It sets in a few hours. (*Search: https://www.nu-heat.co.uk/)*

### How does underfloor heating work?

Most underfloor systems run off gas boilers, feeding warm water through the pipework to gently warm the screed, but they also pair up nicely with solar panels, where the heat is generated by the panels, and then transferred to the underfloor system.

Electric underfloor heating is not widely used but can work just as well. It comprises a mat, with electric elements fitted to it, which is laid across the floor and then has a thin screed laid over the top. It is more expensive to run, but can suit some installations better than water based systems.

So, why is underfloor heating worth thinking about for your project?
**Simply**: It is nice to have!

It is nice to have the touch of luxury of a gently warm floor underfoot, especially when you get up on a cold winter's morning. It also gives the area where it is used, a pleasant even air temperature, which may not sound particularly exciting, but again, it just adds to a generally pleasant feeling within the building. It also frees up wall space for furniture: How many times have you been in houses that have radiators dotted all over the place, usually right where you would put a settee, shelf unit, table, wall units or other furniture? It is almost as if some of the commercial house designers *purposely* pick the daftest places they can, to position them. With an underfloor heating system installed, you don't have that problem, and can put *what you want, where you want it.*

The system can also add value to your home: If you sell a house that has underfloor heating, the selling agent will want to promote *that feature*. It is very popular with buyers, and could possibly pay for itself, by increasing the potential selling price of the house.

One slightly negative comment: Underfloor heating is a great idea for the ground floor, but I wouldn't usually install it upstairs. Why not? Due to the different ways the ground and first floor are constructed, it costs a lot more to install on higher floors. Also, on the upper floors, radiators tend to be better positioned, often under windows, so don't cause as many problems when it comes to furnishing the rooms.

One question I am regularly asked about this system is: "*What happens if it gets a leak?*"

**Answer(s):** The pipework has very few joints, and the ones it has tend to be above floor level, at the manifold (*the control centre*), so leaking joints in the floor are unlikely. If it is installed in a 75mm thick sand and cement floor screed, the chances of it being damaged after laying are minimal.

The Nu-Heat screed is thin, but very hard and strong, so I don't foresee much chance of damage being caused to pipework, unless something fairly major happens (*I am not, however speaking from experience here*).

The electric systems are slightly more likely to be damaged and, whereas a leak in a pipe within a water fed floor screed will be obvious by the screed developing a damp area on its surface, with an electric system you can't *see* where the problem is. There are however fairly simple ways to locate and fix it. If the system went faulty, you would call the installer back to find the problem and fix it.

> If you are interested in installing underfloor heating, first talk to your plumbers. They may be able to install it and be happy to give you a price. If not, they may know of, or work with companies who specialise in installing the systems.

## THING 104: BUILDING REGS AND WARRANTY INSPECTIONS

(**Note**: *I have touched on this subject a few times already, but because it is important that this subject is dealt with professionally on site, it also justifies having its own section*)

Before you start work on site, you need to sort out how the Building Regulation and Warranty inspections are going to be organised, whether you will look after it, or whether you will delegate the job to someone on site.

The inspections are usually required at the following stages:

1. After the foundations have been excavated but prior to concrete being poured.
2. After the slab has been formed, but before the concrete is poured.
3. After the roof structure has been constructed, but before it is covered.
4. After the insulation and first fixes have been installed, but before the plaster boarding commences.
5. Before the drainage is backfilled.
6. On completion.

The intervals between the inspections may vary from region to region of the UK, and between different warranty companies, but they all follow the same basic principle of inspecting at important points throughout the project.

Before you start work on site, make sure you check your Building Regs and Warranty paperwork to find out:

a) When you need inspections to be made.

**b)** The process you need to follow to book the inspections.

Building Inspectors usually book inspections 24 hours ahead, whereas warranty Inspectors usually need more notice, especially if they are travelling long distances to attend.

Also, you need to make sure that the job is ready for the inspection. Building Inspectors do not like having their time wasted on aborted inspections. They may not get too annoyed if they find a small problem once, but if there is something wrong every time they come to site, which requires them to make a second visit once it has been dealt with, they can start to get a bit miffed. If this happens, often their reaction would be to start to make surprise visits when you are not expecting them. The reason could be that they have become a bit nervous about whether you are going about everything correctly, or it could just be them saying *"This is what happens if you mess me about"*!

You may decide to delegate the responsibility for booking the inspectors. If you are not going to be on site all the time, it may be that your Project Manager, Foreman Groundworker or Trades Foreman is given the job of booking them. That is fine, just make sure that *just one* person on site is responsible, and that he / she has the correct contact details.

Overall however, this is a job that if possible, you should try to do yourselves. Chinese whispers can often occur on site, so if you are looking after booking all the inspections, there is only one person who can mess up (*even if you are working full time somewhere else, you will be speaking to the people on site regularly, so should be able to keep fully up to speed with what is going on day to day, and even hour to hour*).

The Building Inspector tends to be someone who the people on site can see as a bit of a threat. In the odd case I would agree, this is normally where an inspector can get a bit carried away with their own power (*usually the younger inspectors*), but in general, I see the inspectors as being a useful watching eye over the job. If we forget something, or get something wrong, it is actually quite reassuring to know that we are going to have someone coming round every now and then, who can cast their eye quickly over everything, and if there is anything wrong, making sure it is fixed. I would rather have that scenario, than finding potentially serious faults later, once the house is inhabited.


## THING 105: DRAINAGE, SUDS & SOAKAWAYS

Drainage for housing can be quite complicated, probably deserving of a book being written just on this one subject. However, that book would be an incredibly boring read to most people and I certainly will not be writing or reading it!

In reality, 99% of self-build projects will use a Professional Groundworker to install the drainage system and do all the groundworks necessary to get the services connected.

What I want to cover in this section, are the basics of what happens underground, the types of systems used, how they are installed and what you need to watch out for.

Residential drainage systems in the UK are designated as: Surface Water, Foul Water, or Combined. The names are self-explanatory. Local Authorities do not provide public drainage systems everywhere. Many houses in rural areas have private drainage systems installed and are not connected to the main drainage system.

## 1. Foul Drainage:

All Local Authorities work to the same basic principles for foul water drainage: Wastewater enters the *Private* part system from the house (*usually via 4" pipe from the house, garage and any other buildings*).

At any point where the drainage flow needs to change direction, a manhole must be constructed, so that blockages or other problems can be accessed for unblocking, via a straight length of pipeline.

Depending on the design of the individual system, other fittings may be needed on the private section of the drain, such as rodding eyes, catch pits, and occasionally none return valves. Your House Designer will usually specify the details of the system on the drawings, which then have to be checked and passed by the Building Regulations Inspector, prior to installation work commencing.

The waste runs through the private part of the system to join up with the public system. Before you can legally connect into a public sewer, you need to have a *Section 104 agreement* in place. This gives you the permissions you need. Once that is all done and inspected, the system is adopted. From then on, you will be liable for paying Water Rates, which help to pay for the general upkeep of the UK wide system.

Most individual houses use plastic pipework and manholes for their drainage systems, however, in some circumstances, there may be the need to use concrete or brick manholes and clay pipework (*clay is a lot more expensive than plastic*). Some Architects (*generally the older generation*), prefer clay pipework to plastic, and may automatically specify it for your project. If they do, and if you want to save money, ask why they have done so, and ask if it is possible to change to plastic. In all my years on general housing or self-build sites, I have never used a clay drainage system, however, I have regularly used them on commercial building projects.

## 2. Soakaways:

Where the foul water is disposed of via the Local Authority drainage system, the surface water is often dealt with by installing soakaways in the gardens of the house being built. Simply described, a soakaway is a large hole, usually measuring around 2m x 2m x 2m (*or about 4 cubic metres*) in ground that drains reasonably well (*larger if the ground is found to drain poorly, for example in clay areas*).

The hole is partly filled with clean stone (*around 40mm diameter*), then the surface water drainage pipes (*again usually 4" plastic*) from the buildings, are installed so that they will outfall into the stoned area of the soakaway. The hole is then filled with more clean stone, covered with plastic sheeting, and backfilled with soil (*or whatever the ground surface is going to finished with*), to complete the installation.

The efficiency of the soakaway depends on how much water is can contain. The plastic sheeting laid over the top of the stone stops soil, leaves and other debris from being able to enter the stoned area from above, eventually clogging it up and reducing its performance.

The volume of the soakaway is designed to allow it to receive average amounts of rainwater throughout the year. After it enters the soakaway, the water drains through the stone, and is slowly dispersed into the surrounding ground. Theoretically the ground around the soakaway will be porous enough to absorb the water, without becoming saturated and causing surface flooding. To ensure that that is the case, before work starts, porosity tests have to be carried out on the ground around soakaway. This is done by excavating a hole (*to Building Regs specifications*), filling it with water, and recording the time it takes to empty. The slower the emptying, the larger the soakaway will need to be. However, even after installing the system correctly, in periods of heavy rain, it may be temporarily unable to cope, and areas of local ponding can occur.

### 3. SUDS Systems (Sustainable Drainage Systems)

This is another *"new-fangled gadget"* of a system, that we are presently having to learn about. From what I have learned so far about the SUDS system, I would describe it pretty much as a *posh soakaway*.

We have a development starting, which will be made up of 4 reasonably large 4 bed detached homes, with a private driveway serving all 4 houses. We have been told that we will have to install a SUDS system to cater for all four houses and any other surface water drainage.

The design of the SUDS system has to show that, by its storage capacity and water dissipation potential:

- It reduces to zero, the likelihood of rainwater "run off" on to the adjoining main road.
- It reduces to a minimum, the outfall into an adjacent watercourse, and that any outfall into a watercourse will be uncontaminated.
- That it deals with the surface water in an ecologically sound manner, such as storing it and using it for watering gardens, washing cars etc.

On this development, we have agreed to install a surface water storage tank with a pump, and electrical supply, on each property. Water from the SUDS system will be fed (*pumped*) to a tap, fixed to the external wall of each house. A hose can then be connected, enabling the water to be used for watering the garden, the windows, the car etc.

You may not need to install a SUDS system. The project for 3 houses that we started previously was passed for Building Regs with a basic soakaway system. However, as things change rapidly these days, this may be a subject that you would be advised to do some research on. If you find that you do need to use a SUDS system, it will probably increase your build cost by a few thousand pounds.

## THING 106: **BRICKWORK**

An attractive facing brick adds a visual air of quality to the appearance of a house. It suggests traditional values, strength, and longevity. However, despite those facts, facing brick façades to both residential and commercial buildings have become less popular in recent years. Here are a few of the reasons why, along with a few other comments:

- Facing bricks are becoming very expensive. For an average sized, 4 bed self-build house of 2000 sq ft, you could need anywhere between 10,000 and 14,000 bricks. Prices vary from around £500 / 1000 for a basic brick, up to well over £1,000 / 1000 for a nice, handmade brick. A few years ago, the prices were roughly half of these figures. These high costs, together with the fact that you need a lot of them, can cause severe stress to your build budget. For that reason, we are seeing a lot more render finished houses being built.
- Always try to buy bricks in full loads. Full loads come direct from the manufacturer and work out a lot cheaper than buying individual packs from a builder's merchant. However, if you choose a brick that the merchants keeps in stock for your *full load* deliveries, as you near completion of the brickwork, if you then find that you only need a couple of hundred more bricks to finish the job, you should be able to pick up whatever you need, from the merchant, without having to pay high *part load* charges to get them from the manufacturer.
- Bricklaying is a slow process and is vulnerable to being regularly halted by rain. A four bed self-build house can take anything from three weeks to three or four months to complete, depending on the weather and numerous other factors.
- The speed of bricklaying is partly dependant on how the bricklayer's gang is set up. Bricklaying teams tend to come in 2 & 1 gangs, 3 & 1 gangs and 4 & 2 gangs (*those figures relate to the number of brickies versus the number of labourers in a team*). If I am building a house which involves brickwork, I always try to get a good quality, knowledgeable, 4 & 2 team. That setup tends to keep the build time to the minimum possible, which can save you time and money, and also gives you a good chance of getting a decent job done.
- The longer the brickwork takes, the higher the cost of the scaffolding will be. You will usually get anything from a 6 to 10 week hire period included in your scaffolding

quote, then you will pay a few hundred pounds a week extra after that period expires. It could be 2 weeks after the scaffold goes up that you start bricklaying.

If you take 6 months to build the house, then take a couple of months to get the roof on, tiled, and all the fascias and soffits fitted, you could end up paying around *20 weeks* extra hire charges.

(**Note**: *if you go for timber frame build option, that timescale should be a lot less, due to the fact that the roof is constructed much earlier in the build process. This allows the brickwork <u>and</u> the first fixes inside the building to proceed at the same time, possibly saving a month or two on the scaffold hire charges).*

- Where good quality brickwork can be very attractive, poor quality brickwork can *reduce* the value of the completed house.

- If you get bricks from 2 different batches (*made at different times in the factory*), they can vary in colour, creating unattractive mosaic patterns on the walls. If that happens, the brickies labourers should actively mix the bricks as they take them from the packs, taking a few from *each pack* at a time. If this is done properly, it should even out the finished appearance of the wall.

- The same applies to mortar. If the mortar mix varies, so can the colour / shade of the joints once they dry. This can also create an unattractive mottled appearance to the walls.

- Think about your brickwork joints: There are numerous brickwork joint types (*search: "Types of brickwork joints"*). Different joints suit different styles of brick. A nice *handmade* or *slop moulded* brick, which has a slightly uneven shape, can benefit visually from using a raked out joint, which accentuates the unique shape of each brick. A sharp edged brick can look better with a *bucket handle* (*also called "concave"*) or a *weathered* joint. If you need maximum protection from the elements, a *flush joint* is the best choice for the job.

- There are many different colours of mortar available. They cost quite a bit more than the standard sand and cement mortar, but can add the finishing touch to the appearance of your house. Brick Merchants or Builders Merchants should be able to guide you on this subject. Be aware though, that some colours, once they dry, appear very similar to standard sand / cement mortar, so you could spend a few hundred pounds, but get very little visual benefit.

- **Pre-mixed mortars**: If you want to do away with the on-site mixing of the mortar (*you may not have a water supply, or be short of room to site a mixer*), you can get mortar delivered in tubs, ready mixed, with retarders, that stop it from going off (*setting*) for up to 2 days, depending on the air temperature.

  The downside of the premixed mortars is that, on the same basis that they do not set very quickly in the tub, the same happens once they have been built into the wall. Where a standard mortar sets within a few hours, a premix may take 24 hours or more to gain full strength. This may restrict you to only building maybe two thirds of the normal lift height (*about 4ft - 5ft*), before the weight of the wall starts to squash the lower, still weak joints. This could look terrible once the whole wall has been completed and the scaffold taken down.

- **Finally:** Bricks are not environmentally friendly. We cannot replace the clay ground that their manufacture eats up (*that may be one of the reasons why they are getting to be so expensive*). Bricks also consume a lot of energy in their manufacture and delivery. The clay is moulded then burnt at high temperatures in kilns, in order to give it its strength and appearance. The huge wagons that deliver bricks also create a high carbon footprint, especially if they are being delivered to the far corners of the UK, from where they originate.

I am not against houses with brick facades (*outer skins*). I have built and seen many lovely looking brick-faced houses over the years. However, because of their cost and other negative aspects, I just think that there are now some more modern options available that it may be worth you looking at, before making final decisions for your own project.

## THING 107: BLOCKWORK

In a traditional brick and block house, structurally, the blockwork element is more important than the brickwork element. The blockwork does all the *heavy carrying* work for the house. It takes most of the weight of the roof, the upper floors, and everything that eventually sits on the upper floors. The brickwork usually only creates the cosmetic appearance of the house, as well as physically forming the cavity.

**Standard concrete blocks** are cheap and strong, but are not a particularly attractive building material, nor do they insulate very efficiently. They come in 100mm, 150mm and 200mm widths as standard, and most Builders Merchants stock all three sizes.

With the increasing insulation requirements for new housing, you may find that you need to think about using lightweight thermal blocks instead of solid concrete.

**Thermal (*aerated / lightweight*) blocks** are made using a chemical process which incorporates a high percentage of air into their construction. They still offer the strength characteristics that new housing requires, but the inclusion of the air makes them far better at insulating, as well as being easier to work with and faster to lay.

They cost quite a lot more than standard concrete blocks, so to decide whether they might be a good idea for your build, you need to do some calculations to see which would be the better option to attain the required levels of insulation:

1) Use a standard concrete blockwork external skin and add a lot of insulation.
2) Use an aerated blockwork external skin and add less insulation.

Neither Solid concrete, or nor aerated blocks are particularly environmentally friendly, however aerated blocks are better in this respect, as they do at least help to save energy.

Aerated blocks will also create a slightly smaller carbon footprint on delivery, due to their reduced weight, allowing more of them to be delivered on smaller delivery vehicles.

## THING 108: JOISTS

*Everyone is familiar with standard timber joists; they have been used for centuries in all types of buildings. However, their monopoly on "holding things up" is now severely under threat by a couple of new upstart newcomers.*

I won't need to explain to any reader what a standard joist is, so I will go straight to detailing the two newer alternatives:

**1) I beams:**

A simple but strong alternative to a standard joist, "*I beams*" are lighter than and are made from recycled wood. Like for like, they have similar spanning abilities, but are available in a wider range of sizes, with the larger sections being able to span wider spaces than standard joists. Holes can be drilled through the webs (*the vertical timber*) of *I Beams*, but the positioning and size of the holes is restricted. The manufacturer will supply details of  where and how large and allowed to be. Cost wise, I beams are in a similar price bracket to standard joists, but shopping around is advised.

**2) Easi -joists (also called *metal web joists*):**

I have used both of these products and after some initial scepticism, this is now my first choice for joists (*pushing standard timber joists to third place*). The one huge advantage that they have is that they are, to a large extent "open". There is very little joist in  the way of any of the services, pipes, or cable runs. This one characteristic can save a lot of time and cost when it comes to first fix installations. The trades people much prefer them, to the extent that if I were for any reason not to use them on my builds, I would probably have a mutiny  on my hands!

As well as making things easier for the trades, these joists are similar to I beams, in as much as they are available in a wide choice of sizes, with maximum spanning capabilities *significantly exceeding* that of standard joists. This product *is* the future of floor joists (*until and unless something even better appears*).

**To compare the three joists types, *like for like*, search "Joist span tables" for each one.**

# THING 109 : CLADDING

Over the past few years, I have been noticing a lot more new houses being built with external wall finishes in a mixture of cladding and render, as opposed to traditional brickwork. This is probably partly to do with the high price of bricks and bricklayers, but I also think the trend is partly to do with fashion.

The Scandinavian look of white render is getting popular on new housing, especially with self-builders, who appear to be attracted to its simplicity, clean lines, and attractive appearance. One feature I like about this style, is the way cladding can be used to create visual contrasts of colour, adding a touch of drama, to what could otherwise be a fairly plain building.

The quality and choice of cladding has improved significantly in recent years, as more companies have entered the marketplace. This expanded supply chain has resulted in more competitive pricing, which has created a circular effect of creating *even higher* demand .

As well as the standard timber cladding (*which seems to be, at least temporarily going out of fashion*), there are now products made of plastic, plastic and wood, and also cement. Most of these products are pre-finished, so need little maintenance, come in a wide variety of colours, and are guaranteed for up to 40 years.

The image to the right is from one of our recent builds, where we used a product called *Cedral* (*made by Marley*) for the cladding. It is a pre-finished, cement based product, has a 10 year warranty and a 50 year expected lifespan. We used the *slate grey* colour on this house, but there are a wide choice of different colours.

**Plastic:**

On our next development, we are going to try out a plastic based product called *"Coastline"*, supplied by *"Eurocell"*, a merchant that supplies a wide range of plastic based products. Coastline costs less than Cedral, has a simpler fixing system, is prefinished, and looks similar to Cedral when fitted. It also has a 10 year guarantee and has a UK certificate for fire safe performance. Whether it is as good a product, I will find out soon.

**Wood / plastic composite:**

Another type of plastic based, pre-finished cladding, is the *wood / plastic composite*. As the name suggests, it is a mixture of wood (recyclable) and plastic, (non-recyclable).

Some of these products can have up to 25 year guarantees (**Note**: *I have not yet tried this type of product. If any reader has, I would be interested to hear how you got on with it*).

**Timber cladding:**

Timber claddings are still a firm favourite with Architects, and the groups of Self-Builders who prefer a more traditional appearance. They are available in different profiles, in both hardwoods and softwoods. There is also a wide choice of preservatives and decorative treatments available, to stylise the finished appearance of a building.

The favourite timber cladding choice for Architects seems to be the *natural look*, where the timber is treated with a clear preservative, which maintains its natural appearance at the time of fitting, but which allows the timber to *age* (*change colour*) over time, eventually giving the appearance and character of an old barn. This can look good in some circumstances, but in others, can simply make the building look old and worn out, especially if the render has gone mouldy (*See next section for more details on mouldy render*)

Personally, I prefer the modern bright external finishes for the houses I design and build, and I want both the render and the cladding to look pretty much the same 10 years down the line, as they did when they were first installed.

If you decide to go for timber cladding, I suggest applying the best quality preservative treatments, making sure that you follow the instructions for application (*like making sure you treat the <u>end</u> <u>grain</u> as well as the face and sides*). If you do this job properly, you should get a couple more years between initial installation and needing to apply a fresh coat.

# THING 110: **RENDERING**

*Where brickwork seems to be getting less popular render seems to be getting more popular. The reasons why are probably the same as they are for the increase in popularity of cladding: It quick to apply, attractive, and can reduces the overall build times and cost.*

**Here are brief descriptions of a few of the most common types of render:**

**Sand and cement:**

This is a widely used, traditional method of rendering. It is applied in two coats, usually mixed on site (*although it can be delivered ready mixed*), and once it has fully dried out, it is painted. It is one of the lower cost rendering options, but you do need to factor in the cost of re-painting every few years to maintain the initial appearance of the building. Over time, this can become quite costly, however, if you use a high quality paint, you should be able to keep the re-painting intervals to about 7 to 10 years.

On a new build, having to leave the scaffold up for longer, whilst the painting is done, could incur three or four weeks extra hire charges, which could at up to a few hundred pounds or more.

Although we have not used a sand and cement render on our latest project, apart from the maintenance aspect, I do like this system, and would not have any hesitation in using it again in the future.

### Lime renders:

Lime render is another traditional rendering system, most popular on refurbishment and renovation projects. It can take a bit longer to apply and costs more than sand and cement render. It also needs to be finished with "Lime wash" (*a lime and water mix with chemical and colour additives*), which tends to require re-applying more often than normal render paint.

One of the benefits of using a lime render is that it is classed as *breathable*, so is useful where damp is a problem, perhaps explaining why it is popular for use on older buildings.

Due to the traditional *Old English* finished appearance produced by the lime paint, it is a good rendering system to consider of you want to get away from the modern look, that most of the other renders offer.

### Polymer Renders:

This render is supplied *ready mixed* and *self-coloured*, in a range of colours, usually in 20kg to 25kg bags. Overall, the system works out more expensive to buy and apply than basic sand / cement, or lime renders, but require less of a labour input to mix and apply, and being self-coloured, they also have the additional advantage of not needing painting, either after initial application, or throughout their lifespan.

We have used the Polymer render system on out most recent project and went with a "scratch coat" finish, which has come out looking very nice (*see the image to right*). I like this finish. It is a bit different from what we normally see, and avoids the slightly amateurish, rough looking finish that can sometimes be obvious when the sun shines across the surface of smooth finished renders.

Overall, apart from a tiny bit of mould growth on the bottom inch or so of the render, 18 months after its application on our project (*which I have not yet found a reason for*), I am pleased with the product. This could be an option worth you looking into for your project, if you like the idea of a render that gives an attractive finished appearance and won't need repainting.

### Acrylic (or "Thin Coat") renders.

This is the product that seems to be taking over the world! It has really caught on in recent years. It is quick to apply, you don't need much of it (*being only a couple of millimetres thick*) and it really makes a *new house* look bright, clean, and attractive. – For a while at least!

At the risk of being attacked by the manufacturers, in my opinion, this is the product that has caused more damage to the reputation of rendering than any other. This is the product that can (*and often does*) go mouldy!

As I drive around the country, I am constantly bemoaning new housing developments which were initially attractive, but have quickly turned into a complete mess.

This image shows such an example:

I have never used this product, but out of interest, have tried to find out what the problem is with it. The best reason I have been able to come up with so far is this: *The texture of the render is fairly open and rough, so when it rains, any particles of grit or dirt in the rain can get caught in tiny voids in the surface, and can eventually turn mouldy. When it rains, this grit, dirt and mould is washed down the surface, discolouring it and giving it a very unattractive appearance.*

As I understand it so far, the render cannot be power washed clean, or painted over. To fix the problem, a chemical solution has to be hand applied, and carefully rinsed off once it has loosened the mould /dirt. How long the surface will *stay* clean, I am not sure. Probably a year or so, similar to when it was first applied.

**Comment:** I spoke to the boss of a local housing developer who uses this product and asked him why he continues to use it with the mould problem. His answer was: *"It is cheap and looks lovely when they buy the house"*.
(*Which doesn't exactly inspire confidence in our builders!*)

*I would like to think that the problem either has now been, or is being attended to by the industry, but I am still seeing developments going up around my area, starting to show symptoms within a few months.*
*If anyone in the know, who reads this and can update me on progress, I will re-edit this section in the next edition.*

**For now, though: Buyers beware!**


## THING 111: **WINDOWS AND DOORS**

Choosing windows and doors for your project, is one decision making process that is perhaps given more attention than it really needs.

Although there are thousands of window companies, and wide choices of designs, colours, handles, types of security, fitting method, guarantees and prices, in reality, there is not a huge amount of difference between most of the products when it comes to what they are made of and how they are made, especially in the *mid-price range.*

In other words, once you have decided between softwood, UPVC and a few other materials for the frames, all the products made from each of those materials are pretty similar. This image is of a UPVC window profile (*or it could be steel, or aluminium*). A softwood or hardwood window would look the same if you couldn't see inside it. You can get UPVC windows with a timber grained finish, or Timber windows with a smooth finish, and all types of windows are available in different*, but basically the same range of* colours, and most use fairly similar types of ironmongery and locking systems.

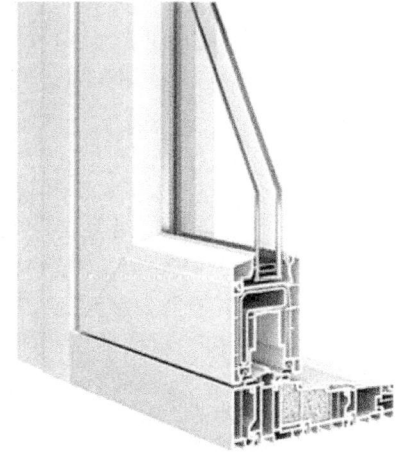

To avoid getting too tied up researching something you don't really need to, I suggest that you look at this subject *twice* before you order: Once at the design stage, to decide what styles, materials, colours etc you would like to go with. When you have made that decision, go out and get prices for either or both *supply* and/or *supply and fit*, so that you can use them in your cost estimating figures. Apart from that, there is no great rush to get everything decided and ordered straight away. It could be a few months before you will be ready to fit windows and the last thing you want is for them to be knocking around on site for weeks, risking damage, before they are fitted.

Most windows are on between 1 – 4 week delivery, so as long as you order them with a week or so to spare (*in case of manufacturing delays*), around a month before you need them is the sort of time you should be placing a deposit with your chosen supplier, and booking a delivery date (*which you should stipulate, will be dependant on how progress is going on site*).

Because the products are so similar, when you shop around, you probably won't notice a huge difference in the price ranges, unless you are going for high end, bespoke products (*which sit in a different sector of the market to standard windows and doors*).

Here are a few pointers to bear in mind as you go about researching and choosing your products and supplier:

1. **Don't believe all the hype:** A window is a window; a door is a door. One can be cheaply made, one can use the best materials, but there is only so much you can do to the basic product, to justify increasing its price past a certain point. If you can buy

one attractive, decent quality window for £400 from one local supplier, while another charges £800 for pretty much the same thing, you need to ask yourself (*and the supplier*) "**Why?**" (*The difference is often simply related to the market they are generally aiming at. If you can show that you are a builder, as opposed to being Joe Public, that one factor could get you an extra 30% off the price.*

2. **Do** believe some of the hype! There have been a lot of improvements made in the design and manufacture of windows and doors in recent years, including in recyclability, strength, glazing, standard of manufacture, longevity, fixtures, and fittings. Some manufacturers have embraced a few of them, some have embraced a lot of them. You might think it is worth paying maybe 15% - 20% extra over the basic price, to get all the bells and whistles, but don't pay much more.

3. **Secured by Design:** I only came across this recently when I went out for window and door quotes for our latest project. A few of the companies I contacted asked if we needed everything to be *Secured by Design* compliant, telling me that some Building Regulations departments are now insisting that all new properties must now meet this standard. There is a brochure online, aimed specifically at the Self-Build market, which you may find useful. Search *"Secured by design for self-build"* to find your way to the brochure. This contact is also in the Self-Build Trade List at the back of the book.

4. **Softwood windows and doors are making a comeback:** In the eighties and nineties, softwood windows were not a product of particularly high quality, they offered poor levels of insulation, were draughty and often started falling apart quite quickly. Most of them were eventually ripped out of older houses in the tens of thousands, to be replaced by the (*then*) newly fashionable product: White UPVC. Unfortunately, these weren't much better than the timber products they were replacing. Now those UPVC windows are being ripped out and replaced with decent widows.

   I was reintroduced to softwood  timber windows about 5 years ago, when an Architect specified them for a job I was looking after. I was impressed. In recent years there have been big improvements in the design, quality of the manufacture, robustness, paints, stains, security, and fittings. The finished product is now light years ahead of the old plastic or wood windows. Wood is obviously also environmentally friendly and recyclable. So, before you make any final decisions for your own project, it might be worth you giving softwood timber windows a look.

5. **Glazing:** Just as with timber, glazing has come a long way over the past few years. 25 years ago, the standard double glazing unit was a "4-6-4". This means that the glazing was 4mm thick and the space between the glass was 6mm. As insulation requirements increased, this changed to 4-12-4 (*slightly, but not much better*).

   Now, depending on how well insulated you want your windows and doors to be for sound and heat, double glazed units can often be up to 32mm (6-20-6). There are also numerous other upgrades available, such as non-reflective glass and thermally efficient glass (*such as "EnergiKare", "K Glass" and others*). Additionally, the double glazing units can be filled with "Argon gas", a dense gas that has significantly better insulating abilities than air. From my own experience, the extra cost of these higher spec glazing units is well worth paying.

6. **Bi-Fold Doors** are now pretty much a must have product for self-builds, and why not, they're great! Here are a couple of things to consider:

   i. **Plastic Bi-fold doors** are liable to expand and contract more than timber, depending on the air temperature, so their installation needs to be given careful attention, most importantly, to make sure that there is adequate clear space around the frames for them to expand into. If the frame is fitted hard up against the blockwork or timber walls, the glazing units could potentially distort as they expand, causing the glazing to crack. Our supplier recommends allowing a 20mm gap all-round the frame, for expansion (*which you will then need to cover over with strips of the same material*).

   Another minor inherent problem is that the doors can sag slightly over time, making them harder to open and close, requiring professional attention to re-align them.

   ii. **Aluminium Bi-fold doors** are stronger than plastic doors and do not expand to the same extent (*although they do still expand a little*). They are also less liable to sagging, so should need less maintenance. However, they are around 10% to 20% more expensive. (*Note: Aluminium is the product we prefer for our own houses*).

## THING 112: **SOLAR PANELS / SOLAR ROOF TILES**

Solar Panel have been around for a long time. Early versions were bulky, inefficient, and expensive and were rarely seen around the UK. A few years ago, things started to change. Technology improved, prices started dropping, efficiency increased, and the UK Government started to offer incentives to tempt more people to install these systems.

The solar panel industry is now huge, but strangely we still seem to be a bit sceptical about them. The main problems seem to be related to their varying and rapidly reducing costs, how the different systems work, how quickly they are evolving and changing (*meaning that if you buy a system, it could be obsolete in 2 years*), and the fact that they only create energy when the sun is, at least partly visible (*or behind very thin clouds*).

I am personally on the fence with regards to solar heating. I have nothing against it, but have not used it on my own houses and probably won't, at least not in the short term. I agree that the system is still evolving, and changing too quickly for me to say, "*That's it, they are as good as they are going to get, I'll use them*". However, given the choice between installing a system that uses sun (*solar panels*), air (*air source heating*), or the heat from the ground (*ground source heating*), I would go for the solar option.

For your own project, if you like the idea of solar power, go for it. Apart from the installation costs and the fact that you usually need a roof that faces in the right direction, there is nothing wrong with the product as it is now (*by the way, you can ground mount solar panels, like they do with the big solar farms, so if your roof aspect is not suitable, you could look at the ground level options*).

*If you do decide to include a solar system as part of your own project, just make sure that you do your homework first.*

There are various types of systems available, and the best system available today may not be the best system in 3 months' time (*which is why I am not talking in detail about the systems here. If I did, the book would probably be out of date before I published it!*)

If you are considering installing a solar system:

1. Make sure that you are fully up to speed with all the latest equipment specs and costs.
2. Try to assess the likely longevity of the various systems, and if possible, chose a system that can adapt and be upgraded over time.
3. Install a system large enough to generate the energy you need to make it a worthwhile investment. The individual companies will suggest the best systems, when they either look at your drawings, or come to the house to sell you their products. As a guide, I did install a system recently on one house, as an extra, requested by the buyer. It was a large 5 bed house and the supplier recommended a 4.5Kw system.
4. Check out the warranty situation. Make sure you are fully covered for problems that you might not even realise exist when you first install the system.
5. Check out what the present and possible future situation is likely to be regarding feed in tariffs. If you think you are going to be able to pay off the cost of the system by selling power back to the grid, you might be disappointed.

*Finally: Shop around. All companies are not the same. As with everything, there are companies who offer high quality service and good value for money, and there are other companies who are "all shop window", who spend a fortune on sales teams and marketing, and add those marketing costs to the selling price of the systems, whilst offering an, at best, average product.*

# THING 113: ECO / ENVIRONMENTALLY FRIENDLY PRODUCTS

I have already mentioned some of the more popular environmentally friendly products generally available (*air source / wind turbine, ground source, solar*) and there are literally hundreds more products that I could write about, the majority of which are interesting, useful, but niche products, which I do not have space to try to cover in this book. However, if environmental considerations are one of the attractions, or even or **the** driving force pulling you towards self-building, there are other books you may be interested in looking at, for example: "**The Green Self-Build Book**" (*available on Amazon*). It has been out for a few years old now and I have not read it, but it should be able to provide you with some good information. You could also have a look at: http://thegreenselfbuilder.co.uk

**Having said that, there are a few things I would like to mention, while we are on the subject:**

As I am with Solar Panels, I am a bit on the fence when it comes to the world of Green / Eco / Environmental thinking, products, and services as they relate to the self-build industry ("*Why am I not surprised?*", you ask).

Having spoken to literally hundreds of self-builders over the years at the shows, I have built up a picture of why people choose to go down this route, and what they want to achieve by doing so. I really admire anyone who is prepared to go out on a limb to get what they want.

What does worry me, however, is that many of the products and services available to Eco Builders, tend to come under the heading of "*shiny things*", they promise a lot but deliver little, and often perform poorly.

Most self-builders seem to have *middle of the road* aspirations when it comes to environmentally friendly thinking. I am in that bracket. I like and want some of the eco features, and want to help to protect the environment, but I also like and want what I already know works and what I am comfortable with.

Despite the fact that the eco industry as a whole is still seen as a niche market within the overall construction industry, its influence is growing and eco product suppliers are fully aware that their main market is very much dedicated to *their type* of products.

This knowledge creates the tendency for some, knowing that competition is not strong, to push their prices up. It can also lead to them feeling less of a need to provide *the best* product they can for the money.

For these reasons, I think it is important that, before you make costly purchase of any products or services that are not mainstream *(not just ecologically)*, that you carry out some research into their strengths and weaknesses. Online is a great place to do this. Just take  a bit of time to read about what previous buyers have thought, *after* they have taken the plunge.

# THING 114: TRUSSES v ATTIC TRUSSES v CUT ROOF

The most common form of roof construction for UK housing is the standard roof truss. It is cheap, strong, quick, and easy to fit, and it does its job well. There are hundreds of thousands of older houses around the UK that were built using standard roof trusses, that have not had any problems with them.

However, having said that, as plots are getting smaller and more expensive, and as building costs rise due to increased regulations and eco awareness, the need use space efficiently increases, so we have now started to consider using the space we have been wasting for decades, up in the roof.

That is where Attic Trusses come into the equation. Offering up to 30% extra living space, on the same building footprint, at a fairly minimal extra cost, compared to standard roof trusses.

In case you are not familiar with this product, here is an attic trussed roof that I installed on the house we built while I was writing this book. It is a large house, over three floors, with five bedrooms on the first floor and two large open areas on the second floor.

Rather than using standard trusses to form a loft, by installing attic trusses I gained a large extra living space.

In the photo, you can see the first floor landing and what was to become be the attic space. The extra living space achieved in the attic measures 4.2m x 14.2m (*just under 60sq.m or 600sq.ft*), which is the equivalent to adding a 2 bedroomed flat to the original floor area, *within the same sized building envelope*.

The way attic trusses work, is by significantly beefing up the standard truss, to make it a lot stronger, and getting rid of the struts that usually fill the middle area. Instead, the bottom timber becomes a floor joists, the two main sloping timbers become rafters, and the thinner sloping struts are replaced by vertical timbers that become internal walls.

With an attic truss, the joist (*the bottom timber*) hangs from the two rafters (*the two main sloping timbers*), using the vertical timbers as hangers. This gives them the extra strength they need to be able to span wide open areas, without needing extra support from underneath.

If there are one or two supporting walls for the attic trusses to sit on, they won't need to be quite as strong, so will work out cheaper to buy (*in other words, if you want to save some money, try to design a couple of supporting walls coming up from below. Your designer should be able to sort this out).*

**Note:** Attic trusses are best suited to simple rectangular buildings. The more you move away from that basic shape, the less effective attic trusses will be as a space creating option.

**Cost:** Attic trusses are not particularly expensive, considering the extra living space they create. A single, standard attic truss of the type and size shown in the photo above would cost around £200, compared to around £70 for a standard truss. You can work out roughly how many trusses you would need, by dividing the length of the building by 0.6 (*the trusses sit at 600mm centres*), and adding one extra truss.

Attic trusses are made by the same companies that make standard trusses, so there would be no problem in you asking for 2 quotes for your house, one using *standard trusses* and one using *attic trusses*. They usually take about 2 – 4 weeks from ordering, to delivery to site, and you will need a crane to lift and position them.

**Increasing your property value:** Even if you don't need to use the extra space that the attic trusses create straight away, or even at all, simply having them there will increase the value of your property noticeably. If you were to then to leave the roof space unfinished / unused, at some time in the future, whoever owns the house (*you or whoever comes after you*) can quickly and cheaply convert it into one or two bedrooms and a bathroom, without having to initially take the entire existing roof off to do so.

**Cut Roof:**

By coincidence, two of the houses we built on our recent development were built using a cut roof method, and one using attic trusses. This allows me to show a direct comparison between the two roof types.

The house in this image is the same size and shape as the one shown above, but instead of using attic trusses, we installed a cut roof. In other words, the carpenters constructed the whole roof shown in this image, by hand.

*"Why didn't you use attic trusses?"* You may ask. Well, without going into detail, when I designed the house, I didn't think it would be possible to build the roof with attic trusses. It was only when we had nearly finished first house, with the roof already on the second, that one day, as I stood looking at the two houses, I suddenly realised that with a few simple design adjustments, attic trusses could have been used.

There is nothing wrong with using a cut roof, it is just slow and labour intensive (*and thus more expensive*). It is how we built most house roofs before trusses were invented.

To build the cut roof, a large, strong timber purlin was fitted to span between the tops of the roof gables at either end of the building, and one supporting wall was added, part way along the length of the building (*you can just see the purlin at the top of the image*). The sloping timbers were then cut and fitted, followed by the short, vertical timber stud walls.

This roof was actually more complicated than the description I have given here. It took two months to complete the whole structure, with fascias, soffits, gutters etc, where the attic trusses took around two to three weeks to get to the same stage.

*My thoughts on the roofing options:*
*Self-builders are generally practically minded people, who like to get their money's worth out of things. Complicated house designs might require cut roofs to be installed, but wherever possible, trusses are a better, faster, cheaper option.*

*If it is practical to do so, designing attic trusses into a self-build project will normally be a practical, and economically sensible thing to do.*

## THING 115: TYPES AND COSTS OF ROOF COVERINGS

Roof coverings, although not a structurally important part of a house build, are important visually. Together with the bricks, render finishes, windows, and doors, they create the style, character, and sometimes charm of the completed building. So, the choices you make will govern where your new home will sit on the scale that goes from *"stunning, head turner"*, to *"dog's dinner"*! Thankfully, self-builders generally have pretty good taste, sour decisions tend to sit towards the top end of that range.

There is a vast array of choice, for tiles, slates, and other products (*such as sheet metals*), and the cost variances from product to product are huge. So, if your budget is limited, it is a good idea to take a bit of time to look at your options.

**Here are some pointers:**

**Roof tiles:**

I will start at the economical end of the spectrum: The image to the right is of a house I built around 15 years ago. The roof tile was then, and still is one of the cheapest, but most popular tiles available in the UK.

Two companies make similar products at similar price points. One is the **Marley Modern**, the other is the **Redland Mini Stonewold**. These are both concrete tiles, which have the appearance of very thick slate. They come in a number of different colours (*search: Marley Moderns* or *Redland Mini*

*Stonewolds*). All three of the houses in the image were tiled with Marley Moderns, in *Anthracite Grey (similar to the colour of slate)*.

Moving to the opposite end of the price spectrum, this image shows an example of **hand-made clay tiles**. Attractive, but also very expensive, both to buy and to fix. One of these tiles can cost about the same as a Marley Modern, but it can take up to nine of them to covers the same area (*sizes vary between manufacturers and ranges*). They also

require three to four times as much treated timber batten, and the same sort of ratio in increased labour and nail costs.

**Natural slate tiles** are attractive, and slot into the price scale somewhere between the previous two products. You can also get fairly realistic *plastic* or *reconstituted* slate, at a lower price than natural slate.

*As a quick, but scary comparison, when you consider that the cost of one Marley modern roof tile is around £1, and the cost of one of some of the small hand-made clay tiles is also about £1, but you might need up to nine of them to cover the same area, when I say that the most recent house we built using Marley Moderns, cost £9,000 for labour and materials, it doesn't take much working out to estimate how much the same roof would have cost to cover if I had used the small, handmade tile.*

**Coated sheet metals:**

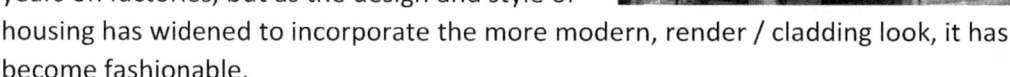

This is a product that seems to be gaining popularity. The image to the right shows a coated sheet metal roof on a log cabin.

This type of roofing has been used for many years on factories, but as the design and style of housing has widened to incorporate the more modern, render / cladding look, it has become fashionable.

Products can be bought as simple plastic coated sheets of steel or can have insulation factory fitted to them. Tata Steel sell coated steel sheeting products for roofs and walls, in many colours.

I like this material for roofing, I am not so sure about it for cladding on housing. If it is not used properly, it can make the building look like it is only going to be there temporarily (*possibly because static holiday caravans are often made using similar looking materials*). However, it is low cost, quick to install and is probably worth having a look at if you are thinking about building a modern looking house. (Have a look at: cladco.co.uk)

# THING 116: **FASCIAS & SOFFITS**

This is usually the last, and a reasonably simple part of the roof construction. It can be fitted by the roofers or the carpenters, and should ideally be installed after the roof tiling / covering has been completed (*if it is fitted earlier it can get in the way of the roofer tilers as they climb on and off the roof to fix battens and lay tiles*).

A couple of decades ago, softwood timber was the standard material used for fascias and soffits, but that gradually changed, when a plastic alternative appeared on the market and quickly started to gain popularity, mainly because it didn't need painting.

When it was first introduced, the plastic was not of particularly good quality and it started to crack and fall apart after a few years. That problem now seems to have disappeared and the modern plastic products offer better solutions, in a wide choice of finishes (*including timber grain*). However, before buying any of these products, it is still a good idea to check the warranty on them. Even if you would not intend to claim on it, it is useful to know how long the manufacturers think their products will last.

The image above shows a standard modern facia and soffit in slate coloured UPVC. This seems to be the colour that has taken the place of white as the most popular colour choice.

The fascia is fitted after the ends of the roof trusses or rafters have been by trimmed back to a line which will form the back of the fascia board itself. Plastic fascia board itself is usually "L" shaped (*occasionally it is rectangular, with a pre-formed groove along its length*). Once it has been fitted, the short part of the "L" forms a lip for the soffit to sit on (*either that, or the soffit slots into the pre-formed groove*). The other edge of the soffit then usually sits on the top brick, or is fixed to a timber batten, which in turn is fixed to the brickwork.

Timber is still used for this job, but not widely. It is now generally used where a traditional visual appearance is required (*as opposed to the slightly shiny, modern appearance of the UPVC).*

If you decide to go for the timber option, be sure to give everything a few generous coats (*especially the open grain at the ends*) of high quality treatment / preservative, or use a good quality paint, to try to avoid the necessity of having to replace them in 15 years or so.

(**Note:** *If you build the house using a timber frame, as a rule, the suppliers don't include the fascias and soffits*).

## THING 117: **GUTTERING AND DOWNPIPES**

The image in the previous section, of fascia and soffit fitted to the corner of a house, shows one of the most popular guttering styles and colours, called *"Black Square line"* in plastic. The older *"half round"* style is not as popular as it used to be, but two other styles you may wish to look at are "OGEE" and "Deep Flow" (*search: Images of guttering to see different styles*).

Although plastic is the now the most popular material for guttering, depending on the style of your house and you budget, there are other more bespoke products made of steel, aluminium or cast iron, which all look good, but come with a hefty price tag.

Gutters and downpipes are usually fitted by either the plumbers or carpenters. It is best to fit them after the surface water drainage has been completed, so the outlets in the guttering can be set accurately above the open end of the newly installed drainpipes, allowing the downpipe to be fitted vertically, and run straight into the gully.

There are different ways to finish the downpipes where they meet the drains. Probably the most common solution is the *45 degree outlet*, which kicks the water away from the house to land on the gully grid. This works fine for average levels of rainfall, but you will probably have witnessed what happens in long periods of very heavy rain, when the water gushes out of the downpipe at such a rate that it misses the gully altogether, and floods the area around it. There are simple ways to combat this:

- Fit the downpipe so that it passes through the gully cover, into the drainpipe itself. The gulley cover will normally be made of plastic, so, all you need to do is mark out the shape of the pipe onto the cover and cut the correct sized opening to allow the downpipe to pass through it. You then cut the downpipe a few inches longer than it needs to be, so it will go through the hole you have cut and continue few inches down into the drainpipe itself.

- Instead of using a standard plastic gully, use a rubber or plastic gasket fitting, that slides over the end of the downpipe and also fits over the open end of the drainage pipe, giving a sealed route for the water to travel from above ground to below ground. This option is useful in times of heavy rain, due to the fact that the water cannot escape, to splash or flood the area around the gully.

-

**Let's take a quick breather here, to ask an important question:**

## THING 118: How are the costs going?

So far, we have so far worked our way through buying the land, designing the house, planning the timetable, and getting stuck into the build. That is pretty much the way most self-builders approach their projects. It is often one mad charge, from day one through to completion, with all the paperwork being left piling up on a table, to be dealt with later (*but rarely actually getting looked at until bills need paying*).

Towards the end of the project, funds and cash flow can start to get tight and you might find yourselves occasionally relying solely on your trade accounts to keep the project supplied with materials until the next stage payment comes in. This is not unusual, but it can get stressful.

### So, where has all the money been going?

What happens on most self-build projects is, as soon as work starts, money starts to get spent in big chunks: Maybe £10,000 for groundworks materials, £20,000 - £30,000 for labour and plant for the foundations, slab, and drainage, £20,000 for the deposit on the timber frame, and so on. At the start of the build, it is easy to think to yourself: *"We've got £150,000 to spend, that's plenty. We don't need to worry!"*.

Then, all of a sudden, usually around two thirds the way through the project, the reality dawns that funds are starting took a bit tight, and the thought process starts to change to working out where all the money went:

*"That problem with the foundations cost us £6,000 extra". The timber frame cost more than we expected. The facing bricks we chose were well over our budget allowance, so were the roof tiles". Etc.*

This is where panic can start to set in, and you immediately contact the lenders to see if you can borrow some extra money.

If this is the first project you have taken on, it is a good idea to stop for minute at some point, not too far into the build, to check that things are moving along as they should be, and that you are not at risk of grinding to a halt before the project has been completed, due to cash flow or any other problems. Just doing this might stop any knee jerk reactions when cash flows does start to show signs of strain.

As I mentioned earlier in the book, the groundworks and drainage will usually be where the lion's share of any overspend will be concentrated. I would guess that probably 80% of construction jobs that go over budget do so, due to something happening underground, in the first couple of months of the job.

After you get past the foundation and drainage phase, the rest of the costs are more predictable. You can choose how much you pay for your bricks and roof tiles and it is a lot easier to estimate costs using a calculator, rather than "best guess".

So, if something comes in over budget (*for example, the timber frame*), as long as you are keeping track of the ongoing costs of everything, and comparing them all to your original estimates, it is easier to catch the problems areas sooner. If you can do that, you will at least have a chance to do something about it straight away.

If you do find yourselves getting tight on funds mid project, here are three ways to help cope with, and hopefully get over the problem:

1) **Try to reduce the remaining costs:** Can you reduce the budget on the kitchen or the bathrooms? Do you really need that £2000 range cooker, or all those fancy towel radiators? Is that expensive shower really something you must have, and the wood burner might have to wait until you have moved in, and have saved up some more money. Then there are all the external works. You have allowed £15,000 for lawns, decking, a hot tub, garden lighting and a garden shed. Can they wait until after you move in, so you can see where you are financially at that time? (*and so on*).

2) **Go back to the lender** to ask if you can borrow some extra on the mortgage. Unless you borrowed yourselves up to the hilt at the outset, they might have a little bit of float in the maximum they can lend, while keeping within their standard lending parameters. Where £10,000 - £20,000 didn't seem much at the start of the job, you would be very grateful to have it to spend now!

3) **Borrow from relatives**. I would use this as your last option. Borrowing from family is usually quite easy to do if they have spare money and want to help you where they can. But think twice about putting *money* and *family* into the same financial equation. It may be fine at the outset, but when they suddenly want the money back to go off on a world cruise for 3 months, and you haven't got it to give them, things can get a bit strained. If you do need to borrow from relatives, keep the amounts as low as possible and try to have a definite plan (*which is better if it is put in writing*), for paying it off asap.

*If all self-builders built one or two brief pauses into their build programmes, just to give some time to look through the "already spent" figures, "the programme" and the "still to be spent" figures, the number of projects that run into financial difficulty would be significantly reduced.*

*Your stress levels almost certainly would be.*

OK, back to it:

## THING 119: DON'T BUDGET TO USE YOUR VAT REFUND AS PART OF YOUR BUILD BUDGET

All I want to do here is make a point that, unless you are in such a tight corner that there is no alternative, you should do your utmost to leave the VAT refund out of any financial calculations, before, or while you are building.

We are all aware that we will get a nice chunk of cash back once the work has all been completed and have moved into the house. It is like a carrot dangling at the end of a piece of string, always in our vision but we can't quite touch it. **YET!**

It is very tempting to have a guess at how much the refund will be, and then plan what we are going to do with it well before we get it!

**For a number of reasons:**
## Just Don't!

### Why not?

If you watch Grand Designs on TV, you will know that one of the things that happens to the people building these houses, is that they nearly always run out of money before the end of the build. However, because the programme doesn't usually stay around until they actually move in, you don't normally see or hear first-hand, about the financial problems they had at towards end of the job, and just after they moved in (*instead, Kevin calls back some months later, to see how it is all going, by which time the drama has usually calmed down a bit, and things are getting back on a reasonably even keel*).

If an episode details how funds and cashflow were getting short towards the end of the build, you can bet that, in most cases things didn't get any better, as the build got nearer to completion. You can also bet that the self-builders were probably still struggling to get to grips with a financial debt problem when Kevin made his return visit. (*I know for a fact that this was the case for at least one couple who appeared on the show. I spoke to them at one of the live events, and they told me that it took them a year or so to sort out paying the last bills off after they moved into the house*).

In the previous section, I talked about trying to find ways to save money, as when you realise it is getting tight. I am sure you will do that, but what if _all_ you can do isn't enough? Wouldn't it be good to have an emergency buffer for _if all else fails_, waiting for you after you have finished the job? *Something that you can always be sure will be there?*

### Something like a few thousand pounds of a VAT refund?

*(If you don't need it to pay off the last of the bills, I am sure you will be able to find something useful to do with it).*

## THING 120: DON'T BUY KITCHENS AND BATHROOMS TOO SOON

**Keeping with the theme of not spending money if you don't need to:**

As housing developers, all the houses we build are *custom finished*, with the buyer being able to choose a lot of the finishing items. When a house is reserved, the buyer gets a list of priced options and, as long as they choose and pay for those options upfront, they become part of the standard build.

One thing we try to be strict about, is a rule that *"Once we have started work, there can be **no more** alterations"*. Pretty much 100% of the time, we fail to meet that target. And what parts of the project do we fail on? The Kitchens and the Bathrooms.

That happens because, at the point when you can *actually, physically* stand in a room, and can start to imagine how it will look completed, all the ideas you previously had for it, often go straight in the bin.

Going back to the start of the job, here is a scenario I have come across a number of times with self-builders (*including me, in my younger years*).

*As you get ready to start work, you want to get as much of the project as possible, planned and costed. That includes the kitchens and bathrooms. So, one weekend, you head off to various suppliers, to get some ideas and prices, and low and behold, one supplier has a kitchen that you immediately fall in love with, and has it on a "very special once in a lifetime offer". Or, they may have a fantastic demonstration kitchen that they are stripping out of the showroom and selling cheap, but they need a decision from you straight away. So, you have a quick think and a chat, and decide: "Let's go for it. We might not get another chance like this".*

*You have to put the kitchen in storage for two or three months, costing you two or three hundred pounds, then one day, your kitchen is finally plastered, and suddenly changes from being part of a building site, to becoming a real room, - **your kitchen**!*

*Within days, you realise that the kitchen you bought isn't going to look right, or that some of the units won't fit where you wanted them to go. Maybe a tall larder cupboard restricts the light from the main window, or the breakfast bar sticks out too far, and doesn't leave enough room to walk between it and a wall (and so on).*

*All of a sudden, that stunning kitchen you have had stored away for months, doesn't seem to be quite the bargain you thought it was, and you end up spending another couple of thousand pounds trying to make it work to suit your new ideas.*

Exactly the same scenarios can play out if you buy bathroom equipment, wall tiles and floor tiles too early.

**Just remember this:**

*There will always be sales on. There will always be bargains to be found. There will always be lovely kitchens, bathrooms, and tiles available. Just don't buy any of them until you know they are <u>exactly</u> what you want, need, and can afford.*

## THING 121: **SUB-CONTRACTOR CONTRACTS**

Drawing up contracts is not something you are likely to be familiar with unless you are a Lawyer. It is a specialist subject, but one which you need to give adequate attention to, to make sure you are legally protected from *"bad actors"* of one type or another.

As you build your new home, you will be dealing with a lot of different trades and subcontractors, and it is likely that this will be the first time you have dealt with most of them. Large amounts of money are regularly going to be changing hands, and you are going to have to trust people you have never met before, to do what they say they will do, correctly, professionally and for the price they have agreed.

It is therefore common-sense to make sure that you are protected against things going wrong with one or more of these financial relationships. Things like incompetence, non-completion, error, and anything else that could negatively affect your project. The best way to do this is by using simple building contracts.

There are a few ways to make sure you are adequately covered. Here are a couple of them:

i.   You could ask your own Lawyer to draw up a standard contract, specific to your project, giving you the protection you need against potentially negative eventualities. This will probably cost you a few hundred pounds to have drawn up, but at least, once you have it, and are able to get each subcontractor to sign it, you will be protected, should any problems arise.

ii.  You could buy a pre-prepared building contract from one of the law websites, to do the same job. Then make your own amendments anywhere you think they are appropriate (*I would suggest getting your Lawyer to cast an eye over it once you think it is satisfactory. They may charge you £50 or so, but it might prove to be worth it at some time during the coming few months*).
    A company I use for this purpose is called: "The Law Depot", but you will find a few similar companies online, offering the same sort of service. (*Go to https://www.lawdepot.co.uk*)

Just having a contract helps to set you up in the eyes of the subcontractors, as someone who is running a professional project. Once they have signed that piece of paper, they know that if they mess up, you can legally come after them for compensation / reparation.

*Simply knowing that can help keep their minds focussed and reduce the potential for the contract itself ever being required to do its job.*

## THING 122: **FIRST FIXES**

Once the roof is on, and the upper floor floorboards have been fitted, theoretically, all the first fixes can begin. However, if you are building in a location where there is a risk of theft (*which these days is most places*), you should secure the building before fitting or storing anything inside. You will also need to buy, or hire a steel container to store some of the more expensive materials and equipment (*containers are cheap to hire. We pay around £60 / month for a 12' long steel container. Delivery charges are from around £100 upwards, depending on how far you are from the depot*)

For safety, as well as security reasons, the site should be fully fenced off from day one, with lockable gates. You might also think about installing a cctv system or arranging for regular visits from a local security monitoring company (*which can be expensive*).

Once you have taken care of the security issues, you need to decide how to go about the job of first fixing. I find the most efficient working method is to try to get all the trades in at the same time. Joiners, plumbers, electricians (*and now in some areas of the country, sprinkler fitters*). If you opt to go with the same idea, you will somtimes get some sort of push back from one or more of the trades, telling you that they need the whole of the building to themselves while they do their work (*everyone likes to have a free run at the whole building, so they can do what they want, when they want, but this is not an efficient way of building*). Unless there is a very good reason for any particular subcontractor to have the house to themselves, I suggest that you simply tell them all that you don't have time to let them go in one by one, adding: *"If there are any problems, let me know"* (there are very rarely any significant problems).

By having everyone working in the house together, they can talk to each other, to sort out the myriad small problems that always crop up at this stage of the job. This is a far better way of doing it than one trade asking me to contact another trade to explain a problem, then me having to report back to all the other trades. – That kind of set up creates the perfect scenario for *"Chinese Whispers"* to occur.

**Here are a few tips to keep in mind for the first fixes:**

1. **Contract:** Make sure each sub-contractor has signed a contract (see previous section).

2. **Materials purchasing:** Some subcontractors like to buy their own materials, that way they make sure they get what they need, when they need it. That is fine, as long as they are VAT registered. If they are not, and you let *them* buy the gear (*maybe on their own account*), you will pay the 20% VAT and won't be able to get it back later.

**So:**

i)        Suggest setting up an account in your name, at their suppliers.

ii)       Get the supplier to give you at least the same prices that they pay, for everything you will need.

iii)      Agree that the person in charge of each trade will keep all the delivery notes for the materials they buy, and give them to you once a week.

iv)      Check the delivery notes for anything that looks odd. Subbies have been known to occasionally stick a few small tools, or other bits and pieces onto client's invoices. This is not the end of the world, especially when you are saving 20% on everything, however, if you check the delivery notes and mention anything that looks out of place, to them, they'll know they are being watched, so are less likely to repeat the action in the future.

v)       Make sure you claim the VAT back at the end of the job.

## 3. Trades:

**Plumbing: Consider using plastic piping.** The traditional material used for the plumbing and heating pipework is copper. The other option is plastic. I changed to plastic a decade or so ago, for many reasons, including: It is cheaper, it comes in long coils so there are fewer soldered joints (*which could leak*), it is quicker to install, and it is quieter (*you are probably familiar with the sound of copper pipes expanding when they are heating up and cooling down or rattling against each other. Plastic does not make any significant noise*).

**Plumbing: Boiler choice:** There is a huge range of boilers of all types to choose from. Take advice from your plumbing installer as to the best one to suit your project, then do some research on alternative, similar options before you buy any particular model. If there is a better deal available on a similar boiler, check with the installer before ordering it.

**Plumbing:** If you do not have a **gas supply** to your plot, but would like to be able to use gas, you could think about installing a large gas storage cylinder in the garden. *Calor Gas* have a residential system that you could consider. Go to: https://www.calor.co.uk

**Plumbing:** Think about installing a **shower on the ground floor**. It doesn't need to cost much, but allows you and the family to get cleaned up when you come into the house dirty, and could be handy in the future, if anyone has trouble getting upstairs.

**Plumbing:** If you are installing **sprinklers,** the system needs to connect to the water supply *inside the building*, but <u>before</u> it gets to the stop tap. That way the water supply to the sprinkler system cannot be turned off by accident.

**Plumbing:** Think about where you might want **outside taps**, and how many. I installed hot and cold outside taps near the driveway on one of my own self-builds, so that I could connect a hose and wash the car with warm water.

**Plumbing:** As mentioned earlier in the book, think about installing a **rainwater harvesting system** to help you to save water. It can be as simple as using water butts under downpipes, or a more complex system of an underground tank with pumps, to feed stored rainwater to taps which are fixed to the external walls of the house.

**Joinery:** One of the first fix jobs is to provide **pattresses** (*also called noggins*) in the timber stud walls. Pattresses are (*usually*) timber plates, made out of plywood or OSB board, fixed where necessary to support all the fittings (*such as radiators / light switches / wall lights / sockets / kitchen units / wall cupboards etc*). This is a bigger job in timber framed houses than it is in traditionally built houses, where some walls are built in blockwork. You will need to think about each wall in the house, how it is going to be used and prior to plaster boarding starting, make sure every area that needs strengthening, has been. It is a quick job to do at the right time, but a very messy and time consuming trying to cut bits of plaster board out later if a support has been missed.

**Joinery:** I hate squeaky floors. **Floorboards** used to be nailed to the floor joists. That is where the problem originated. At the fitting stage, the board is nailed down tight, however, as the whole building dries out over months and years, the boards can shrink in depth by a couple of millimetres. This allows the board to move up and down the nail when it is stepped on, causing the squeaks. Screws do a better job of reducing squeaks, but I like the latest option of gluing all the boards down using an expanding glue (*we use a product called D4 from Everbuild*). We have not had any squeaky floors since we started using this glue. It also speeds up installation. The downside is that, if you ever need to take a board up, you have to physically *cut it out* (*rather than unscrewing or de-nailing it*), which is a messy job. Then, when you have done what needs doing, you have to frame out the opening, to support the part of the floorboard you have just cut out. A bit of a pain, but not the end of the world, and only very rarely required.

**Joinery:** Most joiners prefer to fit the **door frames** _after_ plaster boarding, rather than before. I agree with the *after* option. It is a tidier way of doing the job. However, don't fall out with the chippies over this, it comes down to personal opinion.

**Joinery:** The same goes for **window boards** (*also known as window cills*). I fit them after the walls have been boarded and plastered (*or taped and jointed*). I then run a bead of silicone around the edges and underneath, to tidy up the joint where the board meets the wall.

**Joinery: Service voids** might form part of your build, especially if you use any of the modular build options. These, as the name suggests, are voids, into which all the services are fitted. They are installed between the external wall and the plaster board. If you can negate the need for service voids, by installing the services within the wall itself, you will save time, money, and materials. Talk to your plumber and electrician about this.

**Electrical:** In larger houses, consider **CAT 6 wiring** and **RJ45's** for boosting broadband performance. Here are links to websites that explain what these two items are used for: https://www.lifewire.com/cat6-ethernet-cable-standard-817553

https://uk.rs-online.com/web/c/connectors/network-telecom-connectors/rj45-connectors

**Electrical:** Carefully consider **socket and switch** positions: There is nothing worse than moving into your new home and finding that half your sockets and switches are in the wrong positions for your furniture, or for ease of use. When you are designing your electrical layout, it can be difficult to accurately decide how you are going to use each room, but once the shell is up, this becomes easier. Before you finalise your service installation drawings, stand in each room and try to imagine how it will eventually be laid out and used. Then check that your socket, switch (*and radiator*) positions are not going to cause problems.

**Electrical:** Consider how you will wire up the **outside of the house**. Will you be installing decking, patios, hot tubs, garden shed etc? What will your outside lighting requirements be for leisure, security (*and maybe an electric car charger*)? Make sure you install all the necessary wiring at first fix stage, to save having to go back later to retro fix any missing items.

**Electrical:** Now is a good time to install the wiring for an alarm system. However, you can also buy wireless systems as an alternative, and install them later.

## THING 123: BUILT IN ENTERTAINMENT / HOME AUTOMATION

From past experience with my own clients, and from talking to families at the self-build shows, this is a subject that normally gets the attention of the men but is not of great interest to women. *"Toys for the boys"* seems to be a fairly accurate description of where this subject sits on the list of priorities of self-builders.

These days, after positioning sockets and switches and choosing light fittings, most of us will have broadband at, or near the top of their list of important fixtures and fittings. That used to be a simple matter to attend to: Plug the router cable into the phone socket, and away you go.

Not anymore: We have now moved into a world where fast broadband service around the house is almost as important as having a fridge! We would struggle to live without it.

So, how does broadband affect the way we plan, equip and set up our new homes, and how does it affect the subject of this section; the provision of Home Entertainment (*which has and probably always will be of great importance to the "self-build lads". Me included*).

**Some of the obvious considerations are:**

- Where only the wealthy used to be able to afford a large TV, now a 60", 72" or larger screens are a lot more affordable.
- Where we used to build expensive hifi speakers into the walls, we now have Bluetooth wireless speakers, and surround sound that costs peanuts for a pretty decent system.
- Most people's visual entertainment comes via Netflix, Amazon, and a host of other networks, not via DVD's or Blue-Rays.
- CCTV security cameras use to be expensive and required a full backup system for monitoring. Now they are cheap, and you can monitor them from your phone. Even doorbells can now have two way cameras.
- You can control your central heating, washing machine, oven, and many other appliances from your phone.
- The list goes on and on and will get longer over the coming years.

So, where does that leave the self-build boys and their toys? – Well, totally spoilt would be one way to describe it.

My thinking on the subject of built in entertainment and home automation is:

*What would be the point of spending money on any piece of technology, when a) It could be out of date in 18 months and b) You wouldn't be able to take it with you, if and when you move.*

*So, I would suggest that where possible, you stick with the broadband and the Bluetooth for everything to do with sound, vision, and specialist systems (like the video doorbells and remotely controlled appliance). That way you will be in a better position to upgrade to the next technological innovation when it appears, probably in about a fortnight!*

**Additional:** The whole family might like this, one little bit of fixed technology. You could call it a gimmick, but I think (*partly from experience*) that it would be a good, low cost investment, that you and your family would make good use of, that could actually help you to sell the house faster, should you ever wish to do so (*I don't think there is a phone operated version of it, yet at least*).

I am talking about remote controlled dimming lights. It is a simple, cheap system, that adds a touch of opulence to a house. For around £300 you could swop standard light switches in three or four rooms, to remote controlled switches, each operated by a small remote controlled handset. Rather than having your lights on or off or having to go to the wall to operate a dimmer, this system allows you to create mood lighting in each room. This is most effective when you have a mixture of wall and ceiling lights / spotlights, and are able to set different light levels around the room. It also allows you to mimic the cinema experience, where you sit down, put a film on and dim the lights right down while you watch it, then back up at the end.

*I installed the system in my most recent self-build project a few years ago. When I came to sell the house, I took the first viewers into the living room, closed the curtains, put Lord of The Rings on the large screen TV, with the sound coming through the built in hi-fi surround sound system. I gave them the remotes and let them have a play with them, setting the ceiling and wall lighting to different levels in different Parts of the room.*

**I accepted a full asking price offer before they left the building that evening!**

*OK, so it is a "toy", but it is a good toy,*
*and your kids would love you for putting it in their rooms!*

## THING 124: MECHANICAL VENTILATION

(This subject was briefly covered earlier)

Talking about toys, this one presently seems to be in favour with both the environmentally aware self-build sector and Local Authority Planners. If you want to live in a house with clean filtered air, 24 hours a day, this is the system for you!

I recently lived for a few months in a house with this system already installed. It might be that I had a bad experience of it, or that it was a cheap system, but I was not particularly impressed. As to whether or not it did its job well, I can't say (*although it broke down once, and was noisy most of the time*). However, what I did find myself subconsciously asking the simple question: "*Why?*"

I wholeheartedly agree with using this system to help anyone with breathing problems (*which it does, by constantly refreshing and filtering the air*), and the constant clean air circulating around the house is great, but consider the way the system works:

With this system, the air inside the house is continually changed. The *old* the air is regularly replaced with *fresh clean* air, but, so that heat from within the building is not wasted, each time the old air is removed, the heat contained within it is transferred, via a heat exchanger, to the clean air, which is then fed back into the house and re-circulated around all the rooms. Sounds good?

**My Question:** Why not just open a window or door for a few minutes?

In the summer I don't want the heat coming back in, I want the fresh cooler air. In the winter, as a fairly healthy person, will I notice the difference between the old air and the new air? Will it help improve my overall state of health, or my life in general?

If the cost of having one of these systems was minimal, I would probably give it a try, but they are quite expensive. They start at around £1,000 for a basic system that would suit an averagely sized 3 / 4 bed house, and the prices go up to £3,500+ for a high spec system.

That sort of money buys you a lot of heat (*Yes, I know: Global warming! But I would rather spend the extra money insulation, upgraded thermally efficient windows, a high efficiency boiler etc, which would probably do more to save the earth than one of these systems.*

As with many of the products available across the self-build industry, this one is a *Must have* for some and a *Nah, no thanks* for others.

**Note:** I do need to repeat the fact that this system does have its uses. I don't know the technical details, but I do know that it can be effective in situations where someone living in the house has breathing problems. In those circumstances it is obviously well worth the investment.

*Comments invited*

## THING 125: MAKE ALL DOOR OPENINGS 2'9" WIDE

A few years ago, it became a requirement of the UK Building Regulations, that all ground floor doors were to be a minimum of 2'9" (838mm) wide. This was to done to take into account the needs of people with disabilities. 2'9" wide door openings make the whole of the ground floor area more accessible for wheelchairs, and allow everyone to have a bit more manoeuvring room.

A useful by-product of this decision was that it helped to make moving to a new house easier. Now settees, table and large appliances have at least a fighting chance of getting through the openings. Unfortunately though, the change did not affect doors on the upper floors, which can still be 762mm (2'6") wide, which to my mind is too narrow.

Before the regs changed ground floor door widths to 2'9", we had already been building our houses with all doors at 2'9" width, on all floors. After all, if it makes life easier on the ground floor, why wouldn't it make life easier on other floors too?

One thing I find, when I show a potential buyer around any of the houses we build, is that they notice the wider doors on the upper floors, generally commenting on it being a good idea. It is, and it is an improvement that would only cost a few £'s per door to include in your own build.

## THING 126: SOUND INSULATE BETWEEN ROOM AND FLOORS.

Building Regulations requirements for sound insulation are steadily increasing. About 20 years ago the regs changed to require sound insulation around bathrooms, shower rooms, en-suites, and toilets.

One of the long term complaints that UK house buyers have against new build homes, is that sound insulation is usually woefully poor. The common statement of "*I can hear people talking at the opposite end of the house*" being one regular complaint, which sadly is often true. Timber frame new builds seemed to get extra condemnation for being poorly sound insulated.

In fact, the lack of soundproofing wasn't the fault of the timber frame, or the poor quality of a traditionally built house. The lack of sound proofing was caused by, well, *the lack of soundproofing*!

If I build a house with timber stud internal walls (*which timber frames use on all floors and traditional builds often use on the first floor, and sometimes on the ground floor*), and if I only use a cheap 12mm thick plaster board on each side of each of the stud walls, and the same board on the ceilings, with an 18mm chipboard floor upstairs, that house is going to be noisy.

However, if you are building your own home, either traditionally or in timber frame, and you want to buck that trend, here is what you can do:

- Install 4" of rockwool, (*or similar*) fibreglass insulation in between every room, on all floors.
- Install 150mm of rockwool insulation between floors.
- Use either 15mm standard plasterboards everywhere, or for even better results use "DB" or "Soundbloc" sound insulated boards. (*Search:* www.siniat.co.uk, or https://www.british-gypsum.com/products/gyproc)
- Use 22mm floorboards instead of 18mm
- Fit solid internal doors.

The cost of that soundproofing operation would probably be couple of thousand pounds, for a decent sized 4 bed house, and at that price, I think is a good investment. It will also be something you can highlight, if ever you come to sell the house. You might also be surprised how much difference it makes to the transmitted noise within the building.

**(Note:** *If I have a flexible budget, I will always go for the 15mm Sound Deadening boards)*

Some years ago, I set up a company manufacturing a closed panel building system, similar to the German products (*unfortunately, we ran out of cash before breaking even*). One of the sales promotion attractions we had in the factory, was a mock-up of a room constructed to the same spec as the panels we sold. The walls were constructed of 100mm CLS timber, with rockwool sound insulation between the plasterboards, and we used 15mm Soundbloc plaster boards for the walls. The outside of the room was covered in 9.7mm OSB board (*the same material used in standard timber frames*). The room had no ceiling but did have joists fitted.

I used to take prospective clients into this room and simply say to them "*What does it feel like in here?*". The answer was always either "*It feels very solid*", or "*It feels very strong*".

I have still never come up with a sensible reason why a room can *feel* solid or strong, but the only difference between the walls of that room, and standard timber frame walls, was that we fully insulated the walls, and used 15mm Soundbloc boards instead of 12mm standard boards. That same *feel* was present in every house we built using our system. I can only put the effect down to the sound deadening effect of the insulation and the special plasterboard working together to remove any echo that might have otherwise be heard (*a bit like knocking on a thick solid oak table, as opposed to knocking on a cheap, oak veneered table*).

All the new houses we now build, include the increased levels of sound insulation in the internal walls and between floors, and we offer an upgrade option to the 15mm Soundbloc plasterboards. If you have the budget to cover both of those upgrades, it could be worth giving the idea some consideration.

## THING 127: **CONSIDER FITTING FIRE DOORS**

The previous section talked about soundproofing the building *solid* internal doors as part of that process. Swapping the solid doors for Building regs compliant fire doors, would further improve the levels of soundproofing, as well as providing increased protection for the building's occupants in the unlikely event of fire.

Fire doors have come a long way over the past few years. Here is an image of the fire doors we installed at our most recent development. This particular one is supplied by Howdens Joinery (*a National supplier*), but similar doors are widely available. These were £99 each, but due to the weight of the door, you will also need to fit three heavy duty hinges to each one, which, depending on what finish you choose (chrome / stainless steel), will cost an extra £10 or so per door (*one extra hinge plus fitting*).

As well as the increased fire protection they offer, the difference in soundproofing between a decent £60 standard door, and a £100 fire door in the same style, is significant. For a 4 bed detached house, you may need 12 to 15 internal doors, so the upgrade costs from standard hollow doors, to fire doors would cost you around £500 to £600.

Whether you are spending extra money to soundproof the house, or if you just like the idea of the extra safety that fire doors offer, this is an option worth considering.

# THING 128: VAPOUR BARRIER

You only need to know about vapour barriers if you are building using timber frame, or some of the other kit build products. It is a moisture impermeable layer, that is fitted between the timber frame and the plasterboard, as a barrier to moisture travelling in either direction.

Until recently, simple plastic sheeting has been the material of choice for this task, bought in rolls, the sheet is simply rolled out and stapled to the timber studs that make up the frame of the external walls. The sheets are overlapped at the joints and taped.

Recently, other vapour barrier solutions have become available, that provide the vapour shield, and also help to insulate the walls. These new products can be significantly more expensive than plastic, but they can potentially allow you to reduce the amount of standard thermal insulation required within the external walls.

We used one of these products on our most recent build: *"Superfoil SF60"* which allowed us to downgrade the rest of the insulation within the walls, from solid foam (*expensive*), to rockwool (*cheap*), and still conform to Building Regs requirements.

External walls in all new homes are now required to achieve high levels of thermal insulation. The levels of the insulation are measured by giving them a "U" value. The lower the "U" value of your external wall, the warmer the house will be. (*you don't really need to worry about what a "U" value is, or how it is calculated. You just have to achieve it*).

At the time I am writing this, the "U" value requirement for an external wall is 0.18 $W/m^2K$, or less. Plastic vapour barrier contributes just about zero to achieve this target.

My reason for trying out the new products, was to see which method is least expensive to achieve the required "U" value: The standard plastic vapour barrier and solid foam insulation, or insulated vapour barrier and mineral wool insulation. The result? Overall, when you include: Labour / materials / waste, I think the new system worked out slightly cheaper on this house, but I suggest that you do your own cost reconciliation before making any decision on which method to use for your own project.

One thing to bear in mind when you consider your choices on this subject, is that, where the solid foam insulation has to be accurately cut to size for each void it has to fill (*not an easy task*), rockwool and similar products are easy and quick to install. So, where you may need to pay a joiner to fit the solid foam, you could probably fit the mineral wool, Superfoil, or one of the other insulating vapour barrier products, yourselves.

To find information on the SF60 vapour barrier, go to:
https://www.superfoil.co.uk/vapour-control

# THING 129: PLASTER SKIM v TAPING AND JOINTING

Whichever type of build you go for, whether it be traditional build, timber frame, or any of the other available systems, the chances are that you will have some walls that need to be plaster boarded, then finished with either a *plaster skim,* or by *taping and jointing.* Skimming is by far the most popular method of the two, but which would be the best choice for your project?

**Plaster skim:**

I have used skimmed plaster finishes on probably 90% of the residential projects I have been involved with, but probably only on around 50% to 60% of the commercial projects.

Skimming is a tried and trusted system, that has been around for a long time. For professionals, it is simple and relatively quick to apply, sets the same day and can usually be painted within a couple of weeks (*depending on the moisture content in the air*). Although the product has no major negative aspects, it does have a couple of minor annoyances:

1) Where the plaster skim covers the screws used to fit the boards, if the screws have not been fully tightened, over time, "popping" can occur, causing a small circular piece of plaster be pushed out of the surface (*see image*). These then need to be removed, filled, sanded down and repainted. If the repair is not done properly, once it is repainted with fresh paint, it can leave a bright spot on the wall, which can look just as bad as the original problem. To minimise the risk of this, try to use the same pot of paint for the repair that was used originally, and use the paint brush to "fade" the new paint out over a larger area, so there is no definite sharp, circular area of fresh paint around the repair.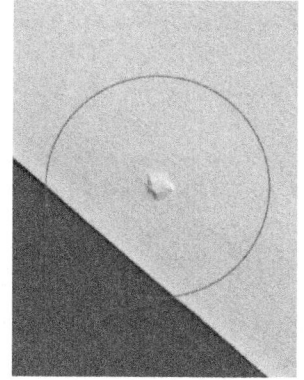

2) When the building becomes inhabited, and the heating system starts being used, everything starts to dry out, in the case of the timber elements (*walls, floors, ceilings etc*), this can lead to slight shrinkages occurring. As the timber shrinks, tiny hairline cracks can start to appear. These can grow to be clearly visible over a couple of months.
To fix this problem, once the house has fully dried out (*after 6 months or so*), we generally go back and do a *6 month snag,* where the cracks all get filled with fine filler, sanded, and repainted.

Apart from those two slight annoyances, nothing else has yet come along that has really threatened the dominance of plaster skimming, at least in the housing industry.

**Tape and Joint:**

Although I have only used this system on around 10% of my residential builds, given the choice, I would probably use it all the time. If set up properly, the application process can be far faster and less labour intensive and the drying out times can be shorter (*which makes it popular on commercial projects*). As with the skim finish, it gives a good quality finished surface, ready to paint.

**How does it work?**

If you are using a tape and joint finish to the walls and ceilings, you will need to use specially made plasterboards. For plaster skimming you will use standard *square edged* boards, for taping and jointing, you will use *tapered edge* boards (*see image*).

Once all the boards have been fitted, a layer of tape and a slurry mix (*similar in texture to a powder mixed filler*) is applied to all the joints, the corners of the walls and the ceilings, using either a wallboard knife, or a specially designed professional applicator. The applicator does the same job as the wallboard knife, but about 5 times faster.

Once that layer has dried, another coat of filler is applied (*this time without the tape*), approximately twice as wide as the first coat. That dries, and a third (*top*) coat is applied. The screw heads also receive a covering of the filler. Once the surfaces are completely dry (*usually after 2 or 3 days*), everything is sanded down to give a smooth finished surface. The result is a surface that can be good as a plaster skim.

**So, why don't I use tape and joint on every job?**

1) Good *Tape and Jointing* contractors are quite hard to find. For every twenty plasterers, there may be one tape and jointer.
2) The system is not something residential house builders are used to using, and when they hear about how it is done, they tend to be a bit nervous of it.
3) Most of the professional tape and jointers that I come across (*the ones who use the professional application equipment*), are not particularly interested in housing. They make good money on the big commercial jobs. The people who tape and joint single houses tend to do the job by hand, which is much slower than using the applicator, and is probably comparable in the time it takes, to skimming.

*You can find taping and jointing videos showing both the hand applied and the professional application methods by searching "Gyproc taping and jointing videos".*

# THING 130: STORAGE CYLINDER SYSTEMS v COMBI SYSTEMS

*If you are not familiar with the different types of domestic hot water and heating systems available for residential installations, it is a good idea to talk to your plumbing and heating installer to get their advice, before you decide which route to go down.*

Here, I am looking at the systems, rather than the boilers. The common residential systems are *Cylinder systems* and *Combi boiler systems*.

**A cylinder system** uses a small boiler and a large storage cylinder. The boiler tops up the cylinder with hot water when it is needed (*or when you programme it to*), so theoretically, you always have a decent supply of hot water for everything you need.

The weakness with this system is that at times of high use, the hot water can run out and you may have to wait for some time before it re-heats.

**A Combi system** uses a larger boiler, and heats water almost instantly as and when you need it. It does not use a cylinder.

The size of the boiler will depend on the anticipated demand for hot water at peak times.

Combi systems are cheaper to install. Although the boiler needs to be larger, there are no costs involved in buying and installing a cylinder (*plus all the pipework and fittings that go with it*). Most combi's can be wall mounted, however, if you are expecting a constantly high level of demand for hot water, the average wall mounted combi can struggle a bit, so you might need to pay more for a large, high capacity floor standing model.

One popular benefit of the combi system is that showers are fed at full pressure, giving a *power shower* experience.

I have used both systems and much prefer the combi boiler system, as much for its simplicity as anything else. If you choose this option, go for a boiler from a manufacturer with a good reputation for reliability.

You may find this link useful: https://www.boilerguide.co.uk/articles/cat/boiler-makes

# THING 131: AIRTIGHTNESS

Again, at the risk of appearing to be very negative about anything new or environmentally friendly, I have to say that I think this is one of the daftest things that has been introduced to the UK building industry in quite a long time (*if you have a different opinion, please feel free to let me know why*).

**Why do I think it is a waste of time and money?**

Every new build house now has to pass an airtightness test. What could be wrong with that? Making sure that warm air is not escaping from the building throughout the year, wasting the finite resources of the planet?

**_This_ is what is wrong with that:**

Here is how it works: Before carrying out an airtightness test, the builder has to spend considerable time going around the building, trying to find anywhere where air could potentially escape through the envelope of the building. Even the tiniest of cracks or gaps can reduce the overall airtightness. Things like tiny bits of plaster missing around spotlight fittings, hairline cracks at plaster joints, tiny gaps behind the skirtings, under the timber frames, poor sealing around the window and door openings, poorly fitting loft hatches, badly patched up holes in walls, that had originally been made for pipework to come in to, or go out of the building……..and so on).

The tester then arrives, and goes around the house, sealing up all the big holes they can find, the ones where noticeable amounts of air will escape while the test is being carried out and thus (*theoretically*) also when the building is in use. Things like letter plates, ventilation duct holes in the kitchen, utility room, bathrooms etc.

Once everything is sealed, using a special pump system, air inside the house is pumped out, causing the inside of the building to have a negative air pressure. The tester then waits for a few minutes and watches his instruments to see if the air pressure is returning to normal, and if so, how quickly. The speed of the increase in air pressure within the building tells him or her whether or not the house passes the test. If it fails, the process will be repeated, and this time the tester and the builder can go round together, listening for "hissing" noises, which would highlight where air is getting back in. If the house fails the test again, any weak spots found will have to be rectified, and the tester will need to come back another day, to do the test again. This could lose up to a week of progress on the completion of the job, and potentially cause problems for the people who may be waiting to move in.

And what happens when the test is all done? The tester goes round and takes all the seals off all the places they were fitted (*the letter plates, the ventilation holes etc*), allowing the air to escape through them, *from that moment on!* So, in fact, the whole process was carried out to find the tiniest of cracks where air could get out, and to fill them, whilst the great big holes such as 4" ventilation ducts in the bathrooms and kitchen, are left open.

My question is simply: ***What is the point?***

The house is never going to be pressurised to an extent where warm air is forced out through hairline cracks, or through a tiny gaps behind the skirting, underneath the timber frame. So, when the doors and windows are all closed, the only place it will escape, will be places such as through the letter plate, and the vent holes that have now all been opened back up!

*And, as final rant: If keeping the air inside the building is so important, why are "they who must be obeyed" enforcing the use of mechanical ventilation, that regularly expels air from within the house, in order to brings fresh air in? How much heat is lost via the heat exchanger each time this happens? Is all the expense, time, and effort in getting the house completely airtight, **really** just to save the tiniest amount of heat loss that could theoretically get out through hairline cracks? Or am I just missing something?*

**Comment invited.**

## THING 132: SPRINKLERS

If you are now expecting me to grumble about yet *another "new-fangled gadget"* that has been landed on us poor, picked upon self-builders, surprise! Having now used sprinkler systems three times, I think this is actually a good idea!

When I first heard that sprinklers were being introduced, and possibly becoming mandatory, like many people, I had visions of houses being flooded with water, and all the furniture and people's belongings being ruined. Thankfully, that is not how the system works.

Sprinklers are not yet mandatory across the whole of the UK, but they probably soon will be. Living in Wales, where they are already mandatory, I am now getting used to installing them.

To explain how sprinkler systems work, the easiest thing for me to do is to run through the system as we have installed it in our new homes.

The sprinklers themselves are set in the ceilings of all levels of the building. Each sprinkler has a maximum coverage radius of about 8', so, allowing a bit of overlap, the maximum spacing of the sprinkler heads is about 15ft, depending on the size and shape of the room, and any obstructions that might restrict this area and require extra sprinkler heads to be fitted.

The sprinklers fittings themselves are fairly unobtrusive. The ones we have installed comprise a simple flat circular metal plate, about 1mm thick, which sits under the ceiling, with a small gap of about 1mm between the top of the plate and the ceiling. *(Note: airtightness weakness alert!)*

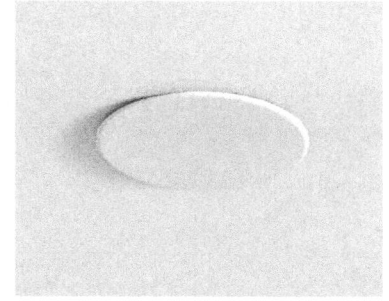

The pipework linking all the sprinklers is permanently filled with water, so there is no delay in delivery once the system is activated.

In the event of the temperature in any part of the building exceeding 30 degrees centigrade above average ambient (*expected*) temperature, the nearest sensor(s) to where that heat is located, will be triggered. *Not the full system*, just the sprinklers that are in the immediate vicinity of the temperature increase (*which means that my initial fears about all my belongings being destroyed were unfounded*).

The system can be quickly turned off once it has done its job, by means of an "on off" lever or valve.

The first system we installed in a large 5 bedroomed house over 3 floors, cost £3,800, but by the time we installed the system in the third house, that price had come down to £3,100. I would imagine the price will continue to drop, as competition between suppliers increases.

Whether or not you are required to install sprinklers, especially if you are building a three storey house (*which needs a fireproof corridor with self-closing doors if you don't have sprinklers, but just standard fire doors if you do*), I think they are worth at least looking into.

## THING 133: SECOND FIX INSTALLATIONS AND STAIRS

We are now moving away from the *build* phase of the project, to the *fit out* phase. This is where you get the chance to add your own design ideas and finishing touches, to create a finished product to be proud of, that meets your needs and suits the lifestyles of you and your family.

After the plastering has been completed, you will move on to the second fix stage of the plumbing, electrical, joinery and possibly the sprinklers. You might also start to think about getting some paint on the walls (*although this work should be left for a while if the walls are not yet dry*).

You now need to decide what sort of look and feel you want to achieve for the finished house. Do you want to follow one visual theme throughout, or let each member of the family have a free range of choice in their own personal spaces? The first materials you will need will be the internal doors, skirtings, architraves, and stairs.

So, how do you try to ensure that you make the right choices?

Even if everyone is being allowed to make their own choices for their own spaces, it is a good idea to follow one general visual theme throughout the house, a single style, *such as "Contemporary", "Traditional", or even "Uniquely You"*.

Bearing that in mind, you will have limitless choices of colours, wall coverings, furniture, and other products, and it can all get a bit overwhelming at this stage. The trick here, is to keep everything as simple as possible. One thing that I have found self-builders tend to be fearful of, is making wrong decisions. The decision to build a house was possibly the biggest, most important project you have ever made, and you want to do your utmost best to make sure that you get everything right. So, here is a well meant reality check:

*You will make mistakes. Some of you will make a few, some of you will make many of them. Does it matter in the large scheme of things?* **Very rarely.** *Could the mistakes ruin the project?* **Not unless you do something incredibly stupid** *(which is unlikely).*

I have completed 5 of my own self-builds. I have been proud of each one, but in one way or another, none of them have been perfect. The first thing that happens as soon as I move into a new self-build house, is that I start to see the mistakes I have made, in room sizes, decoration choices, socket and switch positions, furniture choices, carpets, ironmongery, and dozens of other little things. None of that though has taken away *any* of the pleasure I feel every time I enter my own, wonderful, self-designed and built home. You will probably feel exactly the same, even if you do mess up on some finishing details. These are normally easily fixable later anyway.

So, having said that, when it comes to making decisions on your second fix materials, starting with the doors, skirtings, architraves and stairs, just take your time, do some research (*preferably together with the rest of the family*), make a decision on what sort of visual theme you want to achieve, look at your choices, get some brochures and prices and get out and buy some stuff!

**Note:** The stairs possibly need a bit more consideration than a lot of the other items at this stage. Are you ok with a standard set of stairs, or do you want to make a statement with them? This decision will partly depend on your available budget. "*Posh*" stairs are expensive but can add the finishing touch to the whole project. Personally, I stick with standard stairs, on the basis that I only use them to get from one floor to another. If I have got £10,000 spare, I would rather spend it upgrading the kitchen and / or bathrooms.

## THING 134: BRUSH PAINTING v ROLLER PAINTING v SPRAYING

If you watch the self-build programmes on tv, have you noticed how many people paint their houses using paint brushes? Most, it seems. Given all the options available, painting walls with a paint brush would be my last choice.

**Why?** Apart from being very slow, unless you are a professional decorator, the chances are that the finished job will be uneven, with visible bristle stroke lines going off in all directions.

To my mind, paint brushes should be used, only for *cutting in* the corners and for the wall to ceiling intersections, plus detailing around sockets, switches, radiators, and other such fittings. The rest of the wall should be either rolled or sprayed:

**Rolling:** With a bit of practice using a roller and a decent quality paint, you should be able to achieve a high quality finish, quickly and easily. I would suggest kitting yourselves out with the professional tools, as opposed to the DIY options. Instead of using the 9" DIY paint trays and roller sets, visit a Professional Decorators Merchants and get 12" trays, or, if you are feeling brave, one of the large paint buckets. Also get three or four good quality 12" rollers, a couple of roller frames and pick up a professional quality extending pole to fit your roller frame. Using a pole will speed up the job and take a lot of the bending and stretching work away, which on a large project can be a godsend, especially if you have a dodgy back.

That is all the rolling equipment you will need for the main walls and ceilings. If there are two of you doing the job, get two sets, so you don't end up fighting over who gets to use the pole (*by the way, a couple of sets of 2 or 3 step "step stools" stools will be needed for getting up to cut in the wall to ceiling joints*)

Take some time to learn how to load the roller up, so that you get plenty of paint on it and can then get it to the wall without dripping it all over the floor (one hint to help with this is moving the tray or bucket around the floor as you paint, so it is right next to the part of the wall you are just about to paint.

Once you get the hang of rolling using professional gear, you won't want to go back to brush painting for anything other than detailing. I have been roller painting for many years and have come to the point where I actually find it quite relaxing to do! (*No, I don't want to come and paint your house!*)

**Search:** *Paint rolling instructional videos.*

**Spraying:** Just prior to the recession in 2008, I had a house built in Florida. It was quite an eye opening experience. America seem to be miles ahead of us in many ways, but this is especially apparent in the way they build houses. One of the systems regularly used over there, is paint spraying. Not only for standard paint, but also for textured coatings, to both the internal and external walls. The results are good, and it takes a fraction of the time to paint a full house, compared to rolling.

Spraying is now becoming a more available option in the UK. Systems for paint spraying can be either hired, from around £80 / week, or bought, from around £250 (*I actually bought a system from ALDI for less than £200, just to see how good it was. It was OK for smaller DIY decorating jobs, but possibly not to do a full house, and it takes a bit of learning*).

A good spraying job can give an excellent finished surface. In fact, it can be so good that, if you need to repaint anywhere at any time in the future, once you have sprayed an area, the parts of the wall that have been rolled can look a bit amateurish. To avoid the mismatch, our paint spraying company has one person spraying, and one person following on, rolling the sprayed surface with a 12" roller, so that it looks like a normal rolled surface.

**Search:** *Spray painting instructional videos*

## Tools and equipment:

**Brushes:** Whichever painting system you use, you will still need to use brushes for the areas where the rollers can't reach and to do all the fiddly, detailed bits (*tops of skirtings, corners, around radiators, etc*).

As I suggested for buying rollers and trays, it is a good idea to kit yourselves out with a set of good quality, professional synthetic brushes (*why not bristle brushes? No matter how much I pay for bristle brushes, I always seem to get bristle loss, constantly finding the odd bristle in the surface of an area I have just painted, and ending up with paint all over my fingers as I try to extract it. Synthetic brushes seem much less prone to this problem*).

***Note:*** *My favourite paint brush is the "cutting in" brush. I only found out about these when one came free with a pack of mixed brushes. They are great for painting accurately round sockets and switches and cutting into the tops of skirtings. I suggest you get yourselves one of these.*

**Paints:** Using good quality paint can actually save you money, compared to using cheap paint. I discovered this fact about 25 years ago and have bought decent paint ever since. For the walls I usually use *obliterating emulsion*, or similar. As the name suggests, it is thick and covers well. So well in fact, that often it really needs one thick coat, plus a thin coat, to give a professional looking finish.

If you use a cheap paint on a newly plastered wall, the first coat gets sucked into the plaster and almost disappears, and because the paint is normally thin in texture, and of low quality, two more coats can still leave a wall or ceiling looking only half finished.

If you are going to do the painting yourselves, think about the time and effort it will take you to paint *three full coats* on *all the walls and ceilings*. For a four bedroomed house, two of you, working full days, could probably do a coat in four to five days. So, three coats would take you 12 to 15 days (*not including skirtings, architraves, window cills etc*). If you could reduce that to one thick coat, plus a quick top up coat, and free up some more time up to do other things, the extra £15 each, for half a dozen large or so 15 litre buckets of the good quality paint (*maybe around £75 to £100 in total*), would probably represent very good value.

**Other equipment:** When you visit the Decorators Merchants, don't be afraid to pick their brains. Tell them what you are going to be doing, ask them if they will be able to give you their *best* trade prices (*as, for a short period of time, you will be buying the same* *quantities of paint as you would be if you were a professional decorator*), and ask them to show you what equipment they would recommend for the jobs you need to do.


## THING 135: **KITCHENS**

This one, single subject probably gets more attention than any other during a self-build project. The house design is important, so are the materials choices, the bathrooms, the finishes, and the furnishings, but nothing seems to attract the long term attention of self-builders, more than the kitchen. Why is that? Well, it could be that we, as humans tend to be attracted to *shiny things*, and the kitchen is often literally the *shiniest thing* in the house! But it is also the place that often ends up being the social centre of the house, the centre of activity for the family and the natural gathering point when you entertain guests. So, because we want the rooms we are going use most, to be the nicest places in the house, we tend to put a lot of time, effort, and money in to getting the kitchen right.

How do you get the kitchen right? You start by doing a bit of homework:

Grab a pen and paper and stand in the kitchen where you are living now. Write down what you like about it and what don't you like about it. For example:

- Are there enough floor and wall units?
- Are they all big enough, or are some of them too small and basically a waste of space?
- Do you have enough drawer space?
- How does this kitchen cope with all the recycling of waste that you are now having to do?
- Would you change the cooking equipment? Maybe for a waist height, built in double oven, a range cooker, an Aga or a Rayburn?
- What about the extractor fan above the hob? Is it something you would choose again, or would you look for something different?
- Would you like a large American Fridge Freezer with an ice dispenser?
- Where would the sink, washing machine and dishwasher go in your new house? (*usually in the utility room, or if they are in the kitchen, under a window if possible, either side of your sink*).
- What about taps? Have you wanted one of the taps with a rinsing hose that pull out, or the one that boils or chills water instantly?
- Do you like your present style of worktops, or do you fancy something more sleek, slim, and modern?
- What about the cupboard units themselves, do you prefer drawers at the top of the cupboards, or have full height doors and keep all the drawers in one or two units?
- Would you like some subtle "mood" lighting in this room?
- Would you want a TV in the kitchen, on the wall perhaps?

Once you have completed an investigation of your old kitchen go, and have a look at what is available in the shops. Choose two or three kitchen suppliers. If you have plenty of money to spend, maybe one *high end*, one *mid-range* and one reputable *trade supplier* (*we usually get quotes from Wren, Benchmarx and/or one or two of the kitchen suppliers linked to the National Builders Merchants, who have showrooms at their depots*).

**When you visit any of these places, remember this:** Push the fact that you are, to all intents and purposes, a *trade buyer*. Make the most of that fact by doing some hard negotiation on pricing. Also compare prices between the retail and the trade suppliers (*theoretically, there should be no comparison, the trade suppliers should be able to give you both quality and prices that the retails suppliers simply cannot match*).

The other trick I suggest you try, is to visit some of the local and National housebuilder's developments. Tell the salespeople that you are thinking of moving to the area and go and have a look at their kitchens. The builders usually spend a lot of money on their showhouses and make the kitchens look as nice as they can be. If nothing else, you may get a few ideas from the visit.

Once you have spent three or four days doing everything I have suggested above, you should be able to make some definite decisions. If not, give yourself a talking to! – You have got a lot of other things to do as well, so get this sorted soon!

(*Note: As I mentioned earlier in the book, DO NOT order your kitchen too early. It is a good idea to do your research early on, but don't order anything until you need to, and until you know you will be ready for it. There is a good chance that you will change your mind on things as the project proceeds*).

**How much should you pay for your kitchen?** That depends on your overall budget and on the house that it is going in to. Don't spend over £15,000 on a kitchen for a small 3 bed detached house, and don't spend less than £10,000 on a kitchen for a large 5 bed detached.

As an example: The houses we sell are generally large and sell for £300,000 to £400,000 (*in South Wales*), probably more like £800,000 in the South East. We spend around £10,000 - £12,000 on the kitchens, including appliances, via the Trade suppliers. We then let the client ad some upgrades if they wish to. When they do, they will then usually spend an extra £3,000 to £4,000 on more specialist things like "Corian" worktops, specialist splashbacks, Aga's etc.

**A few tips on kitchen design:**

- Try to design kitchen using as many large units as possible. A 1200mm wide unit can cost less than twice the price of a 300mm unit (*in other words less than half the price compared to the space it fills*).
- Beware the "fiddly bits": One trick of kitchen designers, is to keep adding attractive features that you don't need, but which look nice. These items are where they make

their profits, so don't fall for it unless you fully agree that it is a worthwhile extra cost.

- There are many and varied options for worktops, check the prices ranges of all the ones you like. You might like one that would cost you £5000, and another that would cost you £500. Where large sums of money are involved, give yourselves time to consider the options before taking the plunge.

- Design plenty of room for your recycling requirements. Possibly have small recycling bins in the kitchen, and larger ones in the utility room, or maybe a posh, custom finished *under unit* area in the kitchen, with some nice bins.

- Try to keep your boiler away from the kitchen. It can be noisy (*in the utility room and/or in a cupboard if possible*).

- Look at the new styles of wall finishing's for kitchens. There are now some nice alternatives to tiles, at reasonable prices.

- Think about buying your appliances separately from your units. If you do you could save a lot of money. We use companies like "AO" (*Appliances Online*) who have competitive prices to start with and will knock up to 15% off if you spend over a certain amount.


## THING 136: **BATHROOMS**

Thankfully, long gone are the avocado coloured bathrooms, and we have thankfully also moved on from the days where every bathroom had standard white cheap baths and basins, with a pair of basic, chrome and plastic pillar taps, a choice of half a dozen styles of 6" x 6" tiles to choose from, and bidets in every house bigger than 2 bedrooms. And, at last, whirlpool baths also seem to be getting less popular (*no-one use them anyway, after getting over the novelty of having one*).

However, as usual, us Brits don't quite get things right. When the manufacturers realised that people wanted better quality bathrooms and a wider choice of styles, over a few years, everything to do with bathrooms went right to the opposite end of the spectrum, to where no two shops sold the same bathroom equipment, where basins, toilets, toilet seats, taps, showers and shower enclosures came in such a wide range of shapes sizes, with some *built in*, some *wall hung*, some *water saving* and showers that were so powerful it was like being bombarded with thousands of steel pellets.

So, here we are. Bathrooms are probably just behind kitchens when it comes to the money being spent on them as part of a self-build. But are we choosing sensibly, or are we all getting a bit too carried away?

At the end of the day, a bath is a bath, a toilet is a toilet. We all want attractive bathrooms, but we would also like them to do their jobs properly, and not be overpriced. Sadly, a lot of the equipment you will come across doesn't score well in either of those two categories. Unfortunately, it is sometimes hard to tell which is the good stuff, which is vastly overpriced, and which represents good value for money.

Here is a quick look at the individual bits of the bathroom:

## Baths:

Baths are becoming less popular as more people have become used to showering , but for reselling the house at a later date, you should always install at least one bath, ideally in the family bathroom (*as opposed to the en-suite*).

**Size / Shape:** A standard bath measures 1700mm x 700mm, as it has done for decades. With one curved end (*for us to lean back on*), and one flattish end, where the taps are.

There are now many variations on that tried and trusted style, many of which may look pretty, but detract from what the bath is designed to do. Here are a few examples:

- The bath will be wide at one end and narrow at the other, so one end can also be used as a shower. *Problem: It is not always comfortable to lie in.*
- Both ends are flat (*no curved end to lean on*) and sloped. *Problem: If you are not tall enough to jam your feet up against the opposite end, you can constantly slide down the slope into the water. Also, the bottom, flat part of the bath is too short for the length of your body, meaning your feet have to sit halfway up the slope at the other end, probably out of the water.*
- The Taps and pop-up plug hole are halfway down one side: *Problem: When you top the bath up, the (sometimes) very hot water comes out of the tap, straight on to you, so you have to contort yourself to get out of its way before it burns you. Also, as you move around in the bath, you constantly slide over the plug hole, which can have rough edges.*

There are many more design weaknesses to be found in baths, I could fill a page with examples, but instead, here are the things I *look for* when I choose a bath:

➢ Where room permits, I always buy oversized baths at 1800mm x 800mm, curved at both ends, but with both ends almost vertical. The extra length suits taller people better, without using too much extra water. The two curved ends mean two adults or children can easily share one bath. More fun & saves water. The steep ends mean that you don't tend to slide down into the water.

➢ When I can fit 1800mm x 800mm baths, I do go for the centre taps and plug hole because the extra width means that the water doesn't need to fall on to the person in the bath. I just make sure the plug hole is unobtrusive and doesn't have any features that could be uncomfortable to slide over.

➢ I always choose decent quality attractive mixer taps, with a hose and shower head attached (*to allow for hair rinsing and making cleaning the bath easier*). One of my favourite tap styles is the "waterfall" mixer tap, with shower head.

> Unless room is very tight, I don't put the main shower over the bath. If I did, I wouldn't be able to make the other choices I have just listed.

*When it comes to choosing a bath, just make sure you give your shortlisted choices a critical look over. Are they all style and no substance, or will they do the job you want them to do? And are they at the right price (compared to at least 2 other suppliers)?*

## Basins:

When I use a bathroom basin, I don't ask much of it. I want it to be big enough, but not too big. I want it to hold water without it leaking away through an ill-fitting plug, and I want it to empty properly when the plug is pulled out. With some of the basins available, that seems to be too much of an ask.

Some of the fashionable bowls look very attractive. Round glass bowls made of coloured glass or other high quality materials, sitting on top of a vanity unit. Visually, they are lovely, but practically, the bowls are just too small. Any decent rate of water flow from a tap can swirl straight up and out of the opposite side of the bowl. When you use them, you can end up with more water outside the bowl than in it, so they need cleaning more often.

The shape of the bowl is important. Some of the modern basins are nearly flat on the bottom, so the last bits of water sometimes don't drain away, and you have to swill the bowl by hand. How daft is that?

Wall hung basins, with all the pipework hidden inside the wall, again look nice, but what if there is a leak, or you want to change the taps? You can end up having to remove wall tiles and plasterboard to get at the fittings, just to do a relatively simple, quick job.

So, for a basin, this is what I look for:

> A decent oval, "D" shaped, or even rectangular bowl.
> Around 450mm (18") width.
> Steep sides, especially near the rim.
> A base that allows the water to drain quickly and fully.
> Somewhere to put soap and maybe one or two other small items.
> Nice taps that match the bath taps.
> A plug that works and looks like it will do so for a few years.
> If it is wall mounted, the pipework should still be accessible, without damaging the wall.

## WC's:

Toilets are doing their best to look nice, but in doing so are sometimes becoming impractical. There is almost no such thing now, as a standard toilet, unless you buy the £30 versions that landlords chuck into their low rent *buy to let* flats.

As soon as you move away from the standard w.c, the fact that the word *standard* is missing from their description, is where you will find the problems.

Toilets are not complicated. They have four main components, the bowl, the seat, and the cistern, plus the workings that fit inside the cistern. You wouldn't think we could go far wrong with a product that has so few options to mess around with. However, as designers have come up with the multitude of new designs for toilets, to try to make them less utilitarian and more attractive, they have created problems for us (*the public*) for the future.

Seats are now made in dozens of different shapes, but seat sizes and the cistern inner workings are often designed to fit just one particular range. That means that if you ever need to change the seat, or if the flushing mechanism goes faulty, you will need to find exactly the same kit to replace the original. That will probably be fine for three or four years, until that model is replaced, but what about 10 years down the line?

Concealed wc's have similar problems to wall hung basins but are more likely to need maintenance sooner. The two weak points with modern toilets are 1) The seat repeatedly coming loose and being difficult to re-tighten. 2) The flushing system going faulty. The first of those problems is quite easily fixed, but if you have not left an *easy access* cover (*which will often spoil the look of your tiling*), it can be a major job to get at the cistern to fix it.

Here is what I look for  from a w.c:

➢ A standard shape and size of bowl and seat.
➢ A popular make that has been around for a few years, so is more likely to have spares available if and when I need them.
➢ Soft close seat.
➢ Top fix seat (much easier to tighten up and/or change the seat)

## Showers / Shower enclosures:

It is hard to know where to start with showers. The market is so diverse now, with new products and ideas being introduced all the time, that this book cannot do the topic justice.

The best information I can give you for when you are choosing showers and shower enclosures is:

➢ 750mm x 750mm showers are a bit too small. Only use them where there are space restrictions. 900mm x 900mm give a bit of room to move around in. 1200mm x 900mm is as large as you will generally need.
➢ For tight rooms, quadrant shower enclosures are a good choice, as they usually have doors that slide left and right, making it easier to get in and out of the shower in tight spaces. Hinged doors can be restrictive where there is little room for them to swing without hitting walls or equipment.

- Shower enclosure prices can vary greatly, for pretty much the same thing. Check out the same, and similar products online before making final choices.
- Level access shower trays are great if you have mobility problems, but the waste trap has to fitted within the floor space, and that needs to be done at first fix stage (*so you need to make your choice before you get to that part of the build*). With standard shower trays (*where you step up onto the tray*), the waste trap can be above the floorboards.
- Be careful about buying your shower trays from one manufacturer and shower enclosures from another. They can vary slightly in design and shape, which could cause fitting problems.
- Exposed shower valves sit in front of the tiles, concealed valves sit inside the walls. If there are problems with a concealed valve at any time in the future, the tiles will need to be removed (*and later refitted*), to be able to get to and fix the problem. During around 40 years of house building, I have had three concealed showers "blow" soon after the client has moved in (*flooding numerous rooms*). The chance of that happening to you is something you should plan against if at all possible. These days, if I have a choice, I always fit exposed valves.
- If you have a combi boiler system, the showers can run directly off it, so they benefit from the high flow rate it can produce, in other words, you should get the *power shower* experience from all the showers installed in the house. A cylinder system won't necessarily give you the same rate of flow.

## THING 137: TILING

Along with kitchens and bathrooms, wall tiling has become a much more important part of house building in recent years. Floor tiling? Not so much. 15 to 20 years ago, the bathroom wall tiling would often only include a splash back to the sink, and three tiles height above the bath (*or full tiling if there was a shower installed over the bath* ).

I like the modern approach to wall tiling, especially with all the attractive products, styles, materials, and ideas that are now available. A good tiling job can finish a room off spectacularly and can add value to the completed house. However, in the drive to make the most of each bathroom and the kitchen, it is easy to overspend on tiling. Here are some things to bear in mind as you move forward:

- **See before you buy:** Tile prices can vary hugely between local and National suppliers and between shops and the internet. I would personally always recommend buying tiles and accessories from shops, rather than online, so you can see in real life, the tile colours and size, and can feel the texture. A photograph on a computer screen is not the best way to appreciate these details.
- **Shop around:** I normally compare at least three suppliers before making any decisions. For our recent project, we went to one National and two local suppliers.

To get a decent tile from the National suppliers, we were looking at prices of around £40 to £50 / sq m (inc VAT). We negotiated a 5% discount on those prices. We then went to a small local supplier, where the prices were slightly better. Finally, we looked at another local specialist trade tile supplier, with a large warehouse.

For the same quality of tile that would be priced around £40 to £50 / sq m at either of the first two suppliers, here we would pay £15 to £20 / sq m. I cannot guarantee that you would have the same experience where you live, but it is well worth doing some shopping around to check.

- **Beware feature tiles:** Once you have chosen your basic tiles, you will often want to add some feature tiles and/or border tiles, to add a bit of contrast. Be aware that these tiles could sometimes double the overall cost of your purchase.

  Where a nice tile might cost £20 / sq m at the trade shop (at maybe 33 tiles per sq.m), or around **60p each**, feature tiles in the same range could cost upwards of **£4 each**. In other words, you could almost double the overall cost of the *whole job*, just by adding a border, or some other feature. Thankfully, the present trend in tile fashion is towards simplicity, so borders and features are becoming less popular anyway.

- **Be aware of the cost of the fixing materials:** The materials you will need for wall tiling include: Adhesive (*normally waterproof*), edging trims, corner trims, spacers, and grout. You will also need a tile cutter (preferably electric) and probably a diamond drill bit, for making holes in tiles for wires and screws for the various wall fixings you may be including.

  If you go for ready mixed adhesive, try to get the big "trade" buckets, they can work out a lot cheaper. Alternatively, buy the bags of powder, and mix it on site yourselves (*the cheapest option*). Grouts are available in many colours. Ask your supplier what colour they recommend for your choice of tiles. Edging and corner trims come in plastic or metal and can cost from a couple of pounds, to over £10 each. You might need a dozen or so of these, so again, watch the cost.

- **Floor tiling** is slowly getting less popular as new flooring products enter the market. A nice tiled floor can add to the overall attractiveness of a new house, but over time it can start to look a bit tatty, once problems like cracks in the grout and / or the tiles, dirty, stained, mouldy or even missing grout, start to become apparent.

  Before you make your decisions on floor coverings, have a look at some of the mainstream flooring suppliers. There are now some really nice, practical alternatives to ceramic floor tiles that are suitable for use in bathrooms.

- **Plywood upstairs:** If you go for floor tiling onto wooden floorboards, you will first need to fix a sheet of plywood over the original floorboards. This will help to prevent the tile joints moving and cracking. Your joiners should be aware of what they need to do, you will just need to get them the materials they need.

- **Get fixed prices for labour:** Labour costs will vary depending on the type and size of tile, the complexity of the pattern and the amount of any extra feature tiling. Small tiles take a lot more time to fix, borders and features will also add to the labour cost.

If your tiler tells you on the phone, that their fixing rate is £20 / sq m, make sure they see the rooms, and your choice of tiles before you agree to use them. If you don't, once they get to see the tiles, the special tiles, and the borders, they could increase their prices significantly.

- **Silicone all the corners and joints:** Water will escape through the tiniest of holes or thinnest of cracks. Make sure all your bathrooms are properly sealed, using a good quality *flexible* silicone sealant. Don't think that just grouting the edges and corners around the bath will do the job. As the house dries out, and the bath gets repeatedly filled and emptied, the grout will crack and water will be able to escape, potentially over time, causing damage to the tiling, as well as the walls and floorboards.

- **Use anti-mould silicone:** All silicone sealants will be prone to a bit of mould growth. Ask your supplier which products are least susceptible to this problem. It is worth paying a couple of pounds a tube extra, so that you don't have to de-mould the bath and sink as often.

## THING 138: **WET ROOMS**

You might be thinking about incorporating either wet rooms or walk through showers into your new build. Both of these are good options to consider. As well as adding a touch of luxury, they can be especially useful for the elderly, or people with restricted mobility.

If the wet room is to provide facilities for people with any type of disabilities, it is worth thinking about installing it on the ground floor, where it can be accessed without requiring a trip upstairs.

There are various ways to install wet rooms. The whole room can be the wet area, or just one area, with a screen of some description, to divide it from the rest of the room (*this set up is also known as a walk through shower*).

Wet rooms can be installed onto either timber or solid floors, but for them to work, properly there have to be "falls" (slopes) built into the base, to allow water to flow naturally to a drainage outlet.

Installing a wet room is possibly a simpler operation than you might think, but it would be difficult to explain in writing in a couple of pages, so I hunted out a couple of videos that take you through installing either a *part,* or *full* wet room.

Here are three random searches that will take you to some more information on this subject:

For installation on timber floors, go to: "*AKW TuffForm & FormSafe*" then look for the link to the video. Also try: "*Impey Aqua Dec videos*" and again find your way to the videos.

For videos of installation on concrete floors, try: "*CCL Wetrooms, linear screed drain video*".

**Wet room kit prices:** As with kitchens and bathrooms, shop around some local suppliers, including trade suppliers, then compare their  prices to what you can find online.

**Tiling:** Once you have installed the wet room, you will need to fully tile, and then seal the whole area from floor to ceiling, as well as any adjacent areas that could potentially get wet when the room is in use.

If you are on a tight budget, the thought of installing a wet room might not have occurred to you, but you might be surprised. By the time you have bought and fitted a decent power shower, a good sized shower enclosure, a tray, wastes etc and had them all fitted into a standard bathroom layout, then tiled the whole lot, you might find that installing a wet room kit instead, wouldn't cost a lot extra. It would also help to future proof the house and make it more attractive to buyers, should you ever wish to sell.

*Note: If you are installing a wet room, make sure you let the Building Regs people know, and add the installation details to your Building Regs application. If you don't, it could cause delays when they find out, and potentially halt progress until they receive the information they require.*


## THING 139: SNAGGING THE BUILDING

You may be familiar with the term "snagging" as it pertains to construction. If not, it simply means "finding the faults".

Once you are nearing completion of the building works, and thinking about booking your final inspection, it is good practice to have a detailed look around the house for anything that needs finishing, putting right, or that has been missed.

I always carry out a thorough snag at this stage. As well as looking for general faults and problems, I also look for the sorts of thing that the buyer could pick up on, but which are *not* related to Building Regulations or to the structural aspect of the build (*this less formal type of snag is called a "cosmetic snag", and includes things like marks on the paintwork, sockets fitted out of level, rough plastering, gaps in sealing around windows or bathroom equipment, door handles not working smoothly, minor creaks in the floors etc*).

The Structural snag needs to be a bit more technical and comprehensive. If you don't do a thorough job, some of the items you miss could cause the house to fail its final inspections, which could result in you having to call sub-contractors back to put things right, then re-organise the inspections. Not something you want, especially if you are planning on moving on shortly after the first inspection visit.

Here are main items I look for when I carry out a structural snagging inspection:

**Building Regs requirements:**

*All the information you need to comply with the regs will either be on your original drawings, or in the build specification (the one you will have used for your Building Regs application). You should have been checking all of these items as the building work proceeded, so theoretically, the final look around should just be a quick check to make sure you have not missed anything.*

i. **Disabled access:** Does the level access opening conform to regs? Search: https://www.gov.uk/government/publications and look for *"Approved Document M"*.

ii. **Disabled access:** Does the driveway confirm to the disability requirements for landing areas (*where people will get out of vehicles*) and falls?

iii. **Fanned Ventilators** are required in the kitchen / utility / bathrooms. These should include the required delay in the fan actually turning off after being switched off (*to remove dampness from the air in the room*).

iv. **Sockets and switches at the right heights**: Search: https://www.homebuilding.co.uk/electrics-sockets-and-switches

v. **Upper floor window openings installed correctly:** There are regulations governing windows, including cill height on upper floor windows, fire escape openings, security etc.

vi. **Ventilation in windows:** Are vents fitted as required?

vii. **Does all glazing conform to requirements:** These requirements vary from window to window and are also relevant for doors.

viii. **Door openings:** At the moment there should be 2'9" doors downstairs and minimum 2'6" doors for habitable rooms upstairs. However, as you will have read earlier in the book, I recommend fitting 2'9" doors throughout the building.

ix. **Fire doors:** If you build a house higher than 2 storeys, you will need to fit fire doors to habitable rooms. If you are installing sprinklers, you may not need these doors to be self-closing. If you are not installing sprinklers, they *will* need to be. (*These regs are changing, so check your drawings*).

x. **Security:** Are door and window locks specified and fitted as required (*possibly "secured by design"*)?

xi. **Stairs:** Do they conform to the regulations?

xii. **Running water:** The plumbing and heating system should be fully operational.

xiii. **Energy saving light bulbs:** I won't be specific on numbers here, as again, the regs are constantly changing, so check your drawings/specs.

xiv. **Ground floor W.C:** Does the door open outwards? Does the floor space in front of the toilet meet requirements for manoeuvring wheelchairs? (*this information should also be in your specification*)

xv. **Get a copy of your Airtightness test to give to the inspector.**

As the self-builder, you will not usually need to get involved in making sure the regs are being followed to the letter on everything, as you build. Your tradespeople should know what they are doing and if they are not sure of something, the information they need should be on the drawings or in the specifications. Just make sure they have copies of everything when they quote and/or when they started work on site.

## THING 140: FLOOR COVERINGS

Once all the construction work has been completed, your next task is to transform what has been a building site, into your new home (*preferably doing so before you move in. See section 149*). Some floors may have been tiled as part of the building work, but others will still need covering. Reasonable quality floor coverings for a decent sized 4 bed detached house, could cost between £4,000 and £6,000 for underlays, floor coverings, door thresholds, labour etc (*hopefully you will have budgeted for this at the outset*).

At this stage, even if you have budgeted for floor coverings, overspends could have left you short of cash by the time you get to this point. One solution would be to throw some cheap chord carpet and/or vinyl flooring down as a temporary solution, with the thought of changing it later for something decent. This may solve the immediate problem, but is not a particularly good idea for the longer term. From my own experience, and from talking to many self-builders, once you move into the house, whatever stage it is at when you do, that is how it will probably stay for many months (*again, see section 149*). You will have just gone through the exhausting process of building a new house, and if you take your foot off the accelerator now, you will find it hard to go back up through the gears in a few weeks' time. You will have also moved a lot of your furniture in, so the rooms where you have laid the cheap flooring will need to be emptied before you can carry on working on them. This would make each remaining job more complicated and disruptive.

**My recommendation:**

The difference in price between cheap cord carpet and something that will last a few years might not be as much as you would think. They both require underlay, edging strips, door bars and fitting, so those costs will stay about the same whichever you choose. The difference in carpet quality between a cheap cord carpet at £4 / sq m and something that looks and performs reasonably, at around £8 / sq m, for an average sized room of 12 sq m area, is around £50. The advantage of paying the extra £50 is that you won't then need to go back, empty the room, take the cheap carpet up (*probably throw it away*), lay the new flooring, and move all the furniture back in. The better quality floor covering will also probably do a decent job for up three or four years, depending on how much use it gets.

For a simple, attractive solution to floor covering, have a look at the new styles of self-adhesive vinyl flooring. I have recently seen this product in use in show houses and am quite impressed. It is thinner than laminate flooring but comes in similar sized planks and simply sticks down to the floor. You would need to use a decent quality product and make sure that the floor is prepared properly, but this might be a good alternative to laminates or tiles. Because it is permanently fitted, you might also be able to claim VAT back on the purchase, although I am not 100% sure of that. *(If anyone has been successful in claiming VAT back on this product, drop me a quick email to let me know).*

Have a look at flooring.uk.com/luxury-vinyl-flooring, to see examples of the product.

## THING 141: FIXING BOGGY GROUND

**Note:** *I realise that this section is only going to be useful to a limited number of people. I have personally not come across the problem until very recently. It is a problem we will have to deal with on our next development, and if it can happen to me, it can happen to anyone!*

When you carry out your site investigations, you may find that the area you are hoping to eventually turn into the lawn or patio area, is boggy, susceptible to puddling, and would not be suitable to be seeded, turfed or turned into a patio area as it is. The problem might occur only at certain times of the year, but it is something that you will need to attend to. The good news is that this can often be a relatively simple problem to fix.

When you install your surface water drainage pipework, you will usually either link it into a soakaway or a SUDS system. You can use the same process to firm up areas of boggy ground.

To fix the problem, you need to drain the water from the wet area, into a land drain. To do this, you will need to excavate a trench across the lowest part of the boggy land. This trench needs to connect to either an existing soakaway, or SUD's system, or to either of those options that is specially constructed for this particular task.

The trench is then either filled with clean stone or stone *plus* a perforated plastic pipe. A layer of Terram (*or similar*) is laid over the top of the stone (*this will stop topsoil from filtering down into the stone, eventually reducing its efficiency*).

Water runs downhill, so over time the water from the boggy area will drain into the land drain and find its way to the soakaway, where it will be temporarily be stored until it naturally dissipates. The effect won't be instantaneous, depending on the nature of the ground, it could take a few weeks to see a significant difference, but long term, this solution should enable the area to be used for the purpose you intended for it.

*Note: The size of the soakaway needs to be calculated, based on the amount of water it will need to deal with, and the porosity of the ground around it (you don't want to simply pass the problem of boggy ground from one area of your plot, to a different area). You should also include details of any land drainage system in your Building Regs specification, at the initial application stage. If you only discover the problem as you are building, discuss it with your inspector before making any firm plans, and preferably before installing your surface water drainage system.* **See:** https://www.terram.com

## THING 142: RAINWATER HARVESTING

I mentioned this system earlier. It has been around for a long time, but the increased awareness of environmental issues has now significantly raised its profile, which has resulted in some impressive new products coming on to the market.

Until a few years ago, if you wanted to install a rainwater harvesting system, the standard solution was to cut your downpipes off at about 4' above ground level and position a 40 gallon water container, with a tap fitted to it, underneath the pipe. You could then connect a hose to the tap and use the contents of the container to water the garden, wash the car etc. Although that system works perfectly well, we have now made some leaps forward in the technology and range of products that are available to you.

I particularly like the systems that include an underground storage tank, with a built in electric pump, wiring, and a filtration system. The water in the storage tank (*which will have come from your roof and driveway*) is connected, via pipework to an outlet point (*tap*) fixed to the external wall of the house. A standard hose can then be connected and the stored water used on demand, just like a normal water supply, to water the garden, wash the windows, the car and for other similar tasks that would normally use mains tap water (*which these days, usually has to be paid for*).

We are including one of these systems with each house on our new development, partly as a sales incentive, partly because it helps us conform to Build Regs for the overall site drainage, but also because it is a great idea! The system we will be using will cost around £2,500 for the kit, plus installation, but lower cost systems are available.

Here is a link to one company supplying Rainwater Harvesting Systems: *https://www.rainharvesting.co.uk/domestic-rainwater-harvesting*. There are also plenty of other suppliers/installers dotted around the UK. Just search *Rainwater harvesting* and add your location. Once you get to the relevant web pages, you should also find more information, plus some videos showing different systems and installation methods.

## THING 143: GREY WATER SYSTEMS

I am not as convinced about grey water recycling as I am about rainwater harvesting. It sounds like a sensible idea, but when you look at it a bit more closely, you might wonder if it is worth the investment.

These systems work by collecting used water from the house, usually baths & showers, but sometimes also sinks and dishwashers, depending on what sort of use they get (*detergents are hard to filter out, and could damage plants*).

The water from the appliances is cleaned using filtration, UV light and/or chemicals, then stored in a tank, either above ground or below.

The system connects, via plastic pipework, to:

1) A tap on the external wall of the house, to be re-used for cleaning the car, watering the garden etc,

2) Another tap inside the house, to be used for washing clothes and dishwashing. The theory promoted by the manufacturers, is that having this system installed could cut your mains water use by up to 50%.

The main benefits of the system are obviously related to lowering the use and waste of clean tap water, which is getting expensive to produce and which creates its own carbon footprint whilst it is being treated and fed via the mains water system, to wherever it is needed.

The downsides include:

- You are storing water that is not completely clean, and once removed from its storage tank, especially if it has been stored for some time, it could smell.
- You need to have the system designed and installed so that it works side by side with the basic plumbing system inside the house, as well as supplying an outside outlet. There will obviously be an upfront cost to this operation.
- The system uses energy and/or chemicals to clean the water, and also uses electricity to pump the water round the system. It therefore has a cost to run and maintain (*although this is not high, at probably less than £50 a year, according to the manufacturers*).
- The whole kit, plus installation can be quite costly. Systems cost between £3,000 and £6,000 and upwards of an extra £1000 for installation. There are also a maintenance costs over many years, to consider.

The main selling point for this product for you as a potential self-builder, is that the mains water to your new home will be metered. Water is already getting expensive and its cost will continue to increase.

The question is, do you think the cost of mains water will ever reach a point where cost of installing one of these systems is a worthwhile investment?

*With the latest rainwater harvesting systems providing alternative, more practical solutions for water savings, at a lower cost? Possibly not.*


## THING 144: PATIOS v DECKING

Once all the building works are completed, before you sit back and start to enjoy your new home, if you have managed to get to this point and still have some cash left, your thoughts might turn to tidying up the outside areas. A patio or decking area would give you somewhere to sit and  relax in the evenings as you start to unwind and recover from all the stresses and hard work.

So, which do you go for?

In recent years, patios seem to have started to lose some of their appeal and popularity. If you have lived in a house with a patio area that is a few years old, the chances are that some of the slabs are cracked, with weeds growing up through the cracks, some of the mortar joints between the slabs will have broken up and come out, leaving untidy lines between the slabs, through which more weeds are growing, and the slabs themselves are looking the worse for wear, discoloured and with moss growing on their surfaces. Each spring, the pressure washer has to be brought out to try and spruce the area up, to get it ready for summer. A familiar picture?

OK, that may be true of patios, but what about decking? Again, if you have lived in an older house with a timber decking, the stain will have worn away, leaving bear wood in some places. Some of the timbers will have started rotting or warping, moss and mould could have grown on the surface, and every time it rains, or there is ice, you chance breaking your neck by slipping whenever you walk on it. So, again, each spring, the pressure washer comes out to blast off the moss and mould, and every other year you give it a coat of stain, to try to make it look half decent again.

There is a third alternative if you simply want to get yourselves somewhere to sit in the evenings, just for a few weeks or months while you catch your breath after building the house: **Gravel.** A layer of weed barrier, and a ton of gravel can give you a decent sized dry area to put your patio table and chairs on. It is cheap and quick, and as well as being somewhere to sit, it tidies the area up, for a while at least (*until the weed barrier gets ripped, weeds start to grow up around the edges, the gravel gets mouldy, and it is covered in puddles whenever it rains. Oh yes, and it is too uncomfortable to lie on, if you fancied sunbathing*). This is not the best solution but is still an option.

When you give it some thought, none of those three scenarios is a particularly attractive. option.

But wait: There is hope! There have been a lot of improvements in some landscaping products over the past few years, a lot of them related to decking systems. Probably my favourite of which, is *composite decking,* which is created using a mixture of plastic and wood, used to produce a decking system that solves most of the problems that have, until now, come with using timber.

The system includes all the framing and accessories you will need to create a complete decking. Its benefits include: Longevity, minimal maintenance, non-slip, no mould growth, minimal mis-shaping, and recyclability.

There are quite a few companies offering this type of product. We got some samples from: https://www.envirobuild.com, and have decided to use this, or a similar product on out next development, where I have designed an American style veranda across the front of the house.

I will update this section in a future edition once we have tested the product.

## THINGS 145: **TURFING v SEEDING v ARTIFICIAL GRASS**

**Pro's & cons:**

**TURFING:**
- It can be fairly quick and easy to lay: If you have a flat piece of ground, it can take between one and three days to prepare an average lawn sized area (*depending on how much work the ground needs to get it smooth and stone free, covered with a couple of inches of topsoil*). Then half a day to a day, to lay the turf.
- Creates an instant lawn.
- Cheap: From under £2 / sq m in some areas, plus delivery.
- Different qualities available, from "field" to "putting green" qualities available.
- Doesn't need the normal 6" (150mm) of topsoil depth underneath it: Some builders simply level the area, throw the turf down and give it a roll, ignoring what is underneath it. I don't recommend this technique for two reasons: 1) If it is not laid on a decent, stone free surface of sand or soil, it can settle unevenly and look very untidy quite quickly, leading to 2) stones working their way up through the surface, which can be dangerous for kids playing on it. Also, the stones can catch on and damage lawnmower blades.
- Turf is cut and delivered with half an inch or so of topsoil attached, so if you lay 2" of topsoil or sand, or a mixture of the two, over the whole area, and give then give it all a light rolling with a garden roller, that will normally give a satisfactory finish.

- You do not need to be an expert to lay turf. It is quite forgiving if you don't quite get the whole area perfectly level before laying it. As the grass grow and gets cut, the top of the cut grass will, to a certain extent, even out any minor unevenness.
- The area can usually be in use as a lawn within a couple of weeks of being laid.

*Personal opinion: Having turfed and seeded, I think this is the best option, but make sure you prepare the area well, and pay extra for a good quality grass. **Search:** Turf laying videos.*

**SEEDING:**
- Seed is cheap, but preparation is quite a big job if you do it properly.
- An even spread of seed is necessary to get an even growth over the whole lawn. This is not easy to do when you spread the seeds by hand. (*Argos do a seed spreader for around £20*).
- You need a reasonable depth of decent topsoil for the grass to grow well. This may mean buying it in, which is expensive (*up to £100 / tonne for top quality*).
- Fast growing seed may seem like a good idea to get a lawn quickly, but *"fast growing"* does not just apply to when it is seeded (*Which I discovered, the summer after building my first house, having used it for the back garden, which then needed mowing every single, bl\*\*dy week!*).
- Careful preparation can create a lovely lawn, probably better than most types of turf. If you have the time to get a smooth, firm surface, free of stones, it could be well worth the effort put in at that early stage, allowing you to admire your beautiful lawn for many years to come.
- You cannot walk on the new lawn for up to 2 – 3 months, depending on how fast it grows.
- The best seeding time is late Summer to early Autumn, so if you complete your build at any other time, you might need to wait a few months before you can seed, and then another two or three months until you can actually use the lawn, possibly restricting the enjoyment of your first summer in your new home.

*Personal opinion: I seeded the first lawn that I installed as part of my first self-build. After that, I used turf. Enough said!*

**ARTIFICIAL GRASS:**
- Has become popular in recent years.
- Can create a decent looking lawn in a short time, without needing any topsoil.
- As with turf, it needs quite a lot of preparation to get a decent long lasting surface.
- Can look very untidy if it is not laid with care.
- Low maintenance (*not "No" maintenance. Weeds can grow through the turf and around the edges*).
- Relatively expensive, compared to the other 2 options.

- Even though the quality of the product has improved a lot over the past few years, at the time I am writing this, I have not yet seen an artificial turfed lawn that looks 100% real. For this reason, it would probably not appeal to an enthusiastic gardener, or anyone particularly wanting and attractive natural looking lawn.

**Suggestion:** Have a good look as turf samples at your Builders Merchants or Garden Centre, and try to see some lawns that have been completed a while ago, using the product, before you make any decisions on whether to go for it or not.

**My thoughts:** Not yet convinced.


## THING 146: DRIVEWAYS

**Gravel Driveways:**

My first couple of self-builds were on tight budgets, so there wasn't much cash left for gardens, paths, and driveways once the main building work had been completed. I knew before work started that this would probably be the case, so my plan all along was to temporarily gravel the main driveway and then decide what to do as a permanent finish once we had a bit of spare cash available, after we moved in. The gravel from the drive would then be used for footpaths around the house.

The driveway was large, with plenty of room for 2 cars. In those days there were no disability regulations requiring a hard surface to facilitate a simple transfer from a vehicle, to a wheelchair, to the house. So, gravel was an acceptable finish to enable us to get the completion certificates.

There is no reason why, if your budget is tight, or if you simply like a gravel drive, that you cannot still have at least a _part_ gravel driveway. Some people actually prefer them to other finishes because the noise made by the crunch of the gravel when people or vehicles are approaching the house, lets the occupants know that someone is coming up the drive.

If this is something that interests you, speak to your designer to find out which areas of _your_ driveway would need to be solid (for Building Regs) and which could be gravelled.

**Tarmac:**

Tarmac (_also known as macadam_), has been around for a long time, and is still widely used for driveways. It offers good value for money, it is quick to lay, hardwearing (_as long as it is laid properly_) and is now available in a wide range of colours that can create a bright and attractive entrance. You can even _mix and match_ colours, but although that might look good in new town centres (_where you may have seen it and it is getting popular_), it could be a bit over the top on a simple domestic driveway (_have a look at "Images of coloured tarmac" online_).

**Porous Tarmac:**

This is relative newcomer to the list of domestic driveway options. However, with the changes in the way we now have to deal with surface water discharge, it is starting to be a more common choice for housing projects. The main differences between *standard* tarmac and *porous* tarmac are:

1. Water sits on the surface of standard tarmac (*causing puddles*). Porous tarmac is produced in a similar manner to standard tarmac, by mixing *large and small aggregates with tar (hence the name "Tarmac")*, but porous tarmac uses more of the large aggregates and less of the small, which results in voids being created within the mix. These voids allow rainwater to drain through it, into a layer of clean stone, which acts as a storage tank (in *the same way as a soakaway works*), filling up when it rains, and then dissipating the water slowly into the surrounding ground, over a period of time.
2. Porous tarmac drives can also be linked *directly* to a soakaway or a SUDS system, to increase their drainage capabilities.

**Block paving:**

This and tarmac are the two most popular driveway finishes, and have been around for a long time in one form or another. Whether or not you have any knowledge of building, the chances are that you are very familiar with this attractive driveway finish.

There are few negatives to block paving. It is strong, the individual bricks rarely crack, chip or break, there are lots of choices of colours, and basically you can't usually go wrong with it, as long as you lay it properly.

I will just mention a couple of things you may not know about the product:

1. Just as you can choose between standard tarmac and porous tarmac, you can now choose between a solid block, or a porous block driveway. Just as porous tarmac is getting more popular, so is the porous block. Both of the products offer good solutions for dealing with surface water drainage.

The difference between solid blocks and porous blocks is the edge detail. In the image above, you should be able to see small *lumps* on the sides of each block. These have the effect of creating gaps between the blocks, into which water runs down and through into a stone storage area below (*as it does with porous tarmac*), whilst not noticeably affecting their loadbearing quality, or appearance. These blocks cost slightly more than the standard block but, depending on your location, the ground conditions, and the amount of rainfall you can expect. Using them could save you from having to install a more expensive drainage or SUDS system to comply with Building Regulations.

2. The blocks can either be made of concrete or clay. Clay blocks give a more attractive finish but cost considerably more and are often on long delivery times.
3. Block pavings can be laid in a choice of patterns. (Search: *Patterns for block driveways* to find videos and photo's).
4. Block driveways are significantly more expensive than tarmac, but last longer and deliver a higher quality visual appearance, especially if clay blocks are used.

**Resin Driveways:**

I was quite excited when I first saw this product at one of the shows a few years ago.

Although I do like block paving, and some of the new coloured tarmacs, I have been getting a bit bored with the lack of imagination in the choice of driveway materials here in the UK.

When the resin driveway option first started appearing a few years ago, it looked like it could be the answer: A bright, attractive product, that looks simple to lay, comes in various colours, appearing to be made of stone mixed with a glossy resin, to give a slightly shiny, attractive surface. I thought that if the price, strength, and quality turned out to be similar to block paving, this product could potentially take a big slice of the driveway market fairly quickly.

Well, although I still like the product, it didn't turn out to be quite the revelation that I hoped it was going to be. Here are some facts about the product:

- It come in various colours.
- It is made of resin and stone, and also bits of marble, glass, and other recycled substances (*so it scores reasonably high points for being "green"*).
- It is quite quick to lay.
- It can be mixed to be porous.
- It is more expensive than block paving, but that equation will also depend on what type of blocks you would use as its alternative.
- It is not a particularly strong product on its own. It is not recommended that it be laid straight on to hardcore. If it is, it could fail. It can be laid *over* some existing driveway surfaces (*so it can get extra strength from the existing driveway construction underneath it*), or it can be laid onto a newly laid layer of tarmac or concrete.
- If it is laid correctly, the installers say that it can provide a good, strong, low maintenance surface for many years. I have only seen it around in the UK for a few years, so I won't be able comment on that until around edition 10 of this book!

**Concrete driveways:**

This is my least favourite driveway finish. Concrete is concrete, it is strong and cheap, but unattractive and boring and brittle. If the ground underneath it not good, and settlement occurs, where block paved or tarmac drives will be able to move a little to adjust, concrete would simply *crack*. Once that happens and water gets in, which then freezes and expands during the winter months, it could crack more, due to the effects of frost heave.

Concrete is ok for low cost housing, or could be useful to form part of a long driveway, changing to something better and more attractive near the house, but if you are going to spend a couple of years of your lives creating a beautiful new home for you and your family, unless you don't have any other choice, I would suggest that you have a look at the alternatives before you potentially reduce its visual appeal, by putting a big slab of concrete in right front of it! *Just a thought!*

## THING 147: "LEARN" YOUR NEW HOME BEFORE LANDSCAPING.

Something I have come to realise over the years, both from my own self-build experience, and from dealing with custom-build clients, is that making decisions on the external works and landscaping should be left until after moving in.

When you choose your paint colours for the house, or decide where you are going to put your furniture, beds, curtains, blinds, wall decorations etc, you are making decisions that, if you get them wrong, are quite easy to change (*ok, re-painting a room can be a bit of a hassle, but it is not a major task, especially when you compare it to building a house!*). However, if you complete your external works and landscaping as part of the build, you are going to be *kind of stuck with it*.

One question I get asked endlessly by our custom build clients is: "*Would there be any chance of us changing .... add any subject here*". The fact is that, just as the building visually changes during building, causing clients to re-think their choices internally, things change externally too. Not just due to the build process, but also due to the weather, the seasons, the direction of sunlight and shading at different times of day. Noise generated by neighbouring buildings or roads may also affect the way you design your garden.

As the weeks, months and seasons change, the sun changes position in the sky. Sunsets occur at different points on the horizon, shading in the garden changes, wind will blow through certain areas, but not others. You will also find that, once you move in, you might look out through the various windows and come up with ideas that would create an attractive vista from the most frequently used rooms (*the living room, the kitchen, family room, dining room and the master bedroom. Kids are not usually too bothered about views from their rooms, as long as they have all the "stuff" they want **in** the room!*).

So, my advice on this subject would be to first, get the house built and fully completed. Make decisions on the driveway (*which you will need to do for Building Regs*), and temporarily create an area of the garden that gives you somewhere to relax, sit in the sun, set up barbeques and provides somewhere for the kids to play. Then take a breath, and leave the garden until Spring or Autumn, before deciding what you are going to do with it.

The garden area could be temporarily gravelled or laid over with some low cost paving slabs (*on a sand / cement base*), that could easily be broken up and removed later. You could even throw some turf down and take it back up when you complete the permanent works. You can then take your time planning your next "mini project": The garden itself.

## THING 148: FINAL INSPECTIONS

### At last! You are nearly there!

*There is something quite exciting and exhilarating about booking the final inspections. The words themselves sound like they represent the grand climax to the whole project. So, get your hair cut, best clothes on, banners, fireworks and write yourselves a speech along the lines of:*

### "It was hell out there, but we got through it in the end".

If fact, as I mentioned earlier, the final inspection will hopefully be a bit of an anti-climax. Each final inspection (*Building Regs and Warranty*) usually takes between 10 and 15 minutes, carried out by a bored looking inspector, who has already done half a dozen similar inspections that day. Touch wood, I have never got to the final inspection stage and had a house fail.

The reality is that once you get to the final inspections, all the important work has already been inspected and passed. The excavations, foundations, roof and first fixes are all thing things that could potentially cause the problems with house as it gets older. So, the final inspection is basically just checking that all the final bits and pieces have been done properly, and that everything is as it should be .

The warranty inspection is generally even easier than the Building Regs. The warranty is needed to cover potential problems with the structure of the house, not the small details related to the build. The fee you pay to the warranty companies is more like an insurance policy than anything else. The inspectors are not always highly experienced in the industry, but they do have a reasonable level of knowledge about house building generally. If the Building Inspector is happy, the Warranty Inspectors are generally also going to be happy.

**So, what do you need to pay attention to for these inspections?** *(some of these points have been mentioned previously, but are worth repeating here):*

- Are the bathroom fans all installed and working, and do they have a delay before turning themselves off once the switch has been flicked?
- Are the kitchen and utility rooms fitted as required by Building Regs?
- Are the disabled thresholds complete and do they conform to the regs?
- Is there an adequate hardstanding on the driveway area, and does it link to the disabled access?
- Do slopes on the driveway conform to regs?
- Are there enough energy saving light bulbs in the house?
- Are there fire escape windows where there need to be?
- Are the upper floor window cills at the right levels for escape in case of fire?
- Are fire escape windows correctly installed?
- Do fire doors self-close properly (*where they are required to*)?
- Do the windows have the correct ventilation?
- Does the double glazing have the correct kite marks to show it is made of the correct type of glass for its location?
- Are the door locks up to the required standard?
- Do all the taps work as they should?
- Do the appliances work?
- Are socket and switch heights correct?
- Is the boiler working, and piped up correctly?
- Have the stairs been installed to the right specifications, are the handrails at the correct heights and is the head room acceptable?
- Does the ground floor W.C have an outward opening door, and the required manoeuvring space for wheelchair users to enter and exit easily?
- Is there a stop tap at the water entry point, and is it fitted correctly?
- If you have installed sprinklers, are they working, do they have an "off" lever, and are they correctly connected to the water main system? (**Note:** *They need to connect on the supply side of the stop tap, not the house side).*

Each inspector may have his / her own little foibles and be especially strict on one or two parts of the inspection, but generally, they are just making sure everything has been completed to a *reasonable* standard.

Once the inspectors have completed their inspections, if the house passes, a completion certificate will be sent out to you, normally within a few days. If you need it quickly for any reason (*VAT refunds, getting final mortgage payments etc*), just ask the inspector and they will normally try to speed the issuing process up.

## THING 149: DON'T MOVE IN UNTIL THE HOUSE IS COMPLETE

That heading might be a bit confusing. Why would you move in when the house is not complete? Because doing exactly that is another mistake I have been guilty of making, especially on my early self-builds.

You may be living on site in a caravan while you build, or you may be living some distance away, and travelling every day to the site. At some stage, the house is going to have all the services connected, the kitchen and bathrooms installed, all the doors on and the external doors lockable. In other words, it is going to very much resemble a *real* house. But it will not be a *completed* house.

Despite Building Regulations saying that a building should not be inhabited before it has a completion certificate, some self-builders take the house being capable of providing all their basic needs, as their signal to move everyone straight in. This is not a good idea, both from a legal point of view, and especially if there are more than 2 people involved.

What tends to happen is that the decision is made to use a couple or more of the rooms as temporary living space, so that life will be a bit easier, while work continues to get the rest of the house completed. That is not how it usually works out.

Imagine you have been working on the project for a year or so, you have had a *guts full* of being dirty, stressed and doing physical jobs you have never done before, and at which perhaps you are not particularly confident or competent, and you desperately need a break. Now imagine (*again, as I mentioned earlier*), throwing some cheap cord carpet down in a couple of rooms, taking in your settee, TV, a few rugs, some clothes, a bed, bedding, wardrobe, some kitchen equipment, towels and all your important personal bits and pieces. You go shopping and get some food and wine / beer, a bottle of bubbly, you make up the bed, up and you have your first night in your fantastic new home.

*That's it!* You are now officially a retired self-builder!

What often happens next, is that you decide to have a few days off (*now that the pressure is off and all that*). A sensible thing to do, surely? Just to recharge the batteries?

As you are reading this page, you know where this is going: Before you started the project, you probably spent many months gearing yourself up for this huge adventure. You were raring to go. You started work, and it all went reasonably well, but it didn't half knock the stuffing out of you, both physically and mentally, and now it is nearly complete.

If you stop now, it is going to be extremely hard to get going again. The rooms you are temporarily using could end up staying unfinished for months or years, and you will end up endlessly moving your belongings around to get them out of the way of work that still needs doing.

***Just hang on a few weeks more.** If you can, you could get the whole house finished, you won't have to think about trying to rev yourself up again, and you will be able to enjoy your new home as it is meant to be: "**All done and dusted**".*

## THING 150: VAT REFUNDS

**Now you can claim your VAT back:**

Your project has been signed off as being complete and built to the required standards, and you have received your final certificates. So, you are now able to claim back a lot of the VAT that you have paid out during the build.

With this day in mind, and knowing at the outset that building a house was going to involve paying out a lot of VAT, you should have devised a system that collects, keeps and records **every delivery note and invoice** that you have been issued, throughout the job.

(Note: *you should do this whether or not there is a VAT element on the invoice. Sometimes the invoice will also act as your guarantee, and you will also have needed them to do cost reconciliations during the build*).

VAT for self-builders does not work in quite the same way as it does for standard UK VAT registered businesses. We (as a business) are VAT registered, and we can reclaim the VAT element on *anything* that we pay it out for, each month. Self-builders are limited in what they can claim, and can only make one claim, which is made **_after completion_**.

One slightly strange thing about Self-Build and VAT, is that because you can claim VAT back, you would think that would mean that the build is "VAT EXEMPT", in fact it doesn't quite work like that. You cannot claim for all the things on a self-build, that you could as a professional VAT registered builder.

It turns out that Self-Build is actually *liable* for VAT, but the rate at which it is charged is presently "0%". Strange but true! (*maybe because it makes it easier to change the rules if the Government ever decide to*).

To find out all you need to know about self-build VAT reclaims, either go to:

https://www.gov.uk/vat-building-new-home/how-to-claim

or just search *"Claiming Self Build Refunds"* and work your way through to the page with a link to the forms you need to fill in. The form is titled "**431NB**".

The form is 15 pages long, and the process of filling it in can be a bit mind numbing, but you have to do it, and you need to get it right first time, It is a lot simpler now, than it used to be. Now you only have to list the invoices and the details on them, the forms used to ask questions including: "*How many tonnes of sand, aggregate and cement have you used?"* – Imagine trying to work that one out, when a lot of it is all *mixed together* in the concrete!

If you make mistakes, it could significantly increase the time it takes to get the refund. Make sure you carefully read the section at the end of the application form, that describes how to fill the forms in, and what you can and cannot claim for. It is not too difficult to understand, but it is a bit complicated, and some things you might think you should be able to claim for, you cannot.

**Once you have completed this last task, you can really start to think about moving in and getting to know your fantastic new home. Now just take a break before for a couple of years before you start planning your next one!**

## THING 151: TIDY UP THE PAPERWORK, IT MIGHT BE NEEDED

**Just a quick final note:** Once everything has been completed, it will be well worth the effort if you spend some time getting all the paperwork in order. You will have done a lot of this work for the VAT refund, but spending another day or so sorting and filing all the "flotsam and jetsam" could pay dividends in the future, if ever you have a problem related to anything to do with the build. It could also come in handy if, and when you decide to take on another project in the future. You can then use it to help you with your cost estimating, re-issuing sub-contractor contracts, and contacting all the people you used to build your house *first time around*.

### Authors note (and a quick *plug*):

I hope you have found this book to be interesting and useful. If so, you might also find Book 1 in this series: *"Self-Build Simplified"* just as useful.

Where this book is *facts* and *ideas* based, Self-Build Simplified is around 450 pages long and offers a complete, detailed, and thorough A-Z guide, from your first thoughts, through to completion of the project.

Books three and four in the series, will hopefully follow soon.

### Thank you for buying this book.

*Barry S*

# EXTRAS

I have been knocking around some self-build related ideas for a while and have decided to publish them with this book. If they are successful, they will also be included in my future publications, and updated in both this one, and Self-Build Simplified.

I hope readers find these additional features useful

## 1) I am publishing my email address:

In this world of instant contact and social media, everyone seems to be getting accessible. So, as an experiment, here is my personal email address:

**barry.sutcliffe11@btinternet.com**

The reason I am including it here, at the back of the book, is that I would like it to be used *solely* by readers of the book, to ask relevant questions, make comments, and to offer ideas and suggestions on *any* subject elated to self-build.

I am not publishing a social media page just now, because I cannot commit the time that I would want to, to it. This may follow later, or I may go the whole hog and produce a dedicated website, depending on how *these* features are received.

**If you make use of the email facility, I would ask a couple of things:**

i.   That you are patient in waiting for a response. I am usually quite busy, and I could be getting snowed under with questions! – So, it could be a few days, or even weeks before I can reply. However, I will respond to every contact, asap.

ii.  If you do use this service, could you help me, by taking a few minutes to write an honest review of this book? Good reviews obviously help sales, less positive views (*either on Amazon, or preferably to me directly*), can help me to see where I may need to make alterations in the next update of the book.

## 2) Consultancy Service

Over a number of years, appearing as Self-Build Expert at various shows and exhibitions, I have seen how important it is to get relevant, up to date advice, guidance, and information out to potential self-builders. I enjoy taking part in these shows, and talking to people about their dreams, ideas and plans for their own projects. So, as a second experiment (*again, to see how it goes*), I am offering a limited number of bookings for "**Project Consultations**". These will generally be held at the Self-Build Centre at Swindon (J16 off the M4).

This is roughly how I expect the consultation process to be set up:

1) Prior to the meeting, clients can send relevant information and documents over to me, related to their proposed or live projects, which I will review and make notes on, to bring along to the meeting.
2) At the meeting we can discuss the clients thoughts, ideas, funding, finances, hopes, expectations, and anything else related to their project.
3) By the end of the meeting, we will aim to formulate a *draft plan / to do list*, for how the client can move the project forward, either immediately, or when they are ready.

If we meet at the Self-Build Centre in Swindon, time permitting, once we have finished our meeting, I can introduce clients to the centre itself, explain how it works, and demonstrate how to contact the many exhibiting companies.
(*Search "Self-Build Centre Swindon" to see their website*).

A few days after the consultation, I will email to the clients a short report, recapping the meeting, what was discussed, suggested, and proposed, adding any further thoughts or ideas I may have come up with since the meeting.

## Cost:

### *The standard charge for this service will be £475 (no VAT).*

The fee will cover a one full day consultation at Self-Build Centre at Swindon. It will also cover my time prior to the meeting, studying, and making notes on any information sent over to me by the clients. It will also cover my time preparing notes and comments for a brief *post meeting* report, which will be emailed to the client once complete, but hopefully within a few days.

### Notes:
I live in Swansea, South Wales. If the clients live closer to me than the Self-Build Centre and would like me to come to their home, I can arrange do so.
Where that is the case, as part of the consultation, if the client would like me to look at a particular plot with them, that can be arranged. Alternatively, we can arrange to meet at an alternative location, however, where this is the case, extra travel or possibly other associated costs may need to be added.
Payment for the bookings will need to be agreed and paid in advance of the date of the meeting.

**If you have any questions regarding the consultancy service, please email me at the above address.**

# 3) The Self-Build Trade List

This is another idea I have been kicking around for many years. Now seems as good a time as any to introduce it.

One questions I am often asked by self-builders is: *"Where can we find all the people we will need to design and build the house?"*. Despite the fact that there are thousands of self-build related companies right across the UK, self-builders still struggle to find the people they will need, to help them with the day to day building operations.

It is difficult for any *national* organisation to offer good quality *local* information, so the only way a lot of self-builders presently find local contacts, is to use the trade directories and keep their fingers crossed. Either that or they will *"know people who know people"*, but this can sometimes be a risky way of finding tradespeople and suppliers.

This is not an easy problem to solve, especially as much of the building industry is locally based, and many small suppliers and trades people will only cover areas up to around 30 miles or so from their bases. These companies and suppliers can be hard, or even impossible to find via a standard internet search.

The larger self-build related companies covering the whole of the UK will usually deal with the big ticket items, such as timber frames, the windows and doors, kitchen, and bathroom supply etc, so do not help to solve the problems related to finding brickies joiners, plumbers etc.

**It is my hope that the Self-Build Trade List will over time, be able to fill in some of the missing pieces of the jigsaw.**

## How?

I have started the ball rolling by compiling a list of over 200 of the self-build related contacts that have been mentioned in this book. These are for the most part, either companies I have dealt with personally, or know via other people dealing with them. Some, I have just had a look at their web sites and included their links if I think they look like they might be of use to readers.

-----------------------------------------------------------------------------------------------------------

## IMPORTANT:

**I would like readers to send details of any self-build related trades people, local companies or suppliers that they have *first-hand experience* of, who offer a high quality, good value service, that other self-builders from the *same area* may be interested in talking to regarding their own projects.**

**I will compile these contacts in to lists, which will initially be added to the book when each new edition is published (*about once a year*). Over time, I hope that this source of**

contacts will expand to become a valuable tool, eventually enabling all self-builders to find _everyone_ they need for their projects

If this idea proves to be popular, I may eventually consider setting up a web site to publish the contacts, which anyone can then use at any time.

For now, though, I hope you find the list below useful.

........................................... **DISCLAIMER** ...........................................

The web links, search suggestions and any other contacts details listed within this publication are provided for information purposes only. Their inclusion does not in any way suggest that the author has experience of or recommends their products or services.

Users of the index are strongly advised to carry out due diligence as appropriate.

...................................................................................................................

# The Self-Build Trade List

## AIR SOURCE HEATING

**AIR SOURCE SYSTEMS**: http://www.airsourcesystems.co.uk/
**ECO HOUSE SOLUTIONS**: https://www.ecohousesolutions.co.uk/
**THERMAL EARTH**: https://www.thermalearth.co.uk/
**PLUMB CENTRE**: https://www.wolseley.co.uk/
**AIR CRAFT** (EXHIBITING AT THE SELF BUILD CENTRE): http://www.acsouthern.com/

## APPLIANCES

**AO.COM**: https://ao.com/
**APPLIANCES DIRECT**: https://www.appliancesdirect.co.uk/
**MY APPLIANCES**: https://www.myappliances.co.uk/About

**WARNING:** I do not recommend "Robert Dyas". I recently purchased a faulty appliance from this company, and it took them around 6 weeks to sort out a replacement.

## ARCHITECTS / DESIGNERS

**ALLAN COREFIELD** (UK): https://acarchitects.biz/what-is-a-self-build/

**KAST** (AWARD WINNING SELF-BUILD ARCHITECT): https://www.kastarchitects.com/
**ASSOCIATION OF BRITISH ARCHITECTS**: http://www.asba-architects.org/
**ARCHITECTURE ENGINEERED**: http://www.ecohomedesign.co.uk/
**BOB NICHOLLS**: http://www.bobnicholls.co.uk/
**CHARTERED INSTITUTE OF ARCHITECTURAL TECHNOLOGISTS**: http://www.ciat.org.uk/
**ECO DESIGN CONSULTANTS**: http://www.ecodesignconsultants.co.uk/
**EVOLVED DESIGN**: http://www.evolveddesignhomes.co.uk/
**GREEN SPACE**: http://www.greenspacearchitects.co.uk/
**RIBA** (ROYAL INSTITUTE OF BRITISH ARCHITECTS): http://www.architecture.com/
**TONY HOLT DESIGN**: http://www.tonyholt-design.co.uk/

## BALCONIES (JULIET)

**BALCONETTE**: https://www.balconette.co.uk/
**ORIGIN**: https://www.juliet-balcony.co.uk/
**JULIET BALCONY** (*Based in Rochdale but delivery is UK wide*):
https://www.julietbalcony.co.uk/

## BATHROOM EQUIPMENT:

**VICTORIAN PLUMBING**: https://www.victorianplumbing.co.uk/
**B & Q**: https://www.diy.com/
**BATHSTORE**: (*Barter for the best prices, we did and negotiated further reductions*):
https://www.bathstore.com/
**BATHROOM VILLAGE**: http://www.bathroomvillage.com/

## BRICK SLIPS

**BRICK SLIPS** https://brickslips.co.uk/

## BUILDERS MERCHANTS

**JEWSON**:   https://www.jewson.co.uk/working-with-you/for-self-builders/
**BUILDBASE**:   https://www.buildbase.co.uk/self-build
**TRAVIS PERKINS**:   https://www.travisperkins.co.uk/
**ECO MERCHANT**: http://www.ecomerchant.co.uk/

## CAD PACKAGES:

**SMART DRAW**: https://www.smartdraw.com
**SKETCHUP** (*Recommended by self-builders as easy to learn*): https://www.sketchup.com
**CHIEF ARCHITECT** (*I use this system. Expensive but reasonably easy to learn*): https://www.chiefarchitect.com/

## CLADDING:

**EUROCLAD**: http://www.euroclad.com/
**ENVIRO BUILD**: https://www.envirobuild.com/
**CLADCO**: https://www.wpc-decking.co.uk/

## DECKING

**COMPOSITE DECKING**: https://www.envirobuild.com/
**CLADCO**: https://www.wpc-decking.co.uk/

## DESIGN AND BUILD PACKAGE COMPANIES

**D & M Homes**: https://dm-homes.co.uk/
**POTTON**: https://www.potton.co.uk/what-we-do/house-design-service/bespoke-design
**HOUZZ** (A useful contact for various items): https://www.houzz.co.uk/

## DOORS

**DOORSTORE**: https://www.doorstore.co.uk/
**DIRECT DOORS**: https://www.directdoors.com/
**HOWDENS**: https://www.howdens.com/

## DRAINAGE

Keyline are a large drainage materials company, but are not particularly set up for self-build. You could try your nearest branch to see what reaction you get.

We either use our Builders Merchants for our supply or get the groundworkers to supply the materials. They get better discounts than we would get anywhere. Your contacts may be the same. Do some materials price comparisons.

## DRIVEWAYS

Driveway contractors will almost all be found locally. Anyone advertising that they give National Coverage may do so, but their costs are likely to be high and after sales service may be poor.

## ECOLOGICAL SERVICES

**ARBTECH** (VARIOUS SERVICES): https://arbtech.co.uk/
**BAT SURVEYS**: https://batsurveys.co.uk/
**PHLORUM** (VARIOUS SERVICES, INCLUDING KNOTWEED): https://www.phlorum.com/
**EPR** (VARIOUS SURVEYS): https://www.epr.uk.com
**THE ECOLOGY PARTNERSHIP** (SUSSEX BASED): http://www.ecologypartnership.com/

## ELECTRICAL SUPPLIES

**TLC**:  https://www.tlc-direct.co.uk/
**QVS**: https://www.qvsdirect.com/
**ELECTRIC POINT**: https://www.electricpoint.com/
**ELECTRIC CENTRE**: https://electric-center.co.uk/

## EPC'S

**ENERGY  PERFORMANCE CERTIFICATES** : https://energyperformancec ertificates.co.uk/
**NATIOWIDE EPC**: https://www.nationwideepc.com/

## FENCING

**FENCE STORE**: https://www.fencestore.co.uk/
**BUY FENCING DIRECT**: https://www.buyfencingdirect.co.uk/
**JACKSONS FENCING**: https://www.jacksons-fencing.co.uk

Most fencing suppliers tend to be local. Get National prices, then barter locally, using the online quotes. If no-one locally can beat the National prices, use the National suppliers, but check their returns policy and warranty details first.

## GARAGE DOORS

**GARAGE DOORS ONLINE**: https://www.garagedoorsonline.co.uk/
**DOORS DIRECT TO YOU**: https://doorsdirect2u.co.uk/
**JOHN GLEN** (SOUTH WALES): https://www.johnglen.com/

Most garage doors suppliers will be found locally, due to the fitting usually being part of the purchase. Get a couple of on-line prices for the door supply, then negotiate locally for a *fit only*, or *supply and fit price*.

## GAS (non mains)

**CALOR GAS**: https://www.calor.co.uk
**BOC**: https://www.boconline.co.uk

Local camping shops or outdoor centres normally stock bottled gas.

## GATES

**GARDEN GATES DIRECT**: https://www.gardengatesdirect.co.uk/
**B & Q**: https://www.diy.com/
**JACKSON FENCING**: https://www.jacksons-fencing.co.uk

## GREY WATER SYSTEMS

**AQUACO**: https://www.aquaco.co.uk/grey-water-recycling/residential/

**BRECONGATE BUILDING SOLUTIONS**: http://www.brecongate.co.uk

## GROUND SOURCE HEATING

**THERMAL EARTH**: https://www.thermalearth.co.uk/
**WEST WALES HEATING LTD** (WEST WALES): http://www.westwalesheating.co.uk/
**POWER NATURALLY** (DOREST BASED): https://www.powernaturally.co.uk/

## GROUNDWORKS

Groundworks tend to be carried out by local contractors. There are many regional and national groundworks companies, but they tend to work only on large commercial projects.

Search: Groundwork contractors (*plus your location*).

## GUTTERING & DOWNPIPES

**DIRECT PLASTICS**: https://www.directplastics.com/
**ROOFING SUPERSTORE**: https://www.roofingsuperstore.co.uk/
**SCREWFIX**: https://www.screwfix.com/

**EUROCELL**: https://www.eurocell.co.uk/

Most large town and cities will have local companies supplying these products. Builders Merchants will either stock or will be able to order these products.

## HEAT RECOVERY

If you have read the book, you will know I am not a bit fan of this type of system, but have a look and make up your own minds

**ADM SYSTEMS**: http://www.admsystems.co.uk/
**AERECHO**: http://www.aereco.co.uk/
**AIRFLOW**: http://www.airflow.com/
**BPC**: http://www.bpcventilation.com/

## ICF (Insulated Concrete Formwork)

**ICF SUPPLIES**: http://icfsuppliesltd.co.uk/
**BECO WALLFORM**: https://becowallform.co.uk/
**AMVIC**: https://www.amvicbuild.com/
**DURISOL**: https://www.durisoluk.com/
**NUDURA**: http://www.nudura.co.uk/

## INSULATION

National Builders Merchants may get the best deals for insulation. Some insulation companies will not sell direct to self-builders and will only work through merchants

**SUPERFOIL SF650 VAPOUR BARRIER**: https://www.superfoil.co.uk/
**SUPERQUILT**: https://www.superquilt-insulation.co.uk/
**INSULATION SUPERSTORE**: https://www.insulationsuperstore.co.uk/
**ENCON**: https://www.encon.co.uk/
**ROCKWOOL**: https://www.rockwool.co.uk/
**CELLECTA**: http://www.cellecta.co.uk/

## JOINERY SUPPLIES
**HOWDENS JOINERY**: https://www.howdens.com/
**CHESHIRE MOULDINGS** (Sounds local but is National direct delivery):
https://www.cheshiremouldings.co.uk/

**BENCHMARX** (Part of Travis Perkins. They provide kitchens and a wide range of other products): https://www.benchmarxkitchens.co.uk/
**SELCO** (Joinery and many other building products): https://www.selcobw.com/


# KITCHENS
**BENCHMARX** (Part of Travis Perkins): https://www.benchmarxkitchens.co.uk/
**WREN**: https://www.wrenkitchens.com/
**MAGNET**: https://www.magnet.co.uk
**HUNT BESPOKE KITCHENS AND INTERIORS**: http://www.huntbespokekitchens.com/

There probably thousands of local kitchen suppliers across the UK. You will also find them many Builders Merchant's depots. National companies may have more flexibility on price, local companies may provide a higher quality, more bespoke service.


# LIGHTING
**LIGHT SUPPLIER**: https://www.lightsupplier.co.uk/
**LIGHTING SUPERSTORE**: https://www.thelightingsuperstore.co.uk/
**THE LIGHTING COMPANY**: https://www.lightingcompany.co.uk/


# LANDSCAPING
**DANDY'S**: https://www.dandys.com/collections/grow-your-own
**MARSHALLS**: https://www.marshalls.co.uk/
**LANDSCAPING SUPPLIES DIRECT**: https://lsd.co.uk/
**CORE LANDSCAPING PRODUCTS**: http://www.coregravel.co.uk/

Local Builders Merchants will usually stock a good range of landscaping products. Garden centres will also stock landscaping materials but can be expensive.


# LEGAL CONTRACTS

**LAW DEPOT**: https://www.lawdepot.co.uk
**LEGAL CONTRACTS**: https://www.legalcontracts.co.uk/

Solicitors can usually draw up specially customised contracts for your self-build project, but they will be expensive.


# MODULAR BUILD

**NHOUSE**: https://www.the-nhouse.com/self-build/
**HANSE HOUSE**: https://www.hanse-haus.de/en

**SEVEN OAKS MODULAR** (SOUTH WALES BASED): https://somodular.co.uk/products/
**GO MODULAR**: https://www.go-modular.co.uk/

## PAINTING / DECORATING

**DECORATING DIRECT**: https://decoratingdirect.co.uk/
**DECORATING WAREHOUSE**: https://www.decoratingwarehouse.co.uk/
**DECORATING CENTRE ONLINE**: https://www.decoratingcentreonline.co.uk/

Painting and decorating companies will usually need to be locally based to be price competitive. I have found that one of the best ways to find local decorators is using "yell.com". You could ask for labour only prices and buy the materials yourselves, unless they can show that their prices for the materials are cheaper than you can get.

## PLANNING SPECIALISTS

**POTTON** https://www.potton.co.uk/what-we-do/planning-application-service
**RURAL SOLUTIONS** (Yorkshire based): https://ruralsolutions.co.uk/

Search Yell.com for local Planning Specialists. Local knowledge is important here.

## PLANT HIRE

**HSS HIRE**: https://www.hss.com/hire
**SPEEDY SERVICES**: https://www.speedyservices.com/
**SUNBELT RENTALS**: https://www.sunbeltrentals.co.uk/
**NATIONAL TOOL HIRE SHOPS**: https://www.nationaltoolhireshops.co.uk/
**TRAVIS PERKINS TOOL HIRE**: https://www.travisperkins.co.uk/product/tool-hire

There do not presently appear to be any plant hire companies with specialist departments for self-build. Other Builders Merchants, large and small, may have their own plant hire departments or will be able to *cross hire* from local plant hire companies.

## PLASTER BOARDS

Most builders order plasterboards from the local or National Builders Merchants. Manufacturers will not normally sell direct to builders.

# PLOT FINDING WEB SITES

**BUILD STORE**:  https://www.buildstore.co.uk/find-land-or-a-project

**PLOTFINDER**: https://www.plotfinder.net/

**PLOTBROWSER**:  https://www.plotbrowser.com/

We have found that using the big online Estate Agents (*Right Move / Purple Bricks / On the Move / Zoopla*) is as good a way to  search for *immediately available* plots.


# PLUMBERS MERCHANTS

**PLUM NATION**: https://www.plumbnation.co.uk/
**PLUMB BASE**: https://www.plumbase.co.uk/
**CITY PLUMBING**: https://www.cityplumbing.co.uk/
**GRAHAM** (ENGLAND ONLY): https://www.grahamdirect.co.uk/


# PROJECT MANAGEMENT TRAINING

**SELF BUILD ACADEMY** (RUN BY POTTON HOMES) POTTON
https://www.potton.co.uk/self-build-academy-en

**NSBRC** (NATIONAL SELF BUILD & RENOVATION CENTRE): https://www.nsbrc.co.uk/the-self-build-course/


# PROJECT MANAGERS

**SELF-BUILD PROJECT MANAGEMENT** (Seems to be Hertfordshire based):
http://www.selfbuild-projectmanagement.co.uk   (*Note: I do not know this company*)
**CLPM LTD**: http://www.cl-pm.com/


# RAINWATER HARVESTING
**TANKS DIRECT**: https://www.tanks-direct.co.uk/
**RAINWATER HARVESTING**: https://www.rainharvesting.co.uk
**RENEWABLE ENERGY HUB**: https://www.renewableenergyhub.co.uk/

## READY MIXED CONCRETE

**HANSON**: https://www.hanson.co.uk/en
**READYMIX 2GO**: https://www.readymix2go.co.uk/
**CELTIC READY MIX** (South Wales): https://www.celticreadymix.co.uk/
**TARMAC**: http://www.tarmac.com/

Concrete companies don't offer packages or special deals for self-builders. You might be best getting quotes through National Builders Merchants, who should have accounts with the concrete companies and, even with their percentage on top, could be competitive.

Alternatively, try "Yell.com" to find local suppliers

## RENDERING:

**NOTE: *ALWAYS MAKE SURE THE RENDER TO BE USED ON YOUR BUILD IS GUARANTEED AGAINT MOLD FORMATION***

**K REND**: https://www.k-rend.co.uk/
**TEKFLOOR**: http://www.tekfloor.co.uk/products/external-renders-uk/
**SAS EUROPE**: https://sas-europe.com/
**PERMAROCK**: https://www.permarock.com/

External rendering companies will tend to be locally based. They will buy the products they need from a local Builders Merchant. You could ask them to tell you the prices they pay, so that you could see if you can get the materials cheaper elsewhere.

The traditional render is sand and cement, coated with masonry paint. This does not generally go mouldy. You could compare products and prices (*including the labour content*) to see which is best for your project.

## ROOFLIGHTS

**VELUX**: https://www.velux.co.uk/
**FAKRO**: https://www.fakro.co.uk/
**KEYLITE**: https://www.keyliteroofwindows.com/

I have used all three of these makes. They all worked fine, and I had no problems. In my opinion, Keylite are the best, whilst Fakro tended to be the cheapest.

# ROOF TILES

**MARLEY**: https://www.marley.co.uk/
**REDLAND**: https://redland.co.uk/

Roofing companies will normally be locally based and will want to quote for supplying and fitting, complete with underlay and all accessories. I have included these two webs sites as they are two of the largest suppliers in the UK and have images of their products on the web sites

HIGH END ROOF TILES: http://www.dreadnought-tiles.co.uk/

For roofing contractors, try: Yell.com


# SAPS

**ENERGY TEST**: https://energy-test.co.uk/
**SAP CALULATIONS ONLINE**: http://sapcalculationsonline.co.uk/
**APEX HOME AND ENERGY SURVEYORS**: https://www.apexhes.co.uk/
**BUILD ENERGY**: https://www.buildenergy.co.uk/


# SCAFFOLDING

Scaffolding needs to be erected by professionals, so you will need to get quotes for the main scaffold from local companies. However, you will also probably need access scaffolding during the build. This can be bought online or hired locally. Contacts here are for access scaffold purchase online.

**SCAFFOLDING SUPPLIES ONLINE**: https://www.scaffoldingsupplies.co.uk/
**TOP TOWER**: https://www.toptower.co.uk/
**SCAFFOLD TOWERS**: https://www.scaffold-tower.co.uk/


# SECURITY

**ACT EXCEL**: http://www.actexcel.com/
**SECURED BY DESIGN**: http://www.securedbydesign.com/

Most home security equipment can be purchased from electrical suppliers. Your electrician should be able to fit alarm systems. If not, they will probably work with people who do.

## SELF-BUILD FINANCE

**BUILD STORE**: https://www.buildstore.co.uk/mortgages-finance
**MARY RILEY**: https://www.maryrileysolutions.co.uk/
**ECOLOGY BUILDING SOCIETY**: https://www.ecology.co.uk/mortgages/residential-mortgages/self-build
**MONEY SUPERMARKET**: https://www.moneysupermarket.com/mortgages/self-build/


## SELF-BUILD GROUPS

**SELF-BUILD PORTAL**: https://selfbuildportal.org.uk/
**BADSBA** (BATH AND DISTRICT SELF-BUILD ASSOCIATION): https://www.badsba.co.uk/


## SELF BUILD MAGAZINES

**HOMEBUILDING & RENOVATING**: https://www.homebuilding.co.uk/
**GRAND DESIGNS MAGAZINE**: https://www.granddesignsmagazine.com/
**BUILD IT**: https://www.self-build.co.uk/
**SELFBUILD & DESIGN**: https://www.selfbuildanddesign.com/
**I-BUILD**: https://www.i-buildmagazine.com/


## SERVICE CONNECTIONS

There are many service supply companies. When you need to apply for quotes for connections, if you don't already know who provides the different services in your area, simply search "**Gas suppliers – Your area**"

Before you start excavations on site, you need to find out if there are any services crossing the land which you could damage. This company can provide all the information you will need:

National One Call: https://www.national-one-call.co.uk/


## SIPS (Structurally Insulated Panelling System)

**SIPS UK**: https://www.sips.uk.com/
**SIPS ECO PANELS**: https://www.sipsecopanels.co.uk/
**SIP BUILDING SYSTEMS**: https://www.sipbuildingsystems.co.uk/

## SOLAR PANELS

**ENVIRONMENT LOGIC**: http://www.environmentlogic.com/

There are probably thousands of solar panel installation companies around the UK. I found that the easiest way to locate them is to search: "**Solar Panel Installations -** *Your area*"

## STEEL FRAMES

**GLENDALE ENGINEERING**: https://www.glendaleengineering.co.uk/steel-framed-houses
**PRECISION HOMES**:  https://precisionhomes.co.uk/contact

## STRAW BALE HOMES

**STRAWBUILD**: http://www.strawbuild.org/
**STRAW BALE ASSOCIATION**: http://strawbalebuildinguk.com/
**STRAW WORKS**: http://www.strawworks.co.uk/

## STRUCTURAL WARRANTIES

**BUILDSAFE**: https://buildsafe.co.uk/
**SELF BUILD INSURANCE**:   https://www.selfbuild.uk.com/
**SELF BUILD ZONE**:  https://www.selfbuildzone.com/structural-warranty
**PROTECT SELF BUILD**:   https://www.protekselfbuild.co.uk/self-build-warranty/

## SURVEYING EQUIPMENT

**AUTOMATIC LEVEL PACKAGES**: https://www.sccssurvey.co.uk/

## TILES (Floor and wall)

**VICTORIA PLUM**: https://victoriaplum.com/
**TILES DIRECT**: https://www.tiles-direct.com/
**B & Q**: https://www.diy.com/
**TOPPS TILES**: https://www.toppstiles.co.uk/

A lot of the smaller, local tiling suppliers can often be competitive on price and choice. The National suppliers can sometimes be quite expensive.

Tilers tend to operate locally. Search **Yell.com**

## TIMBER FRAMES

**SCOTFRAME**: https://www.scotframe.co.uk/
**BARTRAM**: https://www.bartramselfbuild.co.uk/about-us/
**POTTON**: https://www.potton.co.uk/
**SEVEN OAKS TIMBER FRAME**: (Based in South Wales): https://somodular.co.uk/products
**CARPENTER OAK**: http://www.carpenteroak.com/
**FLEMING HOMES**: http://www.fleminghomes.co.uk/
**FLIGHT TIMBER STRUCTURES**: http://www.flighttimber.com/
**SCANDIA HUS**: http://www.scandia-hus.co.uk/

There are many hundreds of timber frame companies across the UK. Search either **Yell.com**, or **"Timber Frame suppliers – *your area*"**


## TIMBER SUPPLIES

The best place to buy timber is your local Builders Merchants. Timber suppliers usually only deliver wholesale.


## TRUSSES

There are very few if any National roof truss manufacturers. However, there are many to be found locally and regionally. Search **"Roof Truss Manufacturers – *Your area*"**. Also, ask your Builders Merchant if they can get you a quote. On a recent project I got a quote from a truss manufacturer and another from our merchant. Unknown to us, he went to the same supplier, but the quote was calculated by different estimators. The merchants quote was over £1,000 cheaper than our "direct" enquiry.


## UNDERFLOOR HEATING

**NU-HEAT**: https://www.nu-heat.co.uk/
**WARMUP**: https://www.warmup.co.uk/
**RAYOTEC**: https://rayotec.com/
**THE FLOOR HEATING WAREHOUSE**: https://www.thefloorheatingwarehouse.co.uk/
**THE UNDERFLOOR HEATING STORE**: https://www.theunderfloorheatingstore.com/


## WASTE DISPOSAL SYSTEMS

**INSINKERATOR**: https://www.insinkerator.uk.com/

## WINDOWS

**QUICK SLIDE** (UPVC): https://www.quickslide.co.uk/
**HOWARTH TIMBER WINDOWS AND DOORS** (Softwood – Pre Finished):
https://windowsanddoors.howarth-timber.co.uk/
**JELD-WEN** (VARIOUS PRODUCTS): https://www.jeld-wen.co.uk
**BISON FRAMES**: http://genesiscollection.co.uk/
**CRITTALL WINDOWS**: http://www.crittall-windows.co.uk/
**DALE JOINERY**: http://www.dalejoinery.co.uk/
**ECOHAUS**: http://www.ecohausinternorm.com/
**PREMDOR**: http://www.premdor.co.uk/

## WIND TURBINES

**ECO POWER SHOP**: https://www.ecopowershop.com/
**FUTURE ENERGY**: https://futurenergy.co.uk/

## WOODGLUE (expanding)

**D4**: https://www.everbuild.co.uk/product/d4-wood-adhesive/

Printed in Great Britain
by Amazon